A First John Reader

*Intermediate Greek
Reading Notes and Grammar*

S. M. Baugh, Ph.D.

Associate Professor of New Testament
Westminster Theological Seminary in California

P&R PUBLISHING
P.O. BOX 817 • PHILLIPSBURG • NEW JERSEY 08865-0817

Quotations from the Greek New Testament are from *The Greek New Testament*, 4th revised edition, Barbara Aland, Kurt Aland, Johannes Karavidopoulos, Carlo M. Martini, and Bruce M. Metzger, editors, © 1993, United Bible Societies by Deutsche Bibelgesellschaft, Stuttgart. Used by permission.

Printed in the United States of America

Library of Congress Cataloging-in-Publication Data

Baugh, S. M. (Steven M.), 1954–
    A first John reader : intermediate Greek reading notes and grammar / S. M. Baugh.
        p.   cm.
    Includes bibliographical references.
    ISBN-10: 0-87552-095-2
    ISBN-13: 978-0-87552-095-7
    1. Bible. N.T. John I—Translating. 2. Greek language,
Biblical—Translating into English. I. Title.
BS2805.5.B38 1999
227'.94048—dc21

                                                    99-28120

Contents

Preface

This *Reader* (I hardly knew what else to call it) is not quite like any other work for New Testament Greek. There are workbooks, grammars, and commentaries, all of which this work resembles in its various parts. However, the *Reader* is *not* by any means a full grammar or commentary. It is more of a workbook and introduction to intermediate Greek designed as part of an integrated curriculum to go along with my beginning grammar book, the *Primer*. But because of this work's unique character, I would ask the student to read the Introduction which follows carefully; it will guide you in the intelligent use of this book.

The manuscript for this work was thoroughly revised and expanded during a year long sabbatical for the 1997–98 school year granted by the Trustees of Westminster Theological Seminary in California. I am profoundly grateful for their generous provision.

This book emerged out of several drafts of notes provided for various classes of Greek students at Westminster Theological Seminary in California. These dear folk received these notes with wonderful warmth and charity. Thank you, dear brothers and sisters! Special thanks go to Mr. Brian Lee and to Mr. Chris Tennberg who both read through the work in its entirety and made corrections and suggestions.

And, though it may seem commonplace, it is nevertheless so very true that my wife and family deserve my most loving thanks for their patience and encouragement throughout the years taken to write this book. To Kathy, Stephie, Leah, and Isaac: You are and ever remain my little colony of heaven on earth!

Sola Christi gratia
Westminster Theological Seminary
Escondido, California

Introduction

There is no doubt, the study of ancient Greek is a difficult chore, and too many students come to it with unrealistic expectations. After mastering the paradigms, they feel that Greek should then be easy. They invariably expect to just plug an English equivalent into a particular Greek word's slot, and all should be well and clear. I wish it were so easy! Though one can take such an "interlinear" approach with much of First John (though look at v. 2:6), note the result of using this method with a characteristic sentence from First Peter:

1 Peter 4:1–2

Of Christ then of having suffered to/for flesh and you the same mind arm yourselves

Χριστοῦ οὖν παθόντος σαρκὶ καὶ ὑμεῖς τὴν αὐτὴν ἔννοιαν ὁπλίσασθε

Because the one who suffered to/for flesh has stopped of sin unto the no longer of men to/for lusts

ὅτι ὁ παθὼν σαρκὶ πέπαυται ἁμαρτίας εἰς τὸ μηκέτι ἀνθρώπων ἐπιθυμίαις

but to/for will of God the remaining in flesh to live out time.

ἀλλὰ θελήματι θεοῦ τὸν ἐπίλοιπον ἐν σαρκὶ βιῶσαι χρόνον.

Not very clear English is it?[1] You see, the interlinear approach simply *cannot* succeed with Greek. It will go much better for you if you surrender to that notion right now. Part of the reason is that the grammar of ancient Greek is so very foreign to most modern languages because of its inflections (the endings and complex forms). This means that word order, a major requirement of a meaningful English sentence, is very flexible in Greek.

For instance, let's look at the last part of the First Peter passage quoted above: εἰς τὸ μηκέτι ἀνθρώπων ἐπιθυμίαις ἀλλὰ θελήματι θεοῦ τὸν ἐπίλοιπον ἐν σαρκὶ βιῶσαι χρόνον. The first two words, εἰς τό, introduce a result clause and require an infinitive, but the infinitive, βιῶσαι, has been expressed after what seems to the beginner to be a jumble of other words. Here is the connection indicated in bold type: **εἰς τὸ μηκέτι** ἀνθρώπων ἐπιθυμίαις ἀλλὰ θελήματι θεοῦ τὸν ἐπίλοιπον ἐν σαρκὶ **βιῶσαι** χρόνον.

Furthermore, the article and adjective τὸν ἐπίλοιπον modify something. Perhaps the infinitive, βιῶσαι? Infinitives take articles don't they? Yes, they take articles (*Primer* §25.5), but only *neuter* articles, and τόν is masculine.[2] So, you have to train yourself to look ahead and spot the masculine noun which τὸν ἐπίλοιπον modifies: χρόνον; woodenly: "the remaining-in-the-flesh . . . time" (ἐν σαρκί modifies ἐπίλοιπον). But you will ask, "What is the infinitive doing in the middle of this phrase: τὸν ἐπίλοιπον ἐν σαρκὶ **βιῶσαι** χρόνον? It doesn't belong there does it?" Well, that's where the flexibility of Greek word order allows it to be so expressive. This is actually an elegant little[3] clause which would strike the original reader as refined and pleasing. Notice the little inverted parallelism formed by the words in the middle: **ἀνθρώπων** ἐπιθυμίαις ἀλλὰ θελήματι **θεοῦ**.

So the question now begs to be answered, How does a beginner in "interlinear mode" become an accomplished Greek reader? The answer is not hard to give in a general fashion: practice, practice, practice. And when practice is over: *more practice!* Now, for some students whom God has blessed

---

[1]Don't panic. Not all NT sentences are this complex!

[2]To make parsing decisions like this *intuitively* can only come with practice and time. That is why this book assigns a full review of the Greek paradigms and parsing drill.

[3]Greek sentences, called "periods" or "periodic sentences," can be very long and involved; for instance, Eph. 1:3–14 is one sentence in Greek.

with "language genes" or who have solid experience with language study, they will pick up Greek reading with just practice and practice. But for the rest of us (myself included, mind you), we just slog away like persistent miners until Greek yields its riches.

More specifically, though, there is a particular hurdle you must cross in order to read ancient Greek with understanding. That is, you must learn to see certain grammatical constructions like εἰς τό as expecting a possible infinitive somewhere later in the sentence.[4] More than this, however, you will want to learn the range of possible meanings for constructions like εἰς τό βιῶσαι.[5] How does one learn these things? Not always easily.

Can you learn Greek syntax by sitting down and reading through a Greek reference grammar? If you read the long-time standard, Blass-Debrunner-Funk (BDF), here's a sample of what you would find when learning about the dative case:

192. **The ethical dative:** Rev. 2:5, 16 ἔρχομαί σοι could be an ethical dative (likewise BGU IV 1041. 16 [ii AD]; for classical parallels s. Havers 4, 158 etc.; pap. [Mayser II 2, 270] ἐλθέ μοι), unless it reflects incorrectly, like Mt 21:5 OT ἔρχομαί σοι, Hebr. [לְךָ, לָךְ] 'to you' (in Hebrew with verbs of motion). Ἀστεῖος τῷ θεῷ A 7: 20 (speech of Stephen) also is a Hebraism.

Now there is much we can say about this grammatical description, but two things stand out: (1) What in the world is an "ethical dative"? Unless you know ahead of time, BDF does not bother to tell you what it is![6] (2) Even BDF admits that σοι may or may not be an ethical dative in Rev. 2:5. Why use an equivocal example to illustrate the point rather than a *clear* example?[7] This second point is a failing not only of BDF but of many Greek grammars.

Furthermore, we have inherited a very complicated—and sometimes misleading—body of terms to describe the Greek language. Many of these terms derive from Medieval Latin. It's difficult to remember the difference between a first, second, and third class condition. Even "Future Contra-Factual Conditional" is not easy, though it is slightly better. Some grammarians call purpose and result clauses "final" and "consecutive" clauses. And why do some grammars talk about the "ablative" and "locative" cases when they *look* like the genitive and dative cases respectively?

The foregoing illustrates two important hurdles facing anyone learning ancient Greek. Our reference tools are not meant for the uninitiated, and they were never really designed to be read through. They are reference works meant to be consulted on particular, specialized questions.

What we need is a bridge between the study of Greek forms and the intelligent use of reference grammars. This book attempts to be such a bridge. It is not perfect, but it is a sincere attempt to help you along in the vital study of Greek syntax in an innovative and well-considered way.

The theory which produced this book is part of the same theory which shaped my *Primer*: that progress in language acquisition is aided by orderly and specific instruction, examples, and drills in the sub-skills which make up the language reading process. In my opinion, the larger process of reading the Greek NT involves this sequence of skills acquisition: mastery of forms and vocabulary, mastery of syntactical categories, and mastery of Greek style. This *Reader* fits squarely in the second stage ("mastery of syntactical categories"), yet it provides a systematic review of the Greek

---

[4]Unless, of course, the object of the preposition is a noun: εἰς τὸ θαυμαστὸν αὐτοῦ φῶς, "into his marvelous light" (1 Pet. 2:9).

[5]Later you will also want to reflect on why Peter chose to express βιῶσαι in its aorist form rather than in its present infinitive form (βιοῦν). But that is the subject of another book! Let's take it one step at a time for now.

[6]See §56 of the *Syntax Sketch* below for a definition and description.

[7]The σοι in Rev. 2:5, 16 is not an "ethical" dative, but a "dative of disadvantage" (BDF §188; *Sketch* §55). The Lord of the Church warns his errant vassals: "If you do not repent, I am going to come *against you*," or "*to your harm*."

forms and vocabulary and some introduction to Greek style. The student reviews the *Primer* material and advances in Greek grammar through the process of a guided reading of First John and learning an overview of Greek syntax.

This *Reader* contains two major sections: the Reading Notes and a Sketch of New Testament Greek Syntax (*Syntax Sketch* or just *Sketch*). The Reading Notes provide the "base of operations" for each lesson. Begin by following the assignments given at the start of each lesson, which has three parts: (1) Review assigned lessons in the *Primer*. These lessons cover forms which are either relevant for the syntax assignment or forms which occur in the First John passage covered in the *Reader* lesson. You should make sure that you master all the paradigms and vocabulary from those lessons in the *Primer*. You do not need to go over the exercises in the *Primer* unless you have the time and need.

(2) Read through assigned sections in the *Syntax Sketch* in the second half of the *Reader*. This material is certainly not intended to replace a reference grammar or even one of the excellent intermediate grammars we have available today. It is simply provided as an introduction to the subject to use as a jumping off point in the study of this most significant area of NT Greek. In many cases, references are given in the *Sketch* to NT grammars for further study.

(3) Read the assigned passage in First John. This is the passage which the Reading Notes cover in that lesson. The passages are short at first with long reading notes. As the student advances, the passages become longer and the notes shorter. There is also a Vocabulary section at the start of each lesson. This covers two groups of vocabulary: (a) the essential NT vocabulary based on frequency which picks up where the *Primer* left off (from about 49 occurrences down to about 17); and, (b) all words which occur in the assigned First John passage for that lesson. The latter is provided as a convenience for mastering the text of First John.

At the end of the twelve lessons in the *Reader,* the student will have read all of First John and learned intermediate Greek syntax covering everything except the full Greek verb system. The latter should be taken up next through other works. Yet I sincerely hope that this *Reader* will help launch you into a confident journey into the whole Greek Testament.

Abbreviations

BAGD   Walter Bauer, William F. Arndt, F. Wilbur Gingrich, and Frederick W. Danker. *A Greek-English Lexicon of the New Testament and Other Early Christian Literature.* 2d ed. Chicago and London: University of Chicago Press, 1979.

BDF   F. Blass, A. Debrunner, and Robert W. Funk. *A Greek Grammar of the New Testament and Other Early Christian Literature.* Chicago and London: University of Chicago Press, 1961.

Brown   Raymond E. Brown. *The Epistles of John.* The Anchor Bible. Garden City, N.Y.: Doubleday, 1982.

Burton   Ernest De Witt Burton. *Syntax of the Moods and Tenses in New Testament Greek.* 2d ed. Chicago: University of Chicago Press, 1893.

Calvin   John Calvin. *The Gospel According to St. John 11–21 and The First Epistle of John.* Calvin's Commentaries, vol. 5. T. H. L. Parker, translator. Grand Rapids: Eerdmans, 1959.

GNT   Greek New Testament

L&N   Johannes P. Louw and Eugene A. Nida, *Greek-English Lexicon of the New Testament Based on Semantic Domains.* 2d ed. 2 vols. New York: United Bible Societies, 1988.

LSJ   Henry George Liddell, Robert Scott, Henry Stuart Jones. *A Greek-English Lexicon.* 9th ed. Oxford: Clarendon Press, 1968.

MHT   James Hope Moulton, Wilbert Francis Howard, and Nigel Turner. *A Grammar of New Testament Greek.* 3 vols. Edinburgh: T. & T. Clark, 1908, 1929, and 1963.

Moule   C. F. D. Moule. *An Idiom-Book of New Testament Greek.* 2d ed. Cambridge: Cambridge University Press, 1960.

NA^{27} Eberhard Nestle, Kurt Aland, *et al. Novum Testamentum Graece.* 27th ed. Stuttgart: Deutsche Bibelgesellschaft, 1993.

NT   New Testament

OT   Old Testament

Porter   Stanley E. Porter. *Idioms of the Greek New Testament.* Sheffield: JSOT Press, 1992.

Primer   S. M. Baugh. *A New Testament Greek Primer.* Phillipsburg, N.J.: P&R Publishing, 1995.

Sketch   The *Syntax Sketch* comprising Part II of this work.

Smalley   Stephen S. Smalley. *1, 2, 3 John*. Word Biblical Commentary, vol. 51. Waco, Tex.: Word Books, 1984.

Smyth   Herbert Weir Smyth. *Greek Grammar*. Cambridge, Mass.: Harvard University Press, 1920.

Stott   John R. W. Stott. *The Epistles of John*. Tyndale New Testament Commentaries. Leicester and Grand Rapids: Inter-Varsity Press and Eerdmans, 1960.

Trenchard   Warren C. Trenchard. *Complete Vocabulary Guide to the Greek New Testament*. Grand Rapids: Zondervan, 1998 (revised edition).

UBS[4]   Barbara Aland, Kurt Aland, Johannes Karavidopoulos, Carlo M. Martini, and Bruce M. Metzger. *The Greek New Testament*. 4th ed. New York: United Bible Societies, 1993.

Wallace   Daniel B. Wallace. *Greek Grammar Beyond the Basics: An Exegetical Syntax of the New Testament*. Grand Rapids: Zondervan, 1996.

Westcott   Brooke Foss Westcott. *The Epistles of St. John*. 3d ed. Grand Rapids: Eerdmans, 1966 (reprinted from 1892 edition).

Young   Richard A. Young. *Intermediate New Testament Greek: A Linguistic and Exegetical Approach*. Nashville, Tenn.: Broadman & Holman, 1994.

Zerwick   Maximilian Zerwick. *Biblical Greek*. Rome: Pontifical Biblical Institute, 1963.

The Article I

REVIEW: *Primer*, Lessons 2–3, 14
READ: *Syntax Sketch*, §§1–10
STUDY: 1 John 1:1–4

Vocabulary

ἁμαρτωλός, –όν, sinful; (usually substantive, "sinner") (*hamartology*; cf. ἁμαρτάνω)

ἀποδίδωμι, I am repaying, giving away (*apodosis*)

ἄρα, consequently, so then

ἄχρι(ς), until (conjunction and preposition + gen.)

ἔμπροσθεν + gen., before, in the presence of

ἔτος, ἔτους, τό, year

ἡμέτερος, –α, –ον, our (pronominal adjective; cf. ἐμός, *Primer* §16.1)

θεάομαι, I am beholding, viewing (*theater*)

θηρίον, τό, animal, wild beast (*theriomorphic*)

καθίζω, I am sitting (middle); I am causing to sit (cf. κάθημαι)

κοινωνία, ἡ, fellowship (*koinonia*)

κρατέω, I am seizing, grasping

κρίσις, –εως, ἡ, judgment (*crisis*; cf. κρίνω)

μικρός, –ά, –όν, small, little (*microscope*)

οὐαί, woe, alas (*woe*)

οὐκέτι, μηκέτι, no longer, no more (μηκέτι with non-indicative verbs)

παραλαμβάνω, I am taking; I am taking along

ποῦ, where, where?

προσφέρω, I am offering, bringing to

σταυρόω, I am crucifying (*stauro*lite; cf. σταυρός, cross)

φανερόω, I am revealing; I am appearing (pass.) (epi*phany*)

φόβος, ὁ, fear (*phobia*; cf. φοβέομαι)

φυλακή, ἡ, guard, prison (*phylactery*; pro*phylactic*)

χρεία, ἡ, need, necessity

ψηλαφάω, I am touching, handling

Overview

This lesson introduces you to half of the Greek article uses; the second half are covered in the next lesson. Article usage in this 1 John pericope is fairly standard, although ἡ ζωή in v. 2 is of some interest. The passage selected is only four verses long, so that you can ease into the rhythm of reading Greek. There are more notes in this lesson than normal in order to give you plenty of help at the start.

Remember, all vocabulary for the assigned passage can be found either in the *Primer* (which you should have already memorized) or in the Vocabulary section above. Begin by reviewing the assigned paradigms in the *Primer*, then read through the assigned sections in the *Syntax Sketch*. Work through 1 John 1:1–4 with these notes in order to memorize the paradigms, to understand the grammar, and to become expert in reading the Greek NT. There are no tricks to learning these things; just some hard work: "Commit your works to the Lord, and your plans will be established" (Prov. 16:3).

Reading Notes

1 John 1:1

1:1a. In the case of ὅ, as frequently in Greek, the antecedent of the relative pronoun is not expressed in the sentence; it is merely implied (cf. *Primer* §24.3).

The neuter pronoun "is sometimes used with reference to persons if it is not the individuals but a general quality that is to be emphasized" (BDF §138). The antecedent of this pronoun would then be Jesus Christ.[1] Here, though, ὅ is the object of ἀπαγγέλλομεν in v. 3, "What . . . we are announcing," so some commentators take ὅ to refer to the Gospel message, rather than to Jesus. The problem with this approach is that one does not "see" or "handle" messages. I think the best interpretation is provided by Raymond Brown in the accompanying box.

1:1b. The construction of this first sentence is a bit involved, since the main verb, ἀπαγγέλλομεν, "we are announcing," is in v. 3. To rearrange the order, it reads: "We are announcing also to you . . . what was from the beginning, what we have heard. . . ." There is no great mystery in this word order, since the ὅ clauses were brought into the forefront for our particular attention. To call this a "grammatical tangle" (C. H. Dodd; cf. Brown, 152-53) is too severe. It is rather an effective way of expressing emphasis or giving focus. It is a dramatic opening for the Epistle reminiscent of the opening of John's Gospel. Furthermore, the arrangement of some of the verbs has an interesting reversed parallel arrangement:

> "[T]he 'what' [ὅ] is to be equated with no specific noun in the Prologue, but refers to the whole career of Jesus, with the neuter functioning *comprehensively to cover the person, the words, and the works.*" Raymond E. Brown

INTRODUCTION TO THE EPISTLE (1:1-3):
a. ἀκηκόαμεν (1:1)
  b. ἑωράκαμεν
    c. ἐφανερώθη (1:2)
  b. ἑωράκαμεν
    c. ἐφανερώθη
  b. ἑωράκαμεν (1:3)
a. ἀκηκόαμεν
PURPOSE OF EPISTLE I: γράφομεν ἡμεῖς ἵνα . . . (1:4)

A simple reversed parallel construction with an *a b / b a* or an *a b c b a* pattern is called a "chiasm" or "chiasmus." Sometimes, recognition of this pattern can make a significant difference in the interpretation of a passage. In this case, the focus is on ἐφανερώθη, "it has been manifested," or "it was manifested."

---

[1]The neuter phrase πᾶν τὸ γεγεννημένον, "everything born," in 1 John 5:4 has a personal reference. Similar uses of the neuter with a personal antecedent are found elsewhere in John's writings.

1:1c. Parse: ἦν.[2]

1:1d. You will notice that ὅ is repeated four times in v. 1 at the beginning of the first four clauses (and once in v. 3). Notice also that the clauses get gradually longer—this was deliberate. To repeat a word, especially at the beginning of clauses or sentences is called "anaphora" and is a fairly common rhetorical feature of ancient and some modern literature. The longest example in the NT is the word πίστει ("by faith") repeated 18 times in Hebrews 11 (cf. BDF §491).

1:1e. Parse: ἀκηκόαμεν[3] and ἑωράκαμεν.[4]

1:1f. Much can be made of the perfect aspect of ἀκηκόαμεν and of ἑωράκαμεν. For example, J. R. W. Stott says that the perfect suggests "the abiding possession which results from the hearing" (p. 60). But what is abidingly possessed? On the other hand, some scholars assert that the perfect and the aorist are completely interchangeable with no distinction of meaning.[5] It seems to me that the alternation between the perfect and the aorist in v. 1 is explicable as a difference in *tone*. While it is possible that the perfects in v. 1 express intensification of the actions ("What we *listened to intently* . . . what we have *gazed* upon"), it is more likely that the perfect sounded more "dramatic" or "formal" than the aorist. The perfect forms draw the reader's attention to these verbs (cf. Wallace, p. 578; Young, p. 128). Also note that the perfect verbs in v. 1 are repeated in the next verses and give shape to the paragraph (see note 1:1b above).

1:1g. Parse: ὀφθαλμοῖς.[6]

1:1h. The dative case in the phrase τοῖς ὀφθαλμοῖς ἡμῶν is the dative of means, or the "instrumental" use, which specifies the instrument or means used to perform the action (cf. *Sketch*, §58). John is making certain that the reader does not think that the seeing was visionary or imaginary: it was with the physical eye. Likewise, the touching was physically done with the hands, because "the Word *became* flesh" (John 1:14).

1:1i. Parse: ἐθεασάμεθα.[7]

1:1j. With ἐθεασάμεθα, note the switch to the aorist verb from the previous perfect verbs (cf. note 1:1f above). We may wish to find a radical difference in meaning between ἐθεασάμεθα and the earlier ἑωράκαμεν beyond the fact that one is aorist and one is perfect. Use this passage to think about the difference between the following English verbs which are semantically related: "see," "behold," "view," "stare," "study," "look," "cast the eyes upon," "gaze," "peek," and "glance." One difference lies in the length of time the "seeing" occupies: "to gaze" means to see for a long time; "to

---

[2] εἰμί Impf A I 3 sg; see *Primer* §10.2.

[3] ἀκούω Pf A I 1 pl; cf. *Primer* §§14.1, 4.

[4] βλέπω / ὁράω Pf A I 1 pl; cf. *Primer* §14.1.

[5] Brown, p. 161; BDF §343. Compare K. L. McKay, *A New Syntax of the Verb in New Testament Greek: An Aspectual Approach* (Bern: Peter Lang, 1994), §4.5.2, p. 50.

[6] ὀφθαλμός m d pl; see Primer §3.2.

[7] θεάομαι A D I 1 pl. Remember that with deponent verbs, one can express either the aorist *middle* form as here or the aorist *passive* form (ἐθεάθημεν) with no difference in meaning. Deponents have either middle or passive forms with active meaning (see *Primer* §15.6). The principal parts of θεάομαι are: θεάομαι, —, ἐθεασάμην, —, τεθέαμαι, ἐθεάθην; cf. Trenchard, p. 254.

glance" is to see briefly. Another difference is in the formality of the act or a preference for a certain word in certain settings. Cf. BAGD (p. 353) for ideas on the range of meanings for θεάομαι.

1:1k. The article in the phrase αἱ χεῖρες ἡμῶν, "our hands" is normal and unremarkable with a possessive pronoun (review *Sketch* §5). See also the article in the earlier phrase, τοῖς ὀφθαλμοῖς ἡμῶν.

1:1l. Parse: ἐψηλάφησαν.[8]

1:1m. You know ἅπτομαι, a more common word for "touch" than ψηλαφάω (*Primer* §7.1). What is the difference between "touch," "feel," and "handle"? Some scholars believe that Luke 24:39 (ψηλαφήσατέ με καὶ ἴδετε, "touch me and see for yourselves") was behind John's use of ψηλαφάω here.

1:1n. The genitive in the phrase περὶ τοῦ λόγου τῆς ζωῆς ("word *of life*") is an example of what I call the "genitive of connection" (cf. *Sketch* §49) where the word in the genitive specifies the subject matter of a discourse. Stott has a lengthy discussion of this phrase (pp. 66-69).

The reason the article was repeated before both nouns τοῦ λόγου τῆς ζωῆς is explained in the next lesson on article usage (*Sketch* §15), but you may wish to look ahead. Also notice that abstract nouns like ζωή, "life" may take the article in Greek as you discovered in *Sketch* §6. Review that section if needed.

1 John 1:2

1:2a. Verse 2 is a long parenthetical section expanding upon the character of the ζωή mentioned at the end of v. 1 (cf. BDF §465). Notice that some Greek editions and modern translations provide a dash after v. 1 and v. 2 to mark the parenthesis (e.g., NA²⁷; UBS⁴; NRSV; NASB).

1:2b. In §6 of the *Syntax Sketch* you read that abstract nouns like ζωή may take an article as at the start of this verse (ἡ ζωὴ ἐφανερώθη . . .), because "[s]ometimes the article was used for previous reference" (cf. *Sketch* §3). That is the case here. The flow of the text reads: "concerning the word *of life*—now, *this life (I mentioned)* appeared. . . ." Exegetically, we want to notice such connections, and the article shows the way.

1:2c. Parse μαρτυροῦμεν[9] and ἀπαγγέλλομεν.[10]

1:2d. It is possible to regard the present aspect of the verbs μαρτυροῦμεν and ἀπαγγέλλομεν as a mere description of generally occurring events: "And we both testify and announce to you (at one time or another) concerning the eternal life. . . ." We can call this idea the "general" use of the present. Another option, however, is to regard the events as happening concurrently with the writing of the epistle: "And we (hereby) testify and announce to you."[11] This latter interpretation, which I prefer, brings out John's attitude toward his epistle: it is solemn testimony and announcement of the gospel message.

---

[8]ψηλαφάω 1A A I 3 pl; see *Primer* §8.5 for the first aorist of contract verbs.

[9]μαρτυρέω P A I 1 pl (epsilon contract verb; cf. *Primer* §6.2).

[10]ἀπαγγέλλω P A I 1 pl.

[11]See Wallace pp. 517–18 and 521–22.

1:2e. The article in τὴν ζωήν was employed because John was still referring to the same life introduced earlier in the verse ("previous reference"; *Sketch* §3). The second article in the phrase (τὴν ζωὴν **τὴν** αἰώνιον) is an example of a redundant article used to tie an attributive adjective to its noun (look ahead to *Sketch* §13; cf. *Primer* §10.5). The adjective, αἰώνιος, is parsed as feminine even though the ending (–ον) looks masculine. This adjective and others like it have only one ending for masculine and feminine forms (cf. *Primer* §11.1).

1:2f. Recall that ἥτις (ὅς, ἥ[τις], ὅ) is the normal feminine nominative singular relative pronoun "which (life)." By NT times, this form no longer always had the meaning of an indefinite relative pronoun "whatever"; see *Primer* §§24.2, 4.

1:2g. In the phrase, πρὸς **τὸν** πατέρα[12], the article was used because the referent was specific and well-known: *the* Father (*Sketch* §2). The article was not always needed with a definite noun when it acted as the object of certain prepositions (e.g., ἀπ' ἀρχῆς, "from *the* beginning"; see *Sketch* §19). However, the article makes John's meaning explicit.

1:2h. The repetition of the verb ἐφανερώθη[13] at the end of the verse serves three purposes: (1) to mark off the end of the parenthetical idea (above note 1:2a); (2) to add to the parallel structure of the whole paragraph (above note 1.1b); and, (3) to add the following important idea. Earlier in the verse John had said "the life appeared," here he says "it appeared *to us*"; this further clarifies John's eyewitness qualification to testify concerning the life.

> "[B]y speaking of eternal life as 'existing with the Father,' John is not only referring to the exalted content of the apostolic proclamation, but also making a high christological affirmation by alluding to the pre-existence of Christ. . . . Indeed the christological reference is almost certainly primary." Stephen S. Smalley

1 John 1:3

1:3a. John signals an end to the parenthetic v. 2 and a return to the theme begun in v. 1 by repeating the two verbs ἑωράκαμεν and ἀκηκόαμεν (in reverse order from v. 1). For the repetition of these verbs see note 1:1b above.

1:3b. With ἀπαγγέλλομεν we come at last to the main verb in the sentence (see note 1:1b). Long and involved sentences were a common feature of Greek literary style; see BDF §458. Such sentences—the most complicated are called "periods" or "periodic sentences"—were not viewed in antiquity as clumsy or too involved. Rather, the ancients regarded them as signs of elegance and refinement of education. Do not apply today's trend toward "dumbing down" everything to the standards of antiquity.

1:3c. How do you translate καί here? First, it cannot be a mere joiner, "and," because of the word order. To mean "and" we would need this word order: καὶ ἀπαγγέλλομεν ὑμῖν, "*And* we are announcing to you. . . ." So we are left with two other possible glosses: "also" or "even."

---

[12]πατήρ m a sg (third declension with a slight stem change; see *Primer* §12.3). Cf. John 1:1, πρὸς τὸν θεόν, for the same meaning of πρός, "with," "in the presence of," "in the company of" (cf. BAGD III.7; p. 711).

[13]φανερόω 1A P I 3 sg (an omicron contract verb with typical lengthening of the contract vowel in the first aorist passive stem; cf. principal parts of φανερόω in Trenchard, p. 271).

The first option is "also": "Which . . . we are *also* announcing to you." This implies that the act of announcing had already occurred to others and now the announcement is merely repeated to the readers. The two acts would be parallel: "I do this; I *also* do that."

The second option is "even": "Which . . . we are announcing *even* to you." This is an interesting option. It implies that the action is somehow unexpected, unusual, or otherwise notable (cf. BAGD p. 393, §II.2). This meaning would be particularly fitting, for example, if John's original readers were Gentiles. The thought is: "We apostles have borne eyewitness testimony of these things to the Palestinian Jews, but now I, representing the apostles, bear witness and announce these things *even* to you Gentiles." This is an attractive and plausible interpretation which will have repercussions for our interpretation of other passages such as 1 John 2:2 (*q.v.*).

1:3d. There is no mystery to ἵνα and the subjunctive verb, ἔχητε[14]; this is clearly a purpose clause (cf. *Primer* §22.6). A purpose clause indicates an intended result.

1:3e. ὑμεῖς is plain and simple like most nominatives; it functions as the subject of a verb (*Sketch* §22). However, ἔχητε does not require the nominative personal pronoun ὑμεῖς. The personal pronoun can be said to be "implied, 'embedded,' as it were in the verb" (Wallace, p. 38). Why then did John express ὑμεῖς if it was not needed by ἔχητε? The answer is that ὑμεῖς was used for some kind of emphasis. The Gentile idea makes the emphasis explicable: ". . . in order that *even you* (Gentiles) might have fellowship. . . ."

1:3f. For **καὶ** ἡ κοινωνία **δέ** compare these translations: "*And* our fellowship . . ." (NIV); "*And truly* our fellowship . . ." (KJV; NKJV; NRSV); "*And indeed* our fellowship . . ." (NASB). Whence comes "truly" or "indeed"? And why does the NIV not use either? BDF (§447[9]) is not a great help, for they render it only as "and also," which does not quite fit our context. The answer is that καί sometimes introduces a clause which explains or expands upon a previous point: ". . . in order that you also might have fellowship with us, *and, as a matter of fact,* our fellowship is with the Father and with his Son (implying that your fellowship will be with them too)."[15]

> Quite often interpreters identify a form as "emphatic" and stop there; but you must go further. *There are different kinds of emphasis.* One of the most common is to bring out the contrast between two parties or subjects: ἐγὼ ἐβάπτισα ὑμᾶς ὕδατι, **αὐτὸς** δὲ βαπτίσει ὑμᾶς ἐν πνεύματι ἁγίῳ, "I baptized you with water, but in contrast, *He* will baptize you with the Holy Spirit" (Mark 1:8). There is also emphasis to provide the focal point of the statement, or to demonstrate an author's deep conviction. Another function for an emphatic nominative pronoun is to stress the personal involvement of the subject, especially when it was unexpected: ὁ πέμψας με πατὴρ **αὐτός** μοι ἐντολὴν δέδωκεν, "the Father who sent me has *himself personally* (contrary to your expectations) given me a command" (John 12:49). *Don't settle for merely saying that something is emphatic"!*

1:3g. ἡ κοινωνία δὲ ἡ ἡμετέρα μετὰ τοῦ πατρὸς is a predicate sentence with an implied "is" (ἐστίν): "Our fellowship *is* with the Father."

---

[14]ἔχω P A S 2 pl.

[15]BAGD calls this the "explicative" and "ascensive" in meaning of καί (p. 393, I.3 and again in II.2). B. F. Westcott says: "The δέ serves as the conjunction, while καί emphasizes the words to which it is attached" (p. 12).

1:3h. With κοινωνίαν . . . ἡ κοινωνία we have the article of previous reference (*Sketch* §3). A translation which uses the English demonstrative pronoun brings out the reference: "fellowship . . . *this* fellowship. . . ."

1:3i. Why didn't John write: ἡ κοινωνία **ἡμῶν** instead of using ἡμετέρα? It turns out that ἡμέτερος occurs only eight times in the New Testament (two occurrences are textually uncertain) and only twice in John's epistles, so the word is not very common. Perhaps John used this unusual term to heighten the contrast between "your" and "our." To highlight contrasts is a common use of emphasis in Greek (see the box attached to note 1:3e). In English we might underline or italicize words for emphasis. But remember that in John's day the Greek text would have looked like this:

ΙΝΑΚΑΙΥΜΕΙΣΚΟΙΝΩΝΙΑΝΕΧΗΤΕΜΕΘΗΜΩΝ
ΚΑΙΗΚΟΙΝΩΝΙΑΔΕΗΗΜΕΤΕΡΑΜΕΤΑΤΟΥΠΑΤΡΟΣ

Spotting emphatic words and constructions in Greek is often important for insightful exegesis. Read carefully and learn to identify and reflect upon them.

1:3j. Does μετὰ τοῦ υἱοῦ αὐτοῦ mean "with the Son *himself*" (taking αὐτοῦ as adjectival and intensive, modifying the noun υἱοῦ), or merely "with *his* Son" (taking αὐτοῦ as a personal pronoun)? I prefer the second interpretation, but it is important to develop the skill of identifying possible alternative renderings nevertheless. Recall from *Sketch* §5 that the article with the personal pronoun is normal: **τοῦ** υἱοῦ **αὐτοῦ**.

1:3k. The words Ἰησοῦ Χριστοῦ are in apposition with υἱοῦ. In English we can explicitly state apposition by adding "namely": "and with his Son, *namely*, Jesus Christ." Notice that the personal name Ἰησοῦ here does not have an article. This is normal; however, remember that the article can be found with proper names in Greek (*Sketch* §7).

1 John 1:4

1:4a. ἡμεῖς[16] is the subject nominative of the verb γράφομεν even though it follows the verb. Word placement in Greek is more flexible than in English and often functioned to express emphasis or focus (see the box at §1:3e above).

1:4b. In the phrase ἡ χαρὰ ἡμῶν, there is another textual variation with ἡμῶν and ὑμῶν similar to the one noted under note 1:4a. This is a common variation found in the manuscripts (mss.). Do we expect the article in this phrase (**ἡ** χαρὰ ἡμῶν)? Why or why not? Review *Sketch* §5.

1:4c. The two words, ᾖ πεπληρωμένη, create one verbal idea. This is a periphrastic use of the participle in conjunction with εἰμί; both words can be parsed as one: Pf P S 3 sg.[17] (For periphrastics see *Primer* §21.6.[18]) The periphrastic construction was the most common way to express a perfect passive subjunctive in Koine Greek. John 16:24 says: αἰτεῖτε καὶ λήμψεσθε, ἵνα ἡ χαρὰ ὑμῶν ᾖ πεπληρωμένη. Has this passage influenced the reading in 1 John 1:4 perhaps?

---

[16]Many manuscripts have ὑμῖν, "to you," in place of ἡμεῖς (Aᶜ, C, 1739, 𝔐). As is often the case, this textual variation does not significantly alter the meaning of the verse.

[17]ᾖ—εἰμί P A S 3 sg, see *Primer* §§22.2, 4; πεπληρωμένη—πληρόω Pf P Ptc f n sg (agreeing with χαρά), see *Primer* §21.2.

[18]Cf. Wallace, pp. 647–49; Young, pp. 161-62; BDF §352.

The Article II

Vocabulary

ἀγγελία, ἡ, message (cf. ἄγγελος)
ἀδικία, ἡ, unrighteousness
ἀναγγέλλω, I am announcing, reporting (cf. ἀπαγγέλλω)
ἀνάστασις, –εως, ἡ, resurrection (*Anastasia*; cf. ἀνίστημι)
γενεά, ἡ, generation; family (*genealogy*)
δεύτερος, –α, –ον, second (*Deuteron*omy)
δέω, I am binding (cf. δεῖ)
διέρχομαι, I am going through; I am spreading
ἐπιγινώσκω, I understand, know well
εὐλογέω, I am blessing (*eulogy*)
θαυμάζω, I am amazed; I am surprised (*thauma*turgic)
θλῖψις, –εως, ἡ, tribulation, affliction
καθαρίζω, I am cleansing (*catharsis*)
κατοικέω, I am living, dwelling (cf. οἰκία, οἶκος)
ναός, ὁ, sanctuary, temple
ὅμοιος, –α, –ον, similar, like (*homeo*morphic)
ὁμολογέω, I am confessing, professing
πλανάω, I am deceiving (*planet*)
σκοτία, ἡ, darkness (*scotopia*)
σκότος, –ους, τό, darkness (cf. σκοτία)
σπέρμα, σπέρματος, τό, seed (*sperm*; cf. σπείρω)
σωτηρία, ἡ, salvation; health (*soteriology*; cf. σῴζω)
φωνέω, I am calling (*phone*; cf. φωνή)
ψεύδομαι, I am lying (*pseudo*)
ψεύστης, –ου, ὁ, liar (cf. ψεύδομαι)

Overview

We conclude the sketch of Greek article and anarthrous usage in this lesson. The *Syntax Sketch* discusses several "canons" of article usage which have often been understood far too mechanically by all manner of Greek students. In the *Sketch*, I suggest reading Daniel Wallace's treatment of the "canons" in his *Greek Grammar Beyond the Basics*. Actually, this should be required reading for every Greek student. Learn to treat such "rules" of grammar as guidelines which directed a writer's normal pattern of usage; however, such rules normally allowed for variations and exceptions, especially when conflicting situations arose. Notice the section of the *Syntax Sketch* marked "Conflicts of Interest" for examples of the latter.

Reading Notes

1 John 1:5

1:5a. Parse αὕτη.[1]

1:5b. In the abstract, αὕτη can be considered the subject of a predicate sentence; ἡ ἀγγελία would be the predicate nominative (cf. *Primer* §10.4). We would render: "*This* is the message. . . ." However, if John had intended this, the word order would probably be: αὕτη ἐστὶν ἡ ἀγγελία, as found in 1 John 3:11. Much more likely, αὕτη functions as an attributive modifying ἡ ἀγγελία, "*This* message is (that) which we have heard. . . ."

1:5c. Here, ἡ ἀγγελία is obviously articular because the reference is specific (*Sketch* §2). It is not any message, but *the* message "which we have heard from him."

1:5d. Don't confuse the relative pronoun ἥν[2] with ἦν.[3] What is the antecedent of ἥν in this verse? Must a relative pronoun agree with its antecedent in gender? number? case? See *Primer* §24.5.

1:5e. See note 1:1f above for ἀκηκόαμεν.

1:5f. The variation between ἀναγγέλλομεν here and ἀπαγγέλλομεν in v. 3 is simply a matter of style. An author may make slight changes simply to avoid monotony. We grammarians call this by its Latin name, *variatio*. You may too.

1:5g. While it is abstractly possible that John used ὅτι as the causal conjunction "because" here, it would be difficult to justify in this context. After a verb of speaking like ἀναγγέλλομεν, we should more naturally regard ὅτι as the marker for indirect discourse: "We are announcing *that* God is light." I prefer the term "content clause" for this function, since the clause marked by "that" expresses the *content* of the announcing (see also Wallace, p. 678).

1:5h. The article use and non-use with ὁ θεός and φῶς follows the pattern of "Colwell's canon" (*Sketch* §17), because it is a predicate nominative noun which precedes the copulative verb ἐστιν. Notice, though, that in this case the *quality* of the noun's referent is foremost: "God is *light*," not, "God is *the* light." Colwell's canon implies that a predicate nominative preceding the copulative *may* be definite, not that it *must* be so.

1:5i. Here σκοτία is anarthrous to focus upon its quality (review *Sketch* §18). Reflect upon the meaning of this sentence if John had used the article (ἡ σκοτία).

1:5j. To develop an ability to read Greek in a literalistic manner has some advantage: "And darkness in him not is there none at all." This makes difficult reading in English, but it brings out

---

[1] οὗτος, αὕτη, τοῦτο f n sg (the demonstrative pronoun); compare the personal pronoun αὐτή (see *Primer* §16.2 and §§17.2–3).

[2] ὅς, ἥτις, ὅ f a sg.

[3] εἰμί Impf A I 3 sg.

9

the emphatic character of the two negatives οὐκ and οὐδεμία: "There is none whatsoever"; "There's no darkness in him. None!" For a double negative used for emphasis see BDF §431.

Of course, οὐδεμία[4] is used adjectivally to modify σκοτία (f n sg), "*No darkness* in him. . . ." It is separated from the noun for emphasis. The emphasis here functions to express the author's strong conviction in the assertion (cf. the box attached to note 1:3e on emphasis).

> "*In him is no darkness at all.* John very often uses this way of speaking to amplify by a contrary negation what he has affirmed. Hence the meaning is that God is light in such a way that He admits no darkness." John Calvin

1:5k. If we translate this clause: "In him there is no darkness at all" (NASB; NIV), you may wonder where "there" comes from in the basic statement: "*there* is no darkness." This is simply the requirements of English in an impersonal predicate statement, which asserts or denies the *existence* of something: "There is A" or "There is no A" means "A exists" or "A does not exist." (The other main kind of predication states or denies the *equivalence* of two things: "A is B"; "A is not B.") In English, "there" functions technically as the subject of these predicate statements, but Greek does not need any such a word, because the verb ἐστίν itself communicates its third person subject in its personal ending (as εἰμί communicates its *first* person subject and εἶ its *second* person subject).

1 John 1:6

1:6a. The structure of John's paragraph becomes clearer again when we notice the repetition of the central verbs and their constructions:

> THEME: God is light; therefore: (1:5)
> a ἐὰν εἴπωμεν . . . ψευδόμεθα [negative] (1:6)
> b ἐὰν ἐν τῷ φωτὶ περιπατῶμεν [positive] (1:7)
> a ἐὰν εἴπωμεν . . . ἑαυτοὺς πλανῶμεν [negative] (1:8)
> b ἐὰν ὁμολογῶμεν [positive] (1:9)
> a ἐὰν εἴπωμεν . . . ψεύστην ποιοῦμεν αὐτόν [negative] (1:10)
> PURPOSE OF EPISTLE II: γράφω ὑμῖν ἵνα . . . (2:1)

John organizes his thought here around five future conditions (ἐάν . . .) which alternate in an *a b a b a* pattern. The *a* members refer to negative, deceptive professions of faith, and the *b* members are the positive alternatives.

1:6b. Parse εἴπωμεν[5] and περιπατῶμεν.[6]

1:6c. At some point, you will need to consider what guides an author's motive for choosing to use the present or aorist subjunctive. For now, simply notice that εἴπωμεν is aorist and περιπατῶμεν is present. The nature of each action directed his choice, but that's another study.

---

[4]οὐδείς, οὐδεμία, οὐδέν, f n sg.

[5]λέγω 2A A S 1 pl.

[6]περιπατέω P A S 1 pl. See also ὁμολογῶμεν (ὁμολογέω P A S 1 pl) in v. 9.

1:6d. John expressed περιπατῶμεν in its subjunctive form, because it is parallel with ἐὰν εἴπωμεν. Like English, one can leave out certain words in Greek if they are clearly implied by the context. The thought is: ἐὰν εἴπωμεν . . . καὶ (ἐὰν) περιπατῶμεν, "If we say . . . and (if) we are walking. . . ." The two verbs in this clause are part of the apodosis of the future conditional statement (cf. *Primer* §22.6; BDF §§371[4], 373). (The "if clause" is called the *protasis*.)

1:6e. Parse σκότει.[7]

1:6f. Did John express σκότει with the article (ἐν **τῷ** σκότει) because of previous reference to σκοτία in v. 5 (*Sketch* §3)? In this case a paraphrase could read: "we are walking in *that darkness* (of which God has no part)." Or is this a case of article use with an abstract noun in Greek which is not translated in English (*Sketch* §6): "we are walking in *darkness*." You decide!

1:6g. To translate οὐ ποιοῦμεν τὴν ἀλήθειαν as, "We are not doing the truth," is not very clear, because "truth" is not something one generally "does." We *believe* the truth, *know* it, *seek* it, etc., but how does one "do" it? Similarly, this phrase would make little sense to a pagan Greek. John's meaning can only be understood when one looks to the Hebrew Old Testament and its Greek translation, the Septuagint (LXX). ποιέω τὴν ἀλήθειαν is a Hebrew idiom, corresponding to: אֱמֶת־עָשָׂה, "practice or show (covenantal) fidelity." See the following LXX passages:

- ἱκανοῦταί μοι . . . ἀπὸ πάσης **ἀληθείας** ἧς **ἐποίησας** τῷ παιδί σου, "I am not worthy . . . of all the fidelity you have shown toward your servant" (Gen. 32:11 in LXX; v. 10 in English).

- **ποιήσεις** ἐπʼ ἐμὲ ἐλεημοσύνην καὶ **ἀλήθειαν**, "Please show mercy and fidelity to me" (Gen. 47:29). See the context, which is the taking of an oath, a type of covenantal arrangement.

- ὁ ἀσεβής . . . **ἀλήθειαν** οὐ μὴ **ποιήσῃ**, "The impious . . . in no way practices (covenantal) fidelity" (Isa. 26:10).

This phrase shows that the study of words individually is sometimes inadequate. One must often study not individual words but *phrases* as a group. Consider, for example, the meaning of this English statement: "The hood *played it cool* until the squad car went by." "To play it cool" is a colloquial expression meaning that the subject "assumed a nonchalant or innocent manner," but someone studying English could not determine that meaning for this phrase by doing a word study on the verb "to play," the adjective "cool," or the pronoun "it" independently. The whole must be studied as a phrase.

1 John 1:7

1:7a. Recall that δέ is a postpositive conjunction which is placed second (or later) in its clause. Cf. *Primer* Glossary ("postpositive"); BDF §475.

1:7b. Parse φωτί[8] and αἷμα.[9]

---

[7] σκότος n d sg. A third declension variation following the ἔθνος pattern; see *Primer* §12.2.

[8] φῶς n d sg; cf. *Primer* §11.3.

[9] αἷμα n n sg. The form could be accusative as well (cf. πνεῦμα in *Primer* §11.2), but αἷμα functions as the subject of καθαρίζει here.

1:7c. You learned that when a personal pronoun like αὐτός[10] is expressed in the nominative case, it marks some sort of stress or emphasis (*Primer* §16.5; BDF §277[11]). That is true with most verbs. However, with εἰμί and other copulative verbs the nominative pronoun occurs frequently without any emphasis. The author simply felt that the subject of the predicate statement was best expressed to avoid any potential confusion. Hence, this expression may or may not have some minor stress: "As *he* (personally) is in the light"; or simply, "As *he* is in the light" (no stress). Please note this point of style now, because you will not find it in our reference grammars.

1:7d. ἀλλήλων is a reciprocal pronoun, "one another." "It expresses a mutual action, relationship, or interchange between persons" (Young, p. 79) ; see *Primer* §24.6; cf. BDF §287 for synonymous constructions.

1:7e. In the phrase, τὸ αἷμα Ἰησοῦ[12] τοῦ υἱοῦ αὐτοῦ, think about the article usage. Why didn't John write τὸ αἷμα **τοῦ** Ἰησοῦ? (Cf. *Sketch* §7.) And is the article expected with the possessive pronoun in **τοῦ** υἱοῦ αὐτοῦ? (*Sketch* §5). Ὑιός was put into the genitive in this phrase because it is in apposition with another word which happens to be genitive (Ἰησοῦ). Words in apposition are regularly placed in the same case. We will cover apposition more fully in the next lesson (on 1 John 2:1).

1:7f. Does ἀπὸ πάσης ἁμαρτίας mean, "from all sin" or "from every sin"? Is there a difference in meaning? See this OT statement: καθαρίσαι ὑμᾶς **ἀπὸ πασῶν τῶν ἁμαρτιῶν ὑμῶν** ἔναντι κυρίου (Lev. 16:30; cf. Ps. 18:14 and 50:4).

1 John 1:8

1:8a. The translation, "If we say that we have *no sin*" (e.g., NASB), renders the Greek into idiomatic English. (English-like οὐδεμίαν ἁμαρτίαν ἔχομεν is possible in Greek also.) More woodenly, the Greek reads: "We do not have sin"; the verb rather than the noun is negatived. You will observe this phenomenon often in Greek translation. There is no special emphasis, Greek simply has a different way of expressing the idea.

1:8b. Here the anarthrous noun ἁμαρτίαν is obviously the opposite of an articular noun referring to something specific: "We do not have *sin* (in general)" (see *Sketch* §18).

1:8c. Don't confuse indicative πλανῶμεν[13] with its subjunctive form (also πλανῶμεν [see *Primer* §22.5]). The only way to decide on the correct parsing here is from the context. A subjunctive by itself here would have a hortatory sense: "Let us deceive ourselves," which is clearly *not* what John intended!

---

[10]αὐτός, αὐτή, αὐτό 3 n sg.

[11]BDF §277(4) mentions "oblique cases"—the "oblique cases" are the non-nominative cases (genitive, dative, accusative, and vocative).

[12]Ἰησοῦς m g sg; see *Primer* §28.2.

[13]πλανάω P A I 1 pl; cf. *Primer* §§6.2–3.

1 John 1:9

1:9a. The word order and form of expression of this clause puts some stress upon δίκαιος. Other possible ways to express John's idea in Greek without stress would be: ἐστιν πιστὸς καὶ δίκαιος, or πιστὸς καὶ δίκαιος ἐστιν. Even αὐτός ἐστιν πιστὸς καὶ δίκαιος has no particular stress or emphasis, considering what was said earlier about a personal pronoun used with a copulative verb (see note 1:7c). In this case the emphasis functions to place special *focus* upon δίκαιος for the reader's attention. Why did John place the focus on this word?

1:9b. ἵνα clauses are used to express one of three main ideas: purpose, result, or content. We have already noticed a purpose clause in v. 3 (note 1:3d), and we will describe content clauses later. Here, the ἵνα can only be regarded as a *result* clause (and therefore the equivalent of ὥστε + infinitive in Greek [cf. *Primer* §25.6; Wallace, p. 677; Young, pp. 169–71; BDF §391]. To take this ἵνα clause as expressing *purpose* would be to say that the reason why God is "faithful and just" is with the intention of forgiving our sins. Now, that is truly God's intention, but that is not *why* God is faithful and just. Here John is expressing *result* not an intended result (i.e., purpose): As a result of God's fidelity and justice, he forgives our sins. Forgiveness results from God's character.

> "It is very important to be quite sure that when we have sinned there is a reconciliation with God ready and prepared for us. Otherwise we shall always carry hell about within us."
> John Calvin

Verse 9 is one of the more profound statements in the New Testament, and the Reformation doctrine of imputed righteousness is necessarily implied. Why? Why is God's *justice* mentioned in connection with forgiveness of sins—not his *mercy*? Sometimes the mere reading of a familiar passage *in Greek* allows one to see such profundity for the first time, whereas we tend to read our own language too quickly to observe the obvious. As Holmes would tell Watson: "You *see*, but you do not *observe!* The facts were before you the whole time."

1:9c. One key to parsing the forms of ἀφίημι correctly consists of spotting whether the stem has an iota or not: ἀφίη would be the present subjunctive form (notice the ἵνα; you expect a subjunctive after it) (see *Primer* §27.3). The form here, ἀφῇ, has no iota and is therefore aorist.[14]

1:9d. Parse ἡμῖν.[15]

1:9e. The dative of the personal pronoun, ἡμῖν, is used here to identify either the group who has a "special interest" in the action or who gains "advantage" from it (*Sketch* §§54–55).

1:9f. For τὰς ἁμαρτίας, the article functions in place of a possessive pronoun: *"our* sins" (review *Sketch* §11). To repeat the genitive pronoun here: ἡμῖν τὰς ἁμαρτίας **ἡμῶν**, would be clumsy and repetitious, so the article was used with that meaning as a more elegant option. (Some ancient Greek manuscripts do have ἡμῶν here; e.g., ℵ, C, Ψ, 81, and 614.)

1:9g. The subjunctive καθαρίσῃ[16] is parallel with ἵνα ἀφῇ, so it is a second result clause (cf. note 1:9c above). The idea is: ἵνα ἀφῇ καὶ **ἵνα** καθαρίσῃ. The second ἵνα is clearly perceived from context, so John felt no need to repeat it. Such ellipsis is common in many languages.

---

[14] ἀφίημι A A S 3 sg; see *Primer* p. 240 (Paradigms).

[15] ἐγώ 1 d pl; cf. *Primer* §16.2.

[16] καθαρίζω A A S 3 sg. Note the ζ changing to σ in the simple stem; see *Primer* §7.4.

1 John 1:10

1:10a. This is the last of the five ἐάν clauses that shape this paragraph (cf. note 1:6a above). Recall that 1 John was originally written without any spaces between words or indentations to mark new paragraphs like English. The repetition of words and ideas served to delineate complete ideas into what we would call paragraphs.

1:10b. Parse ἡμαρτήκαμεν.[17]

1:10c. The subtle difference between ἁμαρτίαν οὐκ ἔχομεν (v. 1:8) and οὐχ ἡμαρτήκαμεν in this verse should be noted. Stephen Smalley writes, "It is difficult to see any real difference between the affirmations 'we are sinless' (v 8) and 'we have not sinned' (v 10)" (p. 33), but I cannot agree, primarily because "we have not sinned," although the best English equivalent for οὐχ ἡμαρτήκαμεν, is still not the exact equivalent. The Greek perfect used with a verb like ἁμαρτάνω expressed not only the fact that the act was completed but that there is some implied consequence as well. In this case, οὐχ ἡμαρτήκαμεν says: "We have not committed sin (and thereby have not incurred any guilt)." On the other hand, ἁμαρτίαν οὐκ ἔχομεν in v. 8 merely points to the current condition: "We have no sin (now)," or perhaps "We are not at fault," but says nothing about liability to past lawless acts. (John equates sin with ἀνομία, "lawlessness" in 1 John 3:4. He used ἁμαρτία to refer to a discrete violation of God's commands rather than to a miasmic stain.)

1:10d. Some verbs like ποιοῦμεν[18] here take two accusatives (*Sketch* §30).[19] Now, no one can actually turn God into a liar, so it is best to see this as a hypothetical or intended action. Render the phrase as, "Make him out to be a liar"; or, "Make him (appear) to be a liar."

1:10e. In v. 8, John had stated that the false Christians did not have the truth in them. Is the earlier statement synonymous with what he says here in v. 10? Note this verse's remarkable implications for the biblical doctrine of sin ("Hamartology").

---

[17]ἁμαρτάνω Pf A I 1 pl.

[18]ποιέω P A I 1 pl; cf. *Primer* §6.2.

[19]A double nominative may be used if the verb is passive: ἐτέθην ἐγὼ κῆρυξ, "I was appointed as a herald" (1 Tim. 2:7; 2 Tim. 1:11) (cf. Zerwick §72).

Nominative, Vocative, and Accusative

REVIEW:	*Primer* Lessons 28, 30
READ:	*Syntax Sketch* §§21–34
STUDY:	1 John 2:1–6

Vocabulary

ἀληθῶς, truly (cf. ἀλήθεια)
ἄξιος, –α, –ον, worthy (*axiom*)
ἐργάζομαι, I am working (*ergo*nomic; cf. ἔργον)
ἑτοιμάζω, I am preparing
ἱλασμός, ὁ, propitiation
καινός, –ή, –όν, new, different
κλαίω, I am weeping
μέρος, –ους, τό, part, portion (poly*merous*)
μισέω, I hate (*mis*anthropy)
μνημεῖον, τό, monument, grave (*mnemonics*)
οἰκοδομέω, I am building; I am edifying (cf. οἶκος)
ὀλίγος, –η, –ον, little, small, few (*olig*archy)
ὀφείλω, I ought; I owe
πάντοτε, always
παράκλητος, ὁ, advocate; helper (cf. παρακαλέω)
παρίστημι, I am presenting, approaching
πάσχω, I am suffering, experiencing (*Paschal*)
σήμερον, today
τεκνίον, τό, dear child, little child (diminutive of τέκνον)
τελειόω, I am completing, fulfilling (cf. τέλος)
τέλος, –ους, τό, end, goal; tax (*telic*)
τέσσαρες, –α, four (masculine and feminine share the –ες ending) (*tetra*gonal)
τιμή, ἡ, honor; value
χωρίς + gen., apart from, besides (prep.)

Overview

This lesson covers the main uses of three cases: nominative, vocative, and accusative. The nominative functions the vast majority of times to express the subject of any verb or the predicate with a copulative verb. The other uses of the nominative are much less common. The vocative is used exclusively in direct address, so it is easy to learn. Of the three cases covered in this lesson, the accusative is the most flexible. It is most often used for the direct object of a verb, but you will find its other functions used periodically in the Greek NT.

15

Reading Notes

1 John 2:1

2:1a. As you already learned, Greek nouns modified by a genitive pronoun are usually articular (**τοῖς** ὀφθαλμοῖς ἡμῶν, **αἱ** χεῖρες ἡμῶν, κτλ.). Why, then, doesn't τεκνία μου have an article? The answer is that τεκνία is in the vocative case, and there is no vocative form for the article.[1] Compare the nominative case used as a vocative, which is always articular (*Sketch* §24).

2:1b. Earlier, John had used the first person plural, "*we* are announcing" (1:3, 5) and "*we* are writing" (1:4). "[T]he plural can stand for *one* person" (BDF §141) much like in English usage. Hence, the singular verb γράφω here and the plural verbs earlier may both refer to John alone.

2:1c. ταῦτα, like most substantives in the accusative case, acts as the direct object of a verb (here, γράφω) (see *Sketch* §29).

2:1d. Parse ἀμάρτητε.[2]

2:1e. We saw ἵνα used above to express result (note 1:9b). Here ἵνα introduces a purpose clause; the author's *intended* result is being expressed. John intends something to happen as a result of another action (his writing).

This ἵνα clause takes a subjunctive verb (ἀμάρτητε) as is normal.[3] See especially *Primer* §22.7 for the important distinction between the subjunctive as an *indefinite* action rather than an *uncertain* action. A purpose clause is "indefinite," because it is future from the relative time of the main verb: "I am writing to you in order that (after you read this letter) you might not commit sin." There is a slight imperative note to John's statement implied here: "You should not commit sin."

2:1f. The inspired writer was a realist—God is too, by the way—so John mentions our recourse in the case of sinful failures: ἐάν τις ἀμάρτῃ. . . . Ἐάν, as you learned in the *Primer* (§22.6), marks a future conditional construction, one of the main uses of the subjunctive mood verb. If the condition is fulfilled in the future, then the result follows. In the majority of future conditions, the subjunctive verb in the protasis was expressed in its *aorist* subjunctive form, as here with ἀμάρτῃ.[4] Remember: an aorist subjunctive does not necessarily refer to a *past* event; it is a "simple" event, or has some other nuance. Also notice that the "indefinite" idea for the subjunctive is clearly communicated in combination with the indefinite pronoun τις,[5] "If *anyone* commits sin. . . ." The subject is not definite or specific.

---

[1]τεκνίον n v pl. See *Sketch* §26 for the vocative forms.

[2]ἀμαρτάνω 2A A S 2 pl. Note the *stem change* for the second aorist ἀμάρτητε. (Cf. λάβητε in *Primer* §22.2.) The present subjunctive is ἀμαρτάνητε.

[3]Also notice that the negative used for the subjunctive ἀμάρτητε is μή rather than οὐ. Recall that οὐ(κ) is used almost exclusively with indicative mood verbs and μή with verbs in other moods.

[4]ἀμαρτάνω 2A A S 3 sg. Cf. note 2 above.

[5]τις, τι m n sg. Compare the accented interrogative pronoun τίς; "Who?" (*Primer* §17.2).

2:1g. Not all anarthrous nouns in Greek are indefinite. For instance, many which serve as the object of prepositions are definite requiring an English definite article in translation. For instance, ἀπ᾿ ἀρχῆς, "from *the* beginning" (1 John 1:1; cf. *Sketch* §19). In the case of παράκλητον, however, this noun is best rendered indefinitely, "a paraclete," since we have more than one Paraclete (see John 14:16) (*Sketch* §18).

2:1h. παράκλητον ἔχομεν. . . forms the apodosis of the future conditional sentence (above note 2:1f). Apodoseis (plural of apodosis) can be any number of statements: a statement of what will result after the condition is met ("If anyone commits sin, *he will die.*"); an imperative ("If anyone commits sin, *let him confess!*"); an explanation of the reason why the condition was fulfilled ("If anyone commits sin, *he is not a true disciple.*"); or any number of other ideas. Frequently, the apodosis is a resulting action as in the first example. Here, however, Jesus is not an advocate as a result of someone sinning. He presumably has this function before such sin occurs, so John's statement needs some slight expansion to clarify his point. We could paraphrase: "If anyone commits sin, let him confess and trust in Jesus Christ the Righteous One, for he is our Advocate with the Father." The apodosis as John expressed it serves as the reason for hope should the condition be met.

2:1i. παράκλητος is an excellent subject for a word study. Start with BAGD p. 618.

2:1j. Parse Ἰησοῦν.[6]

2:1k. Ἰησοῦν Χριστόν are in apposition with παράκλητον here. See the accompanying box for explanation and notes 1:3i and 1:7e above for other examples of apposition.

2:1l. δίκαιον is an attributive adjective in Greek (cf. *Primer* §10.5). Its position in the word order carries slight emphasis in order to make it clear that the effectiveness of Jesus as Paraclete with the Father is his righteousness—rather than, say, his oratorical skills. A word order with less stress would be δίκαιον Ἰησοῦν Χριστόν. English translations usually turn this attributive adjective into a substantive, and put it in apposition to the proper name: "Jesus Christ, the Righteous One" (NIV). This is probably an attempt to bring out the stress in the original and seems a good option to me. It does show that we cannot be slavishly wooden in translation.

> APPOSITION. Two or more words, referring to the same person or thing, are said to be "in apposition." The second word or group of words adds further information to the word(s) with which they are in apposition. For example: "I want you to meet my *friend, John.*" "Friend" and "John" are in apposition; they refer to the same person, and "John" adds further information to "friend." Or, "He was speaking to *her, a Samaritan woman*"; "her" and "a Samaritan woman" are in apposition. You can test whether Greek words are in apposition by adding the English word "namely" to your translation. For example: "We have *an Advocate* with the Father, (namely) *Jesus Christ the righteous.*" In Greek, the words in apposition are put into the same case (but there are a few exceptions to this rule—Baugh's Law #3 strikes again; see *Primer*, §23.8).

1 John 2:2

2:2a. Recall that a personal pronoun in the nominative case (αὐτός here) in a predicate statement need not always be emphatic (cf. *Sketch* §67 and note 1:7c).

---

[6]Ἰησοῦς m a sg; cf. *Primer* §28.2.

2:2b. In αὐτὸς ἱλασμός ἐστιν, which word is the subject nominative and which the predicate? See Wallace, pp. 42–46 for discussion of factors bearing on this question.

2:2c. We saw that the anarthrous noun παράκλητος in v. 1 was indefinite in meaning (note 2:1g). Here in v. 2, though, most translations take anarthrous ἱλασμός as definite, supplying "the" in English. To render as, "He is *a* propitiation" would suggest that others exist also, something out of accord with the rest of Scripture. Why then didn't John write ὁ ἱλασμός? The answer is found in the word order: a predicate noun which precedes the copulative verb is usually anarthrous even if it is definite. Do you remember what "canon" this is? (*Sketch* §17).

2:2d. Parse μόνον[7] and explain the use of its case (*Sketch* §32).

2:2e. The combination οὐ μόνον . . . ἀλλὰ καί, "not only . . . but also" or "not only . . . but even," occurs when an author wants to express the inclusion of an idea (cf. BDF §448[1]). It is particularly effective rhetorically when the item included is unexpected, important for a complete viewpoint, or otherwise notable. For example, "*Not only* was he breaking the Sabbath, *but* he was *even* saying that God was his own Father" (John 5:18). You will find οὐ μόνον . . . ἀλλὰ καί fairly often in Paul's letters; for example, the construction occurs ten times in Romans.

2:2f. One of the general characteristics of Koine Greek is the heavy employment of prepositional phrases where earlier Greek writers would have used nouns in various unadorned cases. For instance, the first two uses of περί in v. 2 (**περὶ** τῶν ἁμαρτιῶν ἡμῶν . . . **περὶ** τῶν ἡμετέρων) might have been expressed as simple accusatives (τὰς ἁμαρτίας ἡμῶν . . . τὰς ἡμετέρας). This would be the accusative of "respect" which you just learned (*Sketch* §31). Similarly, the last περί phrase, **περὶ** ὅλου τοῦ κόσμου, could have been expressed as a simple dative, possibly expressing advantage: ὅλῳ τῷ κόσμῳ, "*for the benefit of* the entire world" (look ahead to *Sketch* §55).

2:2g. We discussed the uncommon possessive adjective ἡμέτερος on v. 1:3 above (see note 1:3i). 1 John 1:3 and 2:2 are the only places where this word occurs in John's writings. Why? John's normal style would be to repeat the noun with the article serving in place of the possessive pronoun as in v. 1:9: ἐὰν ὁμολογῶμεν τὰς ἁμαρτίας **ἡμῶν** . . . τὰς ἁμαρτίας. The latter means "our sins" (note 1:9g). Hence, in 1 John 2:2 we expect: οὐ περὶ **τῶν** ἁμαρτιῶν δὲ μόνον, "not only for *our* sins." Therefore, we must consider why John chose to use the emphatic ἡμέτερος instead of the simpler and more common expression.

In my opinion, John wanted to stress the contrast between himself as a member of the apostolic circle (cf. "*our* fellowship" v. 1:3) in conjunction with his readers ("even you [Gentiles]" 1:3), and any other group of people "far off, as many as the Lord our God should summon to himself" (Acts 2:39). The work of Christ is not restricted to Jews, Greeks, or to any ethnic, social, or racial group. And God's saving activity now is no longer restricted to a tiny nation in Palestine as it was under the old covenant. It extends throughout the whole world, wherever Christ's people are to be found (Acts 18:10) and gathered into his one flock (John 10:16). That is John's point, not that every individual who has ever lived or who will ever live has complete (or potential) propitiation of all their sins. "*We* have a Paraclete. . . ."

---

[7]μόνος, –α, –ον, n a sg.

18

Furthermore, notice that the last prepositional phrase is not parallel with the first two: περὶ τῶν ἁμαρτιῶν ἡμῶν . . . περὶ τῶν ἡμετέρων . . . περὶ ὅλου τοῦ κόσμου. The first relate Christ's propitiatory sacrifice to sins, but the third relates it to "the entire world," not to *the sins* of the entire world. In Greek, the pronominal use of the article would have served to communicate that idea easily: περὶ **τῶν** ὅλου τοῦ κόσμου, "on behalf of *the (sins)* of the entire world" (*Sketch* §14; cf. B. F. Westcott, pp. 44–45).

> "John's purpose was only to make this blessing common to the whole Church. Therefore, under the word 'all' he does not include the reprobate, but refers to all who would believe and those who were scattered through various regions of the earth. For, as is meet, the grace of Christ is really made clear when it is declared to be the only salvation of the world." John Calvin

1 John 2:3

2:3a. The structure of the next major section in 1 John is more involved than the previous two, although it is still dependent upon the repetition of words and forms.

EVIDENCE OF TRUE UNION WITH CHRIST (2:3–6).

a ἐν τούτῳ γινώσκομεν ("thus") (2:3)
 b ὁ λέγων . . . μὴ τηρῶν ψεύστης ἐστίν (2:4)
  c ἐν τούτῳ ("this person") (2:4)
  c ἐν τούτῳ ("this person") (2:5)
a ἐν τούτῳ γινώσκομεν ("thus") (2:5)
 b ὁ λέγων . . . ὀφείλει . . . περιπατεῖν (2:6)
  d οὐκ ἐντολὴν καινήν (2:7)
   e ἐντολὴν παλαιάν
   e ἐντολὴν παλαιάν
  d ἐντολὴν καινήν (2:8)
 b ὁ λέγων . . . μισῶν ἐν τῇ σκοτίᾳ ἐστίν (2:9)
   f ὁ ἀγαπῶν . . . ἐν τῷ φωτί (2:10)
   f ὁ μισῶν . . . ἐν τῇ σκοτίᾳ (2:11)

The meaning of the four occurrences of ἐν τούτῳ in the first section is clarified by this structure. In the *a* sections, ἐν τούτῳ means "in this way" or "thus," and points ahead to the conditional statement which follows, while in the *c* sections the phrase means "in this (person)."

2:3b. Parse ἐγνώκαμεν.[8]

2:3c. Interpreters commonly assume that a word must have the same meaning if it is expressed within the same context. I don't know how many times I've read something like this: "The Greek word 'x' must mean 'y' in English because that is its meaning in the previous verse." However, this is not always true. A word in ancient Greek (as well as in modern languages) may very well have different meanings whether uttered in one breath or not. For example, "Israel" in Paul's statement:

---

[8]γινώσκω Pf A I 1 pl (cf. *Primer* §14.1, review section); compare the aorist ἔγνωμεν (*Primer* §9.2).

"They are not all *Israel* who are of *Israel*" (Rom. 9:6) must have different meanings or what Paul said is nonsense.

We find another example of this phenomenon in 1 John 2:3 where γινώσκομεν refers to a cognitive process and conviction ("we recognize this fact") while ἐγνώκαμεν refers to an interpersonal relationship ("that we have come into league with him").[9] The reader intuitively perceives the shift in meaning from the different objects of the verb: the object of γινώσκομεν is a proposition: ὅτι ἐγνώκαμεν αὐτόν, while ἐγνώκαμεν has personal "him" as its object. Interestingly, this subtle meaning would be communicated in modern English in the statement: "We *know* that we *know* the Lord" since "to know the Lord" is Christian idiom for "to be a disciple of Christ" (not an exclusively cognitive event). Secondly, the change in meaning for γινώσκω is also signaled in part by the shift from the present to the perfect tense form.

2:3d. αὐτόν is the simple direct object of ἐγνώκαμεν in v. 3 (*Sketch* §29).

2:3e. Parse τηρῶμεν.[10]

2:3f. Do not be thrown off by the fact that the protasis follows the apodosis in the future conditional clause in v. 3. John has pointed ahead to the condition with ἐν τούτῳ: "In this way we know . . . (namely) if we keep. . . ."

2:3g. One more time: Is the article expected in the phrase **τὰς** ἐντολὰς αὐτοῦ? (*Sketch* §5).

1 John 2:4

2:4a. The articular participle ὁ λέγων is the substantive use of the participle; see *Primer* §20.7. The present participle[11] is frequently found in this construction for someone's characteristic or common action: "He who goes around saying . . ." "The one who commonly says. . . ." Because λέγων is a verb of speech, it introduces direct or indirect statement. In this case, the statement is a *direct* quotation, because the verb used for the reported statement (ἔγνωκα[12]) is first person. Here ὅτι functions in Greek like quotation marks in English. The editors of the UBS Greek edition (but not the Nestle-Aland) help you to interpret statements as direct speech by capitalizing the first character of direct discourse clauses.

2:4b. Parse τηρῶν.[13]

2:4c. It is possible to take τηρῶν as a substantive participle parallel with ὁ λέγων, meaning: ὁ λέγων . . . καὶ τὰς ἐντολὰς αὐτοῦ (ὁ) μὴ τηρῶν, "The one who says and who does not keep." We saw a similar parallel use with subjunctives in 1 John 1:6 (note 1:6d). But if that were what John meant,

---

[9]For the second meaning, see my brief discussion and the references in "The Biblical Meaning of Foreknowledge" in *The Grace of God, the Bondage of the Will: A Case for Calvinism* (T. Schreiner and B. Ware, eds.; Grand Rapids: Baker, 1995), 183–200.

[10]τηρέω P A S 1 pl; cf. *Primer* §22.4.

[11]λέγω P A Ptc m n sg; cf. *Primer* §19.2.

[12]γινώσκω Pf A I 1 sg.

[13]τηρέω P A Ptc m n sg.

he would probably have put μὴ τηρῶν right after καί, and it would have even been clearer if he had repeated the article. Because of these factors, it is best to take τηρῶν as an *adverbial* participle used to bring out the fact that both the λέγων and the μὴ τηρῶν are contemporaneous events; review *Primer* §20.5. This makes John's point quite clear: it is hypocrites he is describing, those who profess Christ *while at the same time* are not keeping his commandments.

2:4d. Parse ψεύστης.[14]

2:4e. ψεύστης is a predicate nominative noun (*Sketch* §23). Since it is anarthrous and precedes the copulative verb (ἐστίν), it could be considered definite according to Colwell's canon learned earlier (*Sketch* §17): "He is *the* liar" (i.e., the liar of liars). Here, however, ψεύστης is clearly indefinite in meaning: "He is *a* liar." John placed ψεύστης before ἐστίν in this instance for emphasis or focus (cf. BDF §472). Colwell's canon states that definite nouns placed in front of the copulative verb are usually anarthrous. This is subtly different than saying that *all* anarthrous nouns placed in front of the verb are necessarily definite. One must determine the specificity of the noun's referent from context. Colwell has helped show from word position that some anarthrous nouns still have a specific referent.

2:4f. As mentioned above (note 2:3a), ἐν τούτῳ means "in this (person)" here: "He is a liar and the truth is not *in this person*."

1 John 2:5

2:5a. ὃς δ' ἂν τηρῇ is a good example of the indefinite relative clause. The elements are: a relative pronoun with no antecedent (ὅς[15]), the indefinite particle ἄν, and a subjunctive verb (τηρῇ[16]); see *Primer* §§22.1 and 24.6. If you think about it, this construction is actually close in meaning to the substantive participle (ὁ τηρῶν), a construction John uses frequently (e.g., ὁ λέγων in v. 4). The participle with πᾶς is virtually equivalent. The phrase: πᾶς ὁ ποιῶν τὴν ἁμαρτίαν, "Everyone who practices sin" (1 John 3:4) is like ὅς ἂν ποιῇ τὴν ἁμαρτίαν, "Whoever practices sin."

2:5b. With αὐτοῦ τὸν λόγον you see the flexibility of Greek word order: "his word." The genitive pronoun in this type of phrase usually follows the noun it modifies: e.g., αἱ χεῖρες **ἡμῶν**, ἡ χαρὰ **ἡμῶν**, ὁ λόγος **αὐτοῦ**, τὰς ἐντολὰς **αὐτοῦ**, κτλ. Hence, we expect τὸν λόγον **αὐτοῦ** here. It is possible either to see a slight emphasis in the word order or merely John's desire for variety of expression. By the way, the order: τὸν **αὐτοῦ** λόγον is also found in Greek (see BDF §271).

2:5c. It is possible to read ἐν τούτῳ as meaning "in this way," "thus," marking the manner in which the love of God is perfected. However, it does seem better to read it as referring to the individual who keeps God's word, "in this (person)." As I mentioned, the structure of the passage may confirm the second reading, although the whole case is admittedly slightly circular. But sometimes circular interpretation is convincing if it provides the most cohesive explanation of the most evidence.

---

[14]ψεύστης m n sg; see *Primer* §§28.2, 4.

[15]ὅς, ἥτις, ὅ m n sg; cf. *Primer* §24.2.

[16]τηρέω P A S 3 sg.

2:5d. The genitive phrase ἡ ἀγάπη τοῦ θεοῦ is a good example of the ambiguity of the genitive relation. Does this mean, "God's love for us" or "our love for God"? It does make a difference and gives commentators *causa vivendi* (or at least *causa scribendi*). We will come back to this example later.

2:5e. Parse τετελείωται.[17]

2:5f. The English translation "is made complete" (NIV) or "has been perfected" (NASB) does not fully capture the meaning of τετελείωται. We sometimes get into trouble with τελειόω when we apply it to moral perfection. Here the idea is that the individual in question has a genuine and full expression of love instead of mere lip service.

2:5g. See note 2:3f for the ἐν τούτῳ . . . ὅτι construction.

1 John 2:6

2:6a. Verse 6 is a difficult verse to translate, so let me go through it step-by-step. As with *all* Greek sentences, begin with the main verb, which is ὀφείλει, and the subject is the substantive participle, ὁ λέγων (cf. *Primer* §20.7). Thus the core is: "The one who says . . . ought to. . . ."

Now we ask, "What does this person say?" The answer is: ἐν αὐτῷ μένειν, "that he remains in him." This use of the infinitive (indirect discourse) will be examined later. It is the equivalent of: ὅτι ἐν αὐτῷ μένει (cf. *Sketch* §94).

Next we ask, "What is it that ὁ λέγων ought to do?" ὀφείλω takes a complementary infinitive (*Primer* §25.6; *Sketch* §87), and the only infinitive left is the last word in the sentence, περιπατεῖν.[18] So far, then, we translate: "The one who says (that) he remains in him, ought to be walking. . . ." Now the rest of the sentence from καθώς to οὕτως is a discrete comparison clause and a reiteration of the subject of the main verb, so we finish our translation: "The one who says (that) he remains in him, ought to be walking just as he walked, so also he (ought to walk)." Easy! Well. . . . Perhaps this illustrates why you need to study Greek syntax so hard!

2:6b. It might be tempting to regard καὶ αὐτός as a hanging nominative (*Sketch* §25), but it is in reality simply a way to stress the personal involvement of the subject in the preceding action (περιεπάτησεν): "as that one walked—even as *he* personally walked, mind you."

---

[17]τελειόω Pf P I 3 sg (the ω in –ωται is lengthening of the contract vowel in the perfect passive form (like πληρόω [πεπλήρωμαι]). See the principal parts of τελειόω in Trenchard, p. 270.

[18]περιπατέω P A Inf.

The Genitive I

REVIEW: *Primer*, Lessons 4–6
READ: *Syntax Sketch* §§35–43
STUDY: 1 John 2:7–14

Vocabulary

ἀληθινός, –ή, –όν, true, genuine (cf. ἀληθής)
ἄρτι, now, just (adverb)
ἄρχων, –οντος, ὁ, ruler (*arch*bishop; cf. ἄρχω)
βούλομαι, I want, wish
διάβολος, ὁ, Devil (*diabolical*)
διακονέω, I am serving (*deacon*)
δικαιόω, I am justifying; I am vindicating (cf. δικαιοσύνη)
ἐκεῖθεν, from there, thence
ἐπιθυμία, ἡ, lust; longing
ἐπιτίθημι, I am putting on; I am adding
εὐχαριστέω, I am giving thanks (*eucharist*)
θύρα, ἡ, door (*door*)
ἱκανός, –ή, –όν, enough; many
ἰσχυρός, –ά, –όν, strong
καλῶς, well (cf. καλός)
καυχάομαι, I am boasting, glorying in
νεανίσκος, ὁ, young man (related to νέος, "young"; cf. *neo*phyte)
παλαιός, –ά, –όν, old, ancient (*paleonto*logy)
παράγω, I am introducing; I am passing away (passive)
πειράζω, I am tempting, testing, trying
πέντε, five (*pent*angle)
πρόβατον, τό, sheep
σκάνδαλον, τό, offense, stumbling block (*scandal*)
τυφλόω, I am blinding (someone); I am blind (passive) (cf. τυφλός)
φαίνω, I am shining, appearing (epi*phany*)

Overview

As the first half of the genitive case sketch looms ahead, I need to say something important. The *Syntax Sketch* follows a traditional format by breaking down the range of each subject's functions into separate paragraphs using labels like "Previous Reference," "Subjective Genitive," and so on. I do not necessarily like this format, but part of my aim is to present those ideas and labels which you will encounter in Greek reference works. I am trying to help you to become familiar with the standard language of Greek grammar as well as with the more important syntactical concepts.

Unfortunately, this method carries one particular danger which you should avoid. Very frequently students of Greek syntax work harder at assigning the proper labels to constructions than they do at *understanding the concepts* which the labeled categories describe. This is a serious problem and one which is particularly frequent when it comes to the genitive case. I often see

23

students agonize over whether a particular genitive phrase should be called a "subjective genitive" or a "genitive of source," but give little thought to what the phrase really means or what bearing this has on the exegesis of the passage where the phrase occurs. As James would say, Τί τὸ ὄφελος, ἀδελφοί μου; (James 2:14)!

My most fervent advice to you, then, is to take the descriptions of usage found in the *Syntax Sketch* as what they are intend to be: brief descriptions of important syntactical concepts. They are designed to help you understand the *meaning* of the biblical text. If you are satisfied with assigning a label to a construction, but do not go beyond this potentially empty exercise, then you have not truly learned Greek grammar. Grammar is a servant of exegesis. I am trying to show you how the two intersect in these 1 John notes (not to provide you with all the answers for you to thoughtlessly regurgitate when needed).

Reading Notes

1 John 2:7

2:7a. The adjective ἀγαπητοί is a substantive in the vocative case which is used for direct address (cf. *Sketch* §27). You learned that substantive adjectives frequently have an article (cf. *Primer* §10.5), but articles are not used with vocatives. Sometimes, ὦ, "O," is used with the vocative for polite or emotional purposes, even with adjectives: ὦ ἀνόητοι, "O you silly people!" (Gal. 3:1; cf. BDF §146).

2:7b. The negative for a verb is usually placed directly in front of it; ἐντολὴν καινὴν **οὐκ** γράφω ὑμῖν is the normal word order if οὐκ were modifying the verb. The word order **οὐκ** ἐντολὴν καινήν focuses the negative upon the commandment: it is "not a new commandment." For further reflection, how does the adjective καινός differ from its synonym νεός? (See BAGD pp. 394 and 535–36.)

2:7c. The conjunction ἀλλά is frequently used to substitute a contrasting idea with a statement which is not true. One idea is stated as not true, and the substitute is given as the truth. "Instead" or "but instead" can be used to render ἀλλά when it has this meaning: οὐ ἦλθον ἵνα κρίνω τὸν κόσμον, **ἀλλ'** ἵνα σώσω τὸν κόσμον, "I did not come in order to judge the world, *but instead* (I came) in order to save the world" (John 12:47). This "substitution" idea is what ἀλλά means in 1 John 2:7: "The commandment I am writing you is not a new commandment, *but instead* it is an ancient commandment." There is also a contrast of antonyms: "new" versus "ancient."

2:7d. There is an ellipsis of γράφω in this clause: οὐκ ἐντολὴν καινὴν γράφω ὑμῖν, ἀλλ' ἐντολὴν παλαιὰν (γράφω). We have seen this common phenomenon before.

2:7e. Parse ἦν.[1]

2:7f. The relative pronoun ἥν agrees with its antecedent (ἐντολήν) in gender and number. Both the antecedent and pronoun are accusative, but this is because both are used as direct objects of their particular verbs: ἐντολήν is the object of the understood γράφω, and ἥν is the object of εἴχετε.

2:7g. Parse εἴχετε.[2]

---

[1] ὅς, ἥτις, ὅ, f a sg; see *Primer* §24.2. Do not confuse with ἦν (εἰμί Impf A I 3 sg; cf. *Primer* §10.2).

[2] ἔχω Impf A I 2 pl. We expect the augment for ἔχω to be eta: ἦχον, but for some reason it augments to εἶχον; see *Primer* §5.4. Recall that the aorist of ἔχω is the second aorist ἔσχον; cf. *Primer* §9.1 (Review).

2:7h. εἴχετε as an imperfect is difficult to put into English. The imperfect and the aorist forms were used in virtually synonymous settings with little perceivable difference in meaning: ἄνθρωπος εἶχεν τέκνα δύο, "A man *had* two children" (Matt. 21:28); Ἀβραὰμ δύο υἱοὺς **ἔσχεν**, "Abraham *had* two sons" (Gal. 4:22). Perhaps the imperfect in 1 John 2:7 simply expresses the continued possession of the commandment: "of which *you have been in possession* from the beginning."[3]

2:7i. We have seen ἀπ᾽ ἀρχῆς before (v. 1:1). Should this be rendered, "from *a* beginning"? (See *Sketch* §19). To what beginning does ἀπ᾽ ἀρχῆς refer here? Commentators, as expected, differ.

2:7j. Notice that the previous uses of ἐντολή are anarthrous and here it is articular. Why? Answer: article denotes previous reference: οὐκ ἐντολὴν καινὴν . . . ἐντολὴν παλαιὰν . . . ἡ ἐντολὴ ἡ παλαιά, "not *a* new commandment . . . *an* ancient commandment . . . *the* ancient commandment (I mentioned previously) is . . ." (*Sketch* §3).

2:7k. What rule does the articular predicate noun ὁ λόγος conform to? (*Sketch* §17).

2:7l. Parse ὅν.[4]

2:7m. The relative pronoun ὅν agrees with its antecedent (λόγος) in gender and number, but not in case. λόγος is a predicate nominative and ὅν is the direct object of ἠκούσατε.

1 John 2:8

2:8a. When there is a contrasting correlation between two items, Greek writers in the classical period used the μέν . . . δέ construction: "On the one hand . . . on the other hand" (cf. BDF §447). The classical period of (Athenian) literature was roughly 500 years prior to New Testament times.[5] Therefore, it seems odd that the authors of BDF (in §447) and others sometimes critique the authors of the New Testament for not conforming to classical style. It is like criticizing a modern author for diverging from Shakespearean English. Now the μέν . . . δέ construction *is* found in the NT, but John communicates the same idea here with πάλιν, "on the other hand," "conversely."[6] We can paraphrase: *"But from another perspective*, the commandment I am writing to you *is* new."

---

[3]Raymond Brown writes: "The imperfect tense of the verb 'to have' is durative. Another suggestion is that it is also an imperfect of incomplete or unaccomplished action sometimes employed with verbs of commanding (BDF 328), implying that while 'you had it from the beginning,' it has not been fully activated" (p. 265). While the first suggestion is at least possible, the second runs afoul of the fact that ἔχω is not a verb of commanding. It denotes *possession* of a commandment—a different kind of event. This error illustrates that commentators (and grammarians) are fallible!

[4]ὅς, ἥτις, ὅ m a sg.

[5]There was a revival of classical, Attic style lasting for several centuries from the late first century BC on (the "Attacistic Period"). The New Testament shows little effect of "Atticism," which was often a bit contrived. Interestingly, the attempt to preserve a "pure" literary style survives today in modern Greek (καθαρεύσουσα, "correct"—the language of the editorial page) in contrast to the ordinary idiom (δημοτική, "the people's"—the language of the sports page).

[6]Cf. Matt 4:7; 1 Cor 12:21; 2 Cor 10:7. Epictetus uses ἀνάπαλιν with the same meaning (e.g., 1.6.4). This is not a common meaning for πάλιν in the NT, though, interestingly, it is found in the classical period (BAGD §4, p. 607).

2:8b. Parse ὅ.[7]

2:8c. The grammar of the clause, ὅ ἐστιν ἀληθές, presents particular difficulties, because it is not clear what the antecedent of the relative pronoun ὅ is.[8] The options are:

(1) The antecedent is the previous action: "The fact that I am, on the other hand, writing a new commandment, this fact is true in him. . . ." While this is grammatically possible, it makes John's point trivial and should be ruled out on that account.

(2) The neuter pronoun explains the newness of the commandment and stands as a neuter "epexegetical" clause to the "new commandment": "On the other hand, I am writing a new commandment, (namely) something which is true in Him . . ." (so Moule, pp. 130–31; ¶4). But this interpretation lends itself to undue moralism, and it makes the next phrase too difficult.[9]

(3) The best option is that the ὅ does not have an antecedent but rather a *postcedent*. Its reference is to something which *follows* it (*post*cedent). In this case the postcedent is the clause begun with ὅτι. In Greek, ὅτι clauses are regarded as neuter singular items, hence neuter singular ὅ agrees with the ὅτι clause.[10]

The meaning of the statement can now be seen as a clarification of how the ancient commandment can also be new: because the eschatological era has begun. Since the darkness was defeated by Christ, and is in the process of being annihilated, the commandment comes to us with greater realization of fulfillment.[11] We can now paraphrase: "On the other hand, I am writing a new commandment to you; what is true in him and in you is that the darkness is passing away and the genuine light is already shining."

2:8d. The force of the present tense of παράγεται is that the action is in progress: "is (currently) passing away." This meaning is part of John's statement that the future, eschatological hope has been inaugurated in Christ (previous note). The same idea is made clearer in the next clause by ἤδη. παράγεται is in the passive voice with an intransitive meaning.[12]

2:8e. Think about the significance of ἤδη ("already") here. For instance: "Are you done with the test *already*?" The action is unexpected because it occurs earlier than anticipated. John says that the light of the last day (cf. Rev. 22:5) is *already* shining.

---

[7] ὅς, ἥτις, ὅ n n sg. The form of ὅ can be either nominative or accusative; it is nominative here as the subject of ἐστιν. Do not confuse ὅ (accented) with the article ὁ (not accented).

[8] The relative pronoun ὅ (neuter) does not agree with feminine ἐντολή, so ἐντολή is not its antecedent. Compare 2 John 5: καὶ νῦν ἐρωτῶ σε, κυρία, οὐχ ὡς **ἐντολὴν** καινὴν γράφων σοι ἀλλὰ **ἣν** εἴχομεν ἀπ᾽ ἀρχῆς, ἵνα ἀγαπῶμεν ἀλλήλους.

[9] E.g., Brown (pp. 266–68) says, ". . . as love becomes real the eschatological victory over darkness becomes apparent" (p. 268). This is not quite the theology of the Bible.

[10] For an example of a ὅτι clause acting as a neuter singular substantive see Gal. 3:11 (neuter singular δῆλον is in agreement as a predicate adjective).

[11] Connected with this point is John's use of ἀληθές ("veritable," "genuine") here and its cognates elsewhere in his writings. See especially, Geerhardus Vos, "'True' and 'Truth' in Johannine Writings," *Redemptive History and Biblical Interpretation: The Shorter Writings of Geerhardus Vos* (Phillipsburg: P&R, 1980), 343–51.

[12] παράγω P P I 3 sg.

1 John 2:9

2:9a. If you think about the meaning of the substantive participle ὁ λέγων, it is virtually the same as ἐὰν εἴπωμεν found in the conditional clauses in 1 John 1:6–10. Although this participial phrase is the mere subject of ἐστίν, it seems clear that a condition is implied. The participle acts as shorthand for: *"If someone says . . . (then) he* is in the darkness. . . ."

2:9b. As we saw in 1 John 2:6, the participle of λέγω, because it is a verb of speech, can introduce indirect discourse. That is why the infinitive εἶναι[13] was used here; it is an infinitive used in indirect discourse (*Sketch* §94). Think of an infinitive as a verbal *noun*, and as a noun it can be used as the direct object of a verb (*Primer* §25.5). Indirect discourse is communicated either with an infinitive clause or with a ὅτι clause that functions as the direct object of a verb of speech or of perception: "The one who says X," where X is the direct object of "says." In English we only use object clauses introduced by "that" in indirect discourse: "The one who says *that* he is in the light." In Greek, John could have used a ὅτι clause with an indicative verb: ὁ λέγων ὅτι ἐν τῷ φωτί ἐστιν. To use an infinitive instead was simply a synonymous option. (Cf. BDF §396–97.)

> "Love and hatred are set in opposition to each other with no alternative, just as we are said to be either *in the light* or *in darkness*, and there is no twilight." John R. W. Stott

2:9c. The article τόν in the phrase **τὸν** ἀδελφὸν αὐτοῦ is the normal use with a noun modified by a genitive personal pronoun (*Sketch* §5). The same phrase also occurs in vv. 10–11 with the article (and see **τοὺς** ὀφθαλμοὺς αὐτοῦ in v. 11 or διὰ **τὸ** ὄνομα αὐτοῦ in v. 12). Get used to this common stylistic feature. Interpretive mistakes have been made because such patterns common to Greek were not learned.

2:9d. Parse μισῶν.[14]

2:9e. Should we take μισῶν as a substantive participle parallel with ὁ λέγων or as an adverbial participle meaning "while at the same time he hates"? Would there be any difference in meaning?

2:9f. The conjunction ἕως sometimes functions like a preposition with the genitive. Here the object of the preposition is an adverb (ἄρτι, "now," "just now," "at present"), found together in other places.[15] The meaning is straightforward: it implies a predication of the action or truth in some previous time period which continues to be true in the author's time: "(previously and) until now," "until the present time," "even to this point in time." They were in the darkness before, and continue to be in darkness into the present time. Can we say by implication that the hypocrite was never truly in the light?

---

[13]εἰμί P A Inf (cf. *Primer* §25.3).

[14]μισέω P A Ptc m n sg; an epsilon contract verb which looks like λύω in this nominative form. Compare the genitive participle where contraction does occur: λύοντος / μισοῦντος.

[15]E.g., "From the days of John the Baptist *until now* (ἕως ἄρτι)" (Matt. 11:12); and, "You have saved the good wine *until now*" (John 2:10). Another way to express this idea in Greek is ἄχρι (or μέχρι) τοῦ νῦν: "from the first day *until now*" (Phil. 1:4). Cf. BDF §216[3].

1 John 2:10

2:10a. Parse ἀγαπῶν.[16]

2:10b. We have seen with ὁ λέγων (1 John 2:4, 6, 9) that John prefers to express substantive participles in their present (versus aorist) forms. Likewise, ὁ ἀγαπῶν here (and ὁ μισῶν in v. 11) is a present substantive participle. Later on we will discuss why the present form was chosen; for now, do you have any preliminary theories?

2:10c. What is the use of the genitive in the phrase τὸν ἀδελφὸν **αὐτοῦ**? (*Sketch* §37).

2:10d. Reflect on the significance of μένει in the phrase ἐν τῷ φωτὶ μένει. Could John have used ἐστιν instead as he does in v. 11 (ἐν τῇ σκοτίᾳ ἐστίν)?

2:10e. The phrase: σκάνδαλον ἐν αὐτῷ οὐκ ἔστιν is a statement of existence similar to one we found in 1 John 1:5: καὶ σκοτία ἐν αὐτῷ οὐκ ἔστιν οὐδεμία. What is different about these statements? Review notes 1:5i–k above.

2:10f. Some people believe that Greek is an exceptionally precise language in which there are few or no ambiguities. This is simply not true.[17] Rather, the ambiguities and precision in the Greek language are different than those in English, so it appears to be more precise sometimes and more ambiguous at other times. For example, the RSV translates καὶ σκάνδαλον ἐν αὐτῷ οὐκ ἔστιν as: "[A]nd *in it* there is no cause for stumbling" (emphasis added); whereas the KJV reads: "[A]nd there is none occasion of stumbling *in him*." The Greek phrase ἐν αὐτῷ is ambiguous here (whereas English "in it" and "in him" are not). Is αὐτῷ neuter referring to τὸ φῶς as the RSV reads, or masculine referring to ὁ ἀγαπῶν? Since there is no difference in form between the two genders, there is ambiguity in Greek solved only through a process of careful interpretation.

2:10g. The term σκάνδαλον is an interesting candidate for a word study (BAGD p. 753).

1 John 2:11

2:11a. Perhaps John returns to the "walking" metaphor in this verse because of the idea of blindness which follows (cf. 1 John 1:6; Ps. 1:1; Matt. 15:14).

2:11b. Parse ἐτύφλωσεν.[18]

2:11c. Most translations render the aorist ἐτύφλωσεν with an English past perfect verb: "has blinded" (NIV; NASB); "hath blinded" (KJV); "has brought on blindness" (NRSV). Why? Why not render every aorist as a simple past: "because the darkness *blinded* his eyes"? The answer: Greek

---

[16]ἀγαπάω P A Ptc m n sg. As in note thirteen above, compare this contract verb's genitive participle with λύω: λύοντος / ἀγαπῶντος.

[17]Actually, if we want to become philosophical, it is possible to defend the thesis that language without some ambiguities is impossible.

[18]τυφλόω A A I 3 sg. Recall that the contract vowel *lengthens* before the sigma in the simple stem: τυφλόω → ἐτύφλωσεν. Likewise: μισέω → ἐμίσησεν and ἀγαπάω → ἠγάπησεν. Review *Primer* §§7.4 and 8.5.

and English, you may be surprised to learn, are not the same.[19] The aorist ἐτύφλωσεν implies in this context that the action is completed, and we can infer from the meaning of τυφλόω that once the event occurs (blinding of eyes), there are enduring consequences (blindness). The English past perfect fits this meaning better than the simple past.

2:11d. The idea of possession does not fit body parts well; nevertheless, we must call the genitive in τοὺς ὀφθαλμοὺς **αὐτοῦ** the "genitive of possession" (*Sketch* §36). You don't *really* want a separate label for this do you? (The "genitive of body parts"??)

1 John 2:12

2:12a. Parse τεκνία.[20]

2:12b. As mentioned earlier, there are ambiguities in Greek. In this verse, ὅτι indicates either the reason that John is writing: "I write unto you, little children, *because* your sins are forgiven you" (KJV; also NKJV; NIV; NASB; NRSV). Or ὅτι can be rendered "that" in a content clause of indirect statement telling the content of John's message plainly to the readers: "Dear children, I am writing to you *that* your sins are forgiven" (BUV).[21] Obviously, the causal meaning is preferred by most authorities (perhaps influenced rightly by v. 2:21), but an interpreter of the Greek text has the opportunity to explore options not available through English translation. English versions may be unanimous *and* unanimously mistaken.

2:12c. ὑμῖν occurs twice here. The first occurrence is a simple indirect object identifying the persons who have a special interest in the action (*Sketch* §54). The second ὑμῖν may be viewed as a dative of advantage: "for you," "for your benefit" (*Sketch* §55).

2:12d. There are times when you may need help parsing Greek verb forms. Kubo's *Reader's Lexicon* has a handy list of difficult verb forms in its Appendix II (pp. 278–84). Although this is certainly not exhaustive, it will help you parse most troublesome forms. For instance, ἀφέωνται in this verse is given on p. 279 (top of column two): "ἀφέωνται (ἀφίημι) pf. pass." While this is not a very complete parsing, it does tell you the lexical form, tense, and mood.[22]

The KJV renders the perfect verb ἀφέωνται with an English present tense: "your sins *are forgiven* you." Why?[23]

2:12e. The KJV renders αἱ ἁμαρτίαι as "*your* sins." Is this allowed? What use of the article is this? (*Sketch* §11).

2:12f. The phrase διὰ τὸ ὄνομα αὐτοῦ needs interpretation. Begin with the meaning of διά here (cf. BAGD pp. 179–81 [esp. p. 181]; BDF §222).

---

[19]See especially Burton, *Moods and Tenses* §52 for a description of the English past perfect in connection with the Greek aorist.

[20]τεκνίον n v(ocative) pl.

[21]"Baugh Unauthorized Version." Not inflicted on the general public yet.

[22]ἀφέωνται = ἀφίημι Pf P I 3 pl. This form occurs six times in the NT (e.g., ἄνθρωπε, **ἀφέωνταί** σοι αἱ ἁμαρτίαι σου, "Man, your sins are forgiven you" [Luke 5:20]).

[23]Stott paraphrases: "they [the sins] have been and remain forgiven" (p. 97). What is the difference? Cf. Young, 126–29; BDF §§340–42.

1 John 2:13

2:13a. Parse πατέρες.[24]

2:13b. Stott remarks on ἐγνώκατε:[25] "literally, 'have come to know' (another perfect tense) God as their Father" (p. 97). To say, "come to know" in English conveys the inauguration of knowledge which was not previously held (called the "inceptive" meaning). Is this John's point?

2:13c. There are two possible interpretations of the article in **τὸν ἀπ' ἀρχῆς**. First, it may be turning the prepositional phrase into a noun phrase (or substantive): "You have known *him who was* from the beginning" (*Sketch* §9). Secondly, the article could be used as a pronoun and the prepositional phrase modifies the verb: "From the beginning you have known him" (*Sketch* §12). The two interpretations are quite different and well illustrates how the interpretation of a phrase may depend solely on the meaning of the article.

2:13d. The noun in the prepositional phrase **ἀπ' ἀρχῆς** is commonly rendered as definite: "from *the* beginning" (NASB), instead of "from *a* beginning." Do you remember why this is allowed (*Sketch* §19)? Don't forget the previous lessons![26]

The phrase ἀπ' ἀρχῆς occurs twelve times in John's writings, but ἀπὸ τῆς ἀρχῆς (with the article) does not occur in John or in any other New Testament writer. Nevertheless, the anarthrous expression is still obviously definite. To what beginning does this phrase refer here since we now know it is a *specific* beginning?

1 John 2:14

2:14a. John's switch from present γράφω in vv. 12–13 to aorist ἔγραψα[27] in v. 14 is sometimes given a more profound interpretation than is really likely. He probably employs the aorist for *variety* in an otherwise repetitious section (cf. BDF §334). The fact that γράφω is used three times and ἔγραψα three times helps delineate the structure of this sub-section. Remember that this sort of thing was used by ancient writers to delineate their discourse before the days of indentation and word spacing.

2:14b. Parse μένει.[28]

2:14c. The second article in the phrase ὁ λόγος **τοῦ** θεοῦ is a good example of what "canon" of Greek article usage? Answer: "Apollonius' canon" named for Apollonius Dyscolus, one of the few ancient Greeks to write anything useful about their grammar. Ancient linguistics was surprisingly primitive in light of their sophisticated studies in other areas and focused on the meaning and etymology of words—studies which were too often quite fanciful and unfruitful.

---

[24]πατήρ m v pl; cf. *Sketch* §26. νεανίσκοι later in the verse is parsed the same way.

[25]γινώσκω Pf A I 2 pl (cf. *Primer* §14.1, review). The epsilon in this form (ἐγνώκατε) is not an augment. It is reduplication found on some forms whose stem begins with two consonants, here –γν– in ἐγνώκατε.

[26]I'll never forget one student's innocent outburst halfway through a Greek reading class. When asked a review question she blurted out: "You mean, we have to *remember* this stuff? I thought this was just for fun!" This *is* fun, but . . . Sigh.

[27]γράφω A A I 1 sg.

[28]μένω P A I 3 sg.

The Genitive II

REVIEW: *Primer*, Lessons 7–8, 15
READ: *Syntax Sketch* §§44–52
STUDY: 1 John 2:15–25

Vocabulary

ἀγρός, ὁ, field; farms (pl.) (*agriculture*)
ἀλαζονεία, ἡ, arrogance, pride
ἀντίχριστος, ὁ, Antichrist (*Antichrist*)
ἅπας, ἅπασα, ἅπαν, all, every (cf. πᾶς)
ἀρνέομαι, I am denying
βιβλίον, τό, book, scroll (*bibliography*)
βίος, ὁ, life; belongings (*biology*)
βλασφημέω, I am blaspheming, reviling (*blaspheme*)
διακονία, ἡ, service, ministry (cf. *deacon*)
ἐπαγγέλλομαι, I am promising (cf. ἐπαγγελία)
ἐπιστρέφω, I am returning, turning (cf. ὑποστρέφω below)
εὐθέως, immediately (adv.) (cf. εὐθύς)
μαρτυρία, ἡ, testimony, witness (cf. μάρτυς)
μάρτυς, μάρτυρος, ὁ, witness (*martyr*)
ὅθεν, from where, whence
ὀπίσω, behind, after (adverb or preposition + gen.)
ὀργή, ἡ, anger, wrath (*orgy*)
οὖς, ὠτός, τό, ear (*otic*)
παραγίνομαι, I am arriving, appearing
περιτομή, ἡ, circumcision
προσευχή, ἡ, prayer (cf. προσεύχομαι)
ὑποστρέφω, I am turning back, returning
χρῖσμα, –ατος, τό, anointing (*chrism*)
ψεῦδος, –ους, τό, lie (*pseudo*)
ὥσπερ, as, just as

Overview

Now we finish up the genitive uses. By covering the genitive in two lessons instead of one, you should have time to review and master all the uses covered in the *Syntax Sketch*. Be sure to review the uses from the last lesson. You will also notice that the comments in the following notes are briefer than before. This is because you are becoming, of course, more proficient in Greek and need less help. If this is not true, review!

Reading Notes

1 John 2:15

2:15a. When we focus more upon verbs, you will learn that Greek makes a basic distinction between "atelic" and "telic" verbs. Put simply, an atelic verb refers to a state of being, condition, relationship, or activity which has no inherent endpoint. (The term *atelic* comes from Greek and means "no terminus," no τέλος). Examples are "I live," "I am healthy," "I have (something)," and "I am walking." Telic verbs have an inherent endpoint; "I fall," "I hit," "I die," "I close" are examples. "Hitting," for example, has an inherent termination when viewed as a discrete event.

The atelic-telic distinction is a critical factor in determining whether imperatives and other forms have certain special nuances. Here, ἀγαπᾶτε is a present aspect imperative.[1] One possible connotation of the present aspect of the imperative is that "something already existing . . . is to stop" (BDF §336[3]). In other words, the present (versus the aorist) of ἀγαπᾶτε may imply that John's readers are in fact loving the world. He tells them: "Stop loving the world."[2] However, to mechanically adopt this interpretation creates problems in many places. And there is no reason to think that John is ordering his readers to quit being so worldly here. He has just expressed his confidence in them in vv. 12–14 and will again (e.g. 2:21). So how do we know whether there is this special nuance or not? The solution is found in the fact that ἀγαπάω is an "atelic" verb, and atelic verbs are normally found in their present forms in the imperative without any special nuance.

2:15b. The commentaries deal with the issue that God "loves the world" in John 3:16, and here we are told not to "love the world." That's why we have commentaries.

2:15c. The article is used with κόσμον because this is a "monadic" noun. What does that mean? (*Sketch* §2).

2:15d. The syntax of the article in the phrase τὰ ἐν τῷ κόσμῳ is straightforward when you realize that the Greek article can turn various parts of speech into nouns. Here the idea is: "the in-the-world things" (covered in *Sketch* §9).

2:15e. ἡ ἀγάπη τοῦ πατρός is an instance where one must decide between two plausible options for interpreting the genitive. Does this mean: "the love which that person has for the Father" or "He loves the Father" (objective genitive; *Sketch* §41)? Or does it mean: "the love which the Father has for that person" or "The Father loves him" (subjective genitive; *Sketch* §38)? The difference is significant. If it means the former, John would be saying that our love has two mutually exclusive objects. Either we love the world or God, not both.[3] If the genitive phrase refers to God's love for us, then John is using this future condition as evidence to form a conclusion. I paraphrase: "If someone loves the world, this is an indication that the Father does not love that person. He is not beloved of God. God first loved us, so only those whom he loves can reciprocate with genuine love themselves"

---

[1] ἀγαπάω P A Impv 2 pl. ἀγαπᾶτε is also the indicative form, but the use of the negative μή here shows that it is imperative in meaning. οὐ would be used with the indicative (οὐ ἀγαπᾶτε, "you do not love"). Remember that the present imperative is used in prohibitions, but the subjunctive is used for prohibitions when the aorist form of the verb was desired; see *Primer* §23.7.

[2] This is presented as the norm for prohibitions by Nigel Turner: "If the tense is the present, prohibition will be against continuing an action which has already begun" (*Grammatical Insights Into the New Testament* [Edinburgh: T. & T. Clark, 1965], 30). And 1 John 2:15 is interpreted in this way by, for instance, R. L. Thomas, *Exegetical Digest of 1 John* (self-published manuscript, 1984), 161.

[3] Cf. Jesus' statement about loving either God or mammon (Matt. 6:24; Luke 16:13).

(1 John 4:10). This is, obviously, an interesting contrast of interpretations, and the Greek genitive can express either meaning. The issue hangs on non-grammatical, interpretive factors.

More pedantically, to understand the concepts of the subjective and objective genitives, turn the lead noun into a verb and determine whether the noun in the genitive relation acts as the subject of the verb ("subjective" genitive), or the object of the verb ("objective" genitive). Like so:

❍ Subjective genitive: ἡ ἀγάπη τοῦ πατρός = ὁ πάτηρ ἀγαπᾷ αὐτόν "The Father loves him." The Father (the word in the genitive) acts like the *subject* of a verb.

❍ Objective genitive: ἡ ἀγάπη τοῦ πατρός = (αὐτὸς) ἀγαπᾷ τὸν πατέρα "He loves the Father." The Father (the word in the genitive) acts like the direct *object* of a verb.

1 John 2:16

2:16a. The use of the first article in πᾶν τὸ ἐν τῷ κόσμῳ has two possible uses, though the difference in interpretation of the whole is negligible. First, we can consider πᾶν to be a substantive adjective, "everything." The article would then simply connect ἐν τῷ κόσμῳ with the substantive. It is like: ὁ ἄνθρωπος ὁ ἀγαθός "the good man," or, ὁ ἄνθρωπος ὁ ἐν τῇ ὁδῷ "the man on the street." If this were the case, though, we would expect πᾶν to be articular: τὸ πᾶν τό. . . . It is more likely that the article turns the ἐν τῷ κόσμῳ phrase into a substantive expression as we saw in v. 15 (above note 2:15d). πᾶν is an attributive adjective modifying this substantive.

2:16b. All three of the genitive phrases in v. 16 are in apposition to the previous phrase "everything in the world, *namely*, the lust. . . ."

2:16c. Decide which of the possible relations of the genitive are represented in these three genitive phrases: ἡ ἐπιθυμία **τῆς σαρκὸς** καὶ ἡ ἐπιθυμία **τῶν ὀφθαλμῶν** καὶ ἡ ἀλαζονεία **τοῦ βίου**.

2:16d. Is Apollonius' canon observed in the three genitive phrases in the previous note? (See *Sketch* §15.)

2:16e. In 1 John 3:17 βίος means "property" or "wealth," and BAGD takes that meaning here in 2:16 also (BAGD §3, p. 142) rather then "life." What do you think? How does βίος differ from its possible synonym ζωή?

2:16f. The subject of singular ἔστιν[4] is the πᾶν τὸ ἐν τῷ κόσμῳ substantive expression. If the subject were the three genitive phrases, the verb would probably be plural. The meaning can be expressed: "Everything in the world . . . is not from the Father." Obviously one must interpret κόσμος here as "that which is hostile to God, i.e., lost in sin, wholly at odds w[ith] anything divine, ruined and depraved" (BAGD, p. 446, §7) or we would have John denying that God created "the (orderly) universe" (BAGD, pp. 445–46, §2–6).

2:16g. In both ἐκ τοῦ πατρὸς and ἐκ τοῦ κόσμου, ἐκ communicates the idea of *source*. Can a genitive without the preposition ἐκ have the same meaning? (*Sketch* §40).

---

[4]εἰμί P A I 3 sg. Review *Primer* §10.2 if needed.

1 John 2:17

2:17a. Parse παράγεται.[5]

2:17b. παράγεται has two subjects, ὁ κόσμος and ἡ ἐπιθυμία αὐτοῦ. παράγεται is singular, despite having plural subjects because of the word order and the use of καί: "The world is passing away *along with* its lust." The second subject is expressed almost as an afterthought, though it tends to receive more focus as a result. See the notes on 1 John 2:8 for the eschatological significance of παράγεται (notes 2:8c–e).

2:17c. εἰς τὸν αἰῶνα, with variations (e.g., εἰς τοὺς αἰῶνας [τῶν αἰώνων]) is an idiomatic expression meaning "forever." See BAGD, pp. 27–28 (under αἰών).

1 John 2:18

2:18a. Why do translations take ἐσχάτη ὥρα as definite ("*the* last hour")? Hint: what rule of article usage deals particularly with predicate statements?

2:18b. Parse ἠκούσατε.[6]

2:18c. Like English, a present tense verb, especially one which denotes traveling, points to a future time reference; see BDF §323(3). (I call this "impending" action.) This is the significance of ἔρχεται here: "Antichrist *is going to come*." John could just as well have written ἐλεύσεται.

2:18d. The phrase καὶ νῦν means "also now" elsewhere in the New Testament (". . . at that time . . . so *also now*" [Gal. 4:29]; ". . . as at all times *also now*" [Phil. 1:20]). And it means "even now" in John 11:22: ". . . *even now* (at this late hour) I know. . . ." What does the phrase mean here? Why?

2:18e. Notice the switch from ἔρχομαι in the previous part of v. 18 to γίνομαι for the many antichrists.[7] Is there any significance to this variation? Compare John 1:9; 3:19; 16:28; 18:37; 1 Tim. 1:15 for Christ's "coming into the world."

2:18f. John is the only author who uses the term "antichrist." In the four passages where this figure is mentioned (1 John 2:18–19; 2:22; 4:3–4; 2 John 7), two important assertions are made about him: (1) The antichrist's influence is already present in this age; and, (2) Although the readers have been taught that one antichrist is to come, there are many as well (e.g., τὸ [πνεῦμα] τοῦ ἀντιχρίστου ὃ ἀκηκόατε ὅτι ἔρχεται καὶ νῦν ἐν τῷ κόσμῳ ἐστὶν ἤδη. . . . νενικήκατε **αὐτούς** [1 John 4:3–4]).

1 John 2:19

2:19a. Parse ἡμῶν (which occurs five times in this verse!).[8]

---

[5]παράγω P M I 3 sg. This form is analyzed as *passive* in our reference works, but it is a clear case of the middle form used with an intransitive kind of meaning (*Primer* §15.8; compare BAGD pp. 613–14, §2.a–b).

[6]ἀκούω A A I 2 pl.

[7]γεγόνασιν—γίνομαι Pf A I 3 pl; cf. *Primer* §§14.1–2.

[8]ἐγώ 1 g pl; cf. *Primer* §16.2.

2:19b. The phrase ἐξ ἡμῶν occurs four times in v. 19 with two different meanings. The meanings are the same as the genitive without a preposition. Identify both (*Sketch* §40 and §46).

2:19c. Parse ἐξῆλθαν.[9]

2:19d. μεμενήκεισαν[10] is a pluperfect form, rare in the New Testament (see *Primer* §14.7).

2:19e. The condition expressed here is labeled either a "second class," "contrary-to-fact," or "unreal" conditional sentence.[11] The marks of this kind of condition are: εἰ and an imperfect or aorist indicative verb in the protasis, and ἄν in the apodosis (although ἄν is occasionally omitted). It is called an *unreal* condition because the condition was not fulfilled. It merely expresses what *would have occurred* if the condition had been met. Here: "For if they were from us, they would have remained with us." Here is another example: εἰ ὁ θεὸς πατὴρ ὑμῶν ἦν ἠγαπᾶτε ἂν ἐμέ, "If God were your father, you would love me" (John 8:42).

2:19f. The combination of ἀλλ᾽ ἵνα is frequently found with an ellipsis of some element from the previous statement. Generically something like "this happened" can be supplied. In v. 19 supply: "But (they went out from us) in order that. . . ."[12] For another instance, see: οὔτε οὗτος ἥμαρτεν οὔτε οἱ γονεῖς αὐτοῦ, **ἀλλ᾽ ἵνα** φανερωθῇ τὰ ἔργα τοῦ θεοῦ, "Neither this man nor his parents sinned, *but* (he was born blind) *in order that* the works of God might be manifested" (John 9:3).

> "John indicates that the schism is part of a divine purpose. The docetic heretics withdrew because they were not in sympathy with the orthodox christology of their colleagues . . . and, by denying the true nature of Jesus (human, as well as divine), they had in any case already severed their *spiritual* connection with the community."
> Stephen S. Smalley

2:19g. Parse φανερωθῶσιν.[13]

2:19h. The passive form of the verb φανερόω (φανερωθῶσιν) can be rendered most intelligibly by an English intransitive verb: "become visible or known, be revealed. . . appear" (BAGD, pp. 852–53), rather than by an English passive.

The subject of this plural verb causes no trouble for most authorities who interpret it impersonally: "that *it* might be shown" (NASB).[14] Grammatically this means that the ὅτι clause is the virtual subject of this verb: "that they all are not of us" was the thing "revealed." This is possibly correct, yet the plural verb is quite unusual since the ὅτι clause must be treated as singular.[15] Perhaps John intended a more active meaning for φανερωθῶσιν than most assume; I paraphrase:

---

[9]ἐξέρχομαι 2A A I 3 pl. This is a second aorist verb with a first aorist ending; cf. *Primer* §27.5.

[10]μένω Plupf A I 3 pl.

[11]See Wallace, pp. 694–96; Young, p. 226; BDF §371[3]; Porter, pp. 259–61; §2.1.2.

[12]See "*their going* showed that" (NIV). BDF §448(7) discusses the idiom.

[13]φανερόω 1A P S 3 pl; cf. *Primer* §22.3.

[14]Cf. BAGD, p. 853, §2b. The King James is more literal but hardly perspicuous: "that they might be made manifest that they were not all of us."

[15]A few Greek manuscripts have singular ἐφανερώθη (notably, 630 and 1505). See the similar phenomenon: **φανερούμενοι ὅτι** ἐστὲ ἐπιστολὴ Χριστοῦ, "You show that you are a letter from Christ" (2 Cor. 3:3; NIV translation).

"that *they might be exposed* (as pretenders)."[16] The idea is at least worth considering; and again, the Greek text reveals options not seen in translations where interpretive decisions are necessarily made for the reader.

1 John 2:20

2:20a. Note the parallelism in: καὶ ὑμεῖς χρῖσμα . . . καὶ ὑμεῖς τὸ χρῖσμα (v. 27). Also note the article in the second occurrence of χρῖσμα; explain the use of this article (*Sketch* §3). Here is a way to present the structure of the passage:

a καὶ ὑμεῖς χρῖσμα (2:20) (inclusio ↓)

b οὐκ ἔγραψα ὑμῖν (2:21) (inclusio ⅋)

c ὑμεῖς ὃ ἠκούσατε (2:24)

d ἀπ᾽ ἀρχῆς

e μενέτω

d ὃ ἀπ᾽ ἀρχῆς

c ἠκούσατε καὶ ὑμεῖς

e μενεῖτε

THEME: καὶ αὕτη ἐστὶν ἡ ἐπαγγελία ἣν. . . (2:25)

b ταῦτα ἔγραψα ὑμῖν (2:26) (inclusio ⋀)

a καὶ ὑμεῖς τὸ χρῖσμα (2:27) (inclusio ↑)

2:20b. To what does ἀπὸ τοῦ ἁγίου refer? Why was the article used? Compare ἀπ᾽ ἀρχῆς.

2:20c. Instead of οἴδατε **πάντες,** "you all know," many early manuscripts have οἴδατε **πάντα,** "you know everything." Which makes the best sense in the context of v. 20?

1 John 2:21

2:21a. Parse ἔγραψα.[17]

2:21b. πᾶν ψεῦδος . . . οὐκ ἔστιν (*"every* lie is *not"*) is a Semitic-style idiom where πᾶς modifies the noun and the negative οὐκ modifies the verb. Paul has a comparable statement: ἐξ ἔργων νόμου οὐ δικαιωθήσεται **πᾶσα** σάρξ, "*All* flesh will *not* be justified from works of law" (Rom. 3:20; Gal. 2:16; drawn from Ps. 143:2). Idiomatic Greek would be: οὐδὲν ψεῦδός ἐκ τῆς ἀληθείας ἐστιν, "No lie is from the truth" (as in English). Hebrew has no word corresponding exactly to οὐδείς "no one" and uses the idiom found here.

---

[16]For the same meaning for this verb see possibly: ἵνα . . . μὴ **φανερωθῇ** ἡ αἰσχύνη τῆς γυμνότητός σου, "that . . . your shameful nakedness *might* not *be exposed*" (Rev. 3:18).

[17]γράφω A A I 1 sg.

1 John 2:22

2:22a. Explain the article with ὁ ψεύστης. Is this specific? generic? or previous reference? (*Sketch* §2–4).

2:22b. At first glance, there is no difficulty with the first statement in v. 22. At second glance there is. If we take the ὅτι clause as indirect discourse, then John is saying, in effect, that the liar maintains that Jesus is the Messiah! The solution is to take ὅτι as introducing *direct* quotation. I paraphrase: "Who is the liar but he who makes the following denial, saying, 'Jesus is not the Messiah.'"

2:22c. One key to John's statements about the antichrist rests on a proper appraisal of the article with ὁ ἀντίχριστος here. It is the article of previous reference, referring back to the same noun in v. 18 (*Sketch* §3). The one, awaited antichrist is, in some sense, already present in those who currently deny that Jesus is the incarnate Messiah.

2:22d. Notice that ὁ ἀρνούμενος[18] is in apposition to ὁ ἀντίχριστος. The antichrist is identified by heretical theology.

1 John 2:23

2:23a. The adjective πᾶς[19] is employed in a different word order in relation with its articular substantive than most attributive adjectives. Normally, an attributive follows the article: ὁ ἀγαθὸς δοῦλος or ὁ δοῦλος ὁ ἀγαθός ("the good slave" for both; cf. *Primer* §10.5). With πᾶς, though, what for other adjectives would be the *predicate* word order, is the attributive position: πᾶς ὁ δοῦλος, "every slave." The reason is that ὁ πᾶς δοῦλος changes the adjective's meaning from "all" to "the whole"; see *Primer* §12.5; BAGD, pp. 631–33.

2:23b. Normally, οὐδέ is found with another form of οὐ meaning "not . . . nor" or "neither . . . nor" (cf. BDF §445). Here the first negative in series with οὐδέ is *implied* in the meaning of ἀρνούμενος. The meaning is something like this: "Everyone who does *not* profess the Son, *neither* has the Father." That ἀρνέομαι can be rendered "to not profess" is clear from the context where it occurs as an antonym of ὁμολογέω here.

1 John 2:24

2:24a. ὑμεῖς is clearly used for emphasis in order to highlight the contrast with the false brothers of v. 19, etc. "But *you* (in contrast to them), what you heard from the beginning, let it remain in you."

2:24b. For now parse all three forms of μένω in v. 24.[20]

---

[18]ἀρνέομαι P D Ptc m n sg. This is one of the few deponent contract verbs in the NT (cf. *Primer* §6.4).

[19]πᾶς, πᾶσα, πᾶν m n sg.

[20]μενέτω—μένω P A Impv. 3 sg (cf. *Primer* §23.2); μείνῃ—μένω 1A A S 3 sg (cf. *Primer* §22.5); μενεῖτε—μένω F A I 2 pl (cf. *Primer* §§18.2, 4).

1 John 2:25

2:25a. Parse ἐπηγγείλατο.[21]

2:25b. Is αὐτός required by the verb ἐπηγγείλατο? What is its significance in v. 25 (cf. *Primer* §16.5)?

2:25c. τὴν ζωήν is in apposition to ἥν, and thereby in apposition to ἡ ἐπαγγελία. ζωήν is in the accusative case because a word in apposition to another is put into the same case as the word upon which it expands.

---

[21]ἐπαγγέλλομαι 1A D I 3 sg. This is a liquid verb (cf. *Primer* Lesson 18), and this variation on ἀγγέλλω happens to be deponent (an old middle voice meaning probably).

6

The Dative

REVIEW: *Primer* Lessons 9, 23
READ: *Syntax Sketch*, §§53–65
STUDY: 1 John 2:26–3:3

Vocabulary

ἁγνίζω, I am purifying (cf. ἁγνός and ἅγιος)

ἁγνός, –ή, –όν, pure

αἰσχύνομαι, I am ashamed; I put to shame

ἀκάθαρτος, –ον, unclean (masc. and fem. share –ος ending) (cf. καθαρίζω)

ἀναγινώσκω, I am reading

ἀσθενέω, I am weak, sick (*asthenia*)

δείκνυμι, I am showing, proving (*deictic*)

διαθήκη, ἡ, covenant; last will

δυνατός, –η, –ον, able; powerful (*dynamite*; cf. δύναμις)

ἐκπορεύομαι, I am going out (cf. πορεύομαι)

ἐχθρός, –ά, –όν, hostile; enemy (substantive)

ἥλιος, ὁ, sun (*helium*)

μέλος, μέλους, τό, member, limb (*melody*)

μετανοέω, I am repenting

μήτε, neither. . . nor, and not (cf. οὔτε)

ναί, yes

οἶνος, ὁ, wine (*oenology*)

οὔπω, not yet

παραγγέλλω, I am ordering, instructing

παρουσία, ἡ, arrival, coming

παρρησία, ἡ, boldness, confidence

ποῖος, –α, –ον, what kind? what?

ποταπός, –ή, –όν, what kind, what manner

πτωχός, –ή, –όν, poor (usually substantive)

ὑπομονή, ἡ, endurance, perseverance; patience (–μονή is from μένω)

Overview

In this letter, John uses the dative almost exclusively as the indirect object of a verb (e.g., γράφω ὑμῖν in v. 2:1). In 1 John 2:26–3:3, the assigned passage for this chapter, datives occur in only two places (2:26 and 3:3—not counting objects of prepositions). This does not give you much practice with the dative. You will encounter some perplexing uses of the dative case in other New Testament writers, so work carefully through the examples in the *Syntax Sketch* to avoid potential problems later.

Reading Notes

1 John 2:26

2:26a. Verses 26 and 27 form the close of an inclusio according to the structure observed in note 2:20a above. An "inclusio" is simply an "envelope" structure enclosing a complete idea and usually marked by the repetition of words. The repetition of χρῖσμα (vv. 20, 27) and ἔγραψα (vv. 21, 26) marks the inclusio in this section. See also note 2:27b below.

2:26b. ὑμῖν is the common dative of indirect object (special interest); *Sketch* §54.

2:26c. Parse πλανώντων.[1]

2:26d. Recall the procedure for assessing the function of participles like πλανώντων. Review *Primer* §20.10 if you are rusty. Remember that one of every twenty words in the Greek NT is a participle.

The present tense form of the participle is common for substantive participles with a "general reference." That is, the action is not necessarily seen as in progress at the time of writing, it merely points to a general or characteristic action of someone: "the ones who deceive" rather than "the ones who are currently deceiving." There is a further consideration. If the context shows that there is resistance to the fulfillment of the participle's action, the present participle may have a *conative* nuance;[2] the action is attempted but not necessarily fulfilled. The translation into English would be: "concerning those who are *trying to deceive* you" (or "who *want to deceive* you"). In a case like this, the fact that the action is only attempted is derived from what is evident from context as here in 1 John. John does not say that his readers are being deceived; just the opposite is clear from v. 27. But someone is *trying* to deceive them. In contrast, an aorist or perfect participle here (περὶ τῶν πλανησάντων or περὶ τῶν πεπλανηκότων) would refer to successful deceivers: "concerning whose who have deceived you."

2:26e. John specified the subject matter of his writing at this point with a prepositional phrase (περί + genitive; see Young, 100). He could also have used either of what two *cases* without a preposition?[3]

1 John 2:27

2:27a. One reason I believe there is an intentional inclusio between vv. 20 and 27 (see note 2:20a and 2:26a) is not only the obvious repetition of words (καὶ ὑμεῖς χρῖσμα . . . καὶ ὑμεῖς τὸ χρῖσμα) but also the use of the article in the second occurrence of χρῖσμα. What is this use of the article called (*Sketch* §3)? Remember that Greek was written in John's day with only occasional and rudimentary punctuation marks, and no standard paragraph breaks or other ways of graphically showing the organization of thought (i.e., ΚΑΙΥΜΕΙΣΧΡΙΣΜΑ . . . ΚΑΙΥΜΕΙΣΤΟΧΡΙΣΜΑ). In this

---

[1] πλανάω P A Ptc m g pl. The omega in the variable vowel slot (πλαν**ώ**ντων) is caused by contraction (πλανα + οντων).

[2] "Conative" comes from a Latin word (*conari*) meaning "to attempt, to try." This is a nuance sometimes communicated by Greek present and imperfect forms. Cf. Wallace, pp. 534–35, 550–52; Young, pp. 109, 114–15 (preferring the term "tendential").

[3] Accusative or dative (*Sketch* §§31 and 56).

system, things like articles of previous reference and repetition of words were used as markers of thought units.

2:27b. Parse ἐλάβετε.⁴

2:27c. ἐν ὑμῖν . . . ἐν αὐτῷ. Both these expressions in v. 27 identify (metaphorical) "location" with the preposition ἐν + dative. Recall that the dative without a preposition can also be used for location; review *Sketch* §63.

2:27d. The ἵνα construction in the statement οὐ χρείαν ἔχετε **ἵνα** τις διδάσκῃ ὑμᾶς, "You do not need anyone to be teaching you," is one of the many places where ἵνα clauses function not to express *purpose* but *content* (often expressed in English by "that"). As such, it is the equivalent of either ὅτι and an indicative verb (οὐ χρείαν ἔχετε **ὅτι** τις **διδάσκει** ὑμᾶς) or a complementary infinitive clause. Here is an example of the infinitive clause: ἐγὼ χρείαν ἔχω ὑπὸ σοῦ **βαπτισθῆναι**, "It is I who have need *to be baptized* by you" (Matt. 3:14; cf. BDF §393[5]).

2:27e. Parse μένετε.⁵

2:27f. The ambiguities in v. 27 are many. In part this is indicated by the large number of variant readings as ancient scribes wrote what they expected to read or smoothed out the sentence to fit a different style. Hence, what is the original reading: τὸ αὐτοῦ χρῖσμα, "his anointing" or τὸ αὐτὸ χρῖσμα, "the same anointing"? Is it μένετε ἐν αὐτῷ, "Remain in him" (an imperative) or μενεῖτε⁶ ἐν αὐτῷ, "You will remain in him" (a promise). And does καθὼς ἐδίδαξεν ὑμᾶς mean, "Just as *he* (the Lord) taught you" or "Just as *it* (the anointing—a metonymy for the Holy Spirit) taught you"? Knowing Greek gives you options which are not normally accessible to the reader of translations, but it does not solve all ambiguities!

1 John 2:28

2:28a. You should now be entirely familiar with the vocative case (τεκνία here). If not, review *Sketch* §26.

2:28b. Parse φανερωθῇ,⁷ σχῶμεν,⁸ and αἰσχυνθῶμεν.⁹

---

⁴λαμβάνω 2A A I 2 pl. As with all second aorist forms, note the stem variance from the lexical form! The imperfect would be: ἐλαμβάνετε.

⁵μένω P A Impv 2 pl (the imperative and indicative share this form; context determines the correct parsing).

⁶μένω F A I 2 pl. Remember that future forms of liquid verbs look like epsilon contract verbs (*Primer* §18.4).

⁷φανερόω 1A P S 3 sg. Notice the characteristic –θη– of the first aorist passive stem (*Primer* §15.4).

⁸ἔχω 2A A S 1 pl. This is the second aorist stem minus the epsilon augment on the indicative form: ἔσχον → ἔ←σχ→ον → σχῶμεν (cf. *Primer* §9.1).

⁹αἰσχύνω 1A P S 1 pl. BAGD (p. 25) identifies this verb as active but found only in the middle and passive in our literature (one could just as easily give it as a deponent verb αἰσχύνομαι). The active meaning would be "to shame (someone)"; middle would be "to be ashamed"; and passive would be "to be shamed (by someone)." The middle has the effect of turning a transitive meaning into an intransitive (see especially *Primer* §15.8).

2:28c. The word order of ἵνα ἐὰν φανερωθῇ σχῶμεν παρρησίαν imbeds ἐὰν φανερωθῇ between ἵνα and its verb, σχῶμεν. We can do the same in English: "in order that, when he appears, we might have confidence." Just make sure you take the ἵνα with σχῶμεν and the ἐὰν with φανερωθῇ and you'll be fine.

2:28d. ἵνα often introduces a purpose clause where the idea of *intention* is in the forefront: "Remain in him, *with the intended result that* we may have confidence." Here, however, ἵνα shows that it may also simply express the result of another action where the idea of intention has receded from view: "Remain in him, *so that as a result* we may have confidence." Result clauses are more often expressed in Greek by ὥστε + infinitive with less ambiguity, but ἵνα has this meaning frequently also (BAGD p. 378, §II.2).

2:28e. Normally, ἐὰν introduces a condition in the future: ἐὰν φανερωθῇ, "If he should appear." In this verse, however, John is not expressing doubt as to whether the Lord will appear. In the common use of Greek (found also in the LXX), ἐὰν doubled in function with the indefinite temporal marker ὅταν, "whenever" or "when," as here and in 3:2.[10] The phrase should then be translated "*when* he appears." Remember, a subjunctive phrase does not necessarily communicate doubt about the fulfillment of an event, but that the author does not know precisely when it will happen. This is the difference between an *uncertain* event and an *indefinite* event; see *Primer* §22.7.

2:28f. καὶ μὴ αἰσχυνθῶμεν is parallel with σχῶμεν and thus dependent upon ἵνα also. The statement without ellipsis would read: καὶ ἵνα μὴ αἰχυνθῶμεν.

2:28g. The prepositional phrase in ἐν τῇ παρουσίᾳ αὐτοῦ expresses the idea of "time when"; the concept is location in time: "at (the time of) his arrival." The dative without a preposition (τῇ παρουσίᾳ αὐτοῦ) could have been used with the same meaning (*Sketch* §64). For example: τῇ τρίτῃ ἡμέρᾳ ἐγερθήσεται, "He will be raised *on the third day*" (Matt. 17:23).

1 John 2:29

2:29a. Parse εἰδῆτε.[11]

2:29b. Why did John switch from οἶδα to γινώσκω (εἰδῆτε . . . γινώσκετε) in v. 29?

2:29c. πᾶς ὁ ποιῶν is a common construction in John. It is the equivalent of a conditional clause: "If someone practices. . . ." English also has a variety of ways to express conditions; for instance, "Anyone who practices righteousness . . ." has a conditional implication. Note the meaning of ὁ ποιῶν τὴν δικαιοσύνην as *practicing* righteousness, a lifestyle. John discusses the opposite lifestyle with the same verb in the next chapter (ὁ ποιῶν τὴν ἁμαρτίαν in 3:4ff.).

2:29d. Explain the use of the article with δικαιοσύνην.

---

[10]See BAGD p. 211, §1d. Many ancient scribes interpreted ἐὰν this way and substituted ὅταν in v. 28.

[11]οἶδα A A S 2 pl. Although this form is parsed as aorist, it has only one stem for its non-indicative forms (sometimes identified as a perfect form from this verb's earlier history). Cf. *Primer*, p. 187.

2:29e. What is the relationship between the verb γεγέννηται[12] and ἐξ αὐτοῦ? (cf. John 1:13).

1 John 3:1

3:1a. Parse ἴδετε.[13]

3:1b. BAGD prefer the rendering "how glorious" rather than "what sort of" for ποταπήν in v. 1 (BAGD pp. 694–95). In either case, the *quality* of God's love is John's focus in this statement.

3:1c. Does ἵνα in v. 1 introduce a purpose or result clause?[14]

3:1d. What is the use of the genitive in τέκνα θεοῦ?

3:1e. διὰ τοῦτο is a common phrase in Greek expressing a conclusion: "hence," "therefore," "for this reason" (e.g., Rom. 5:12; Eph. 1:15). John uses it in v. 1 and elsewhere to refer ahead to a ὅτι clause which expresses the reason for the main statement: "The world does not know us *for the following reason: because* it did not know him." διά in this phrase has its common meaning with an accusative expressing *reason*.

> "Divine childhood is part of the New Covenant. (A related work, Rev 21:7, uses the OT covenant formula for the Christian child of God: 'He who conquers . . . I will be God to him, and he shall be to me a son.') . . . John has rephrased the covenant saying, 'I will be your God, and you shall be my people,' into 'I will be your God, and you shall be my children.' Similarly he has redefined Israel, so that the genuine Israelite is one who confesses Jesus to be God's Son and King of Israel (John 1:47–49)." Raymond E. Brown

3:1f. Parse ἔγνω.[15]

1 John 3:2

3:2a. See note 2:28e above for ἐάν meaning "whenever."

3:2b. Parse ἐσόμεθα.[16]

3:2c. Some adjectives take a dative of respect as ὅμοιοι αὐτῷ does here. The underlying idea can be (awkwardly) paraphrased: "similar with respect to him"; cf. *Sketch* §56. With this dative use, one simply consults a good lexicon like BAGD ("w[ith] dat[ive] of the pers[on] or thing compared"

---

[12]γεννάω Pf P I 3 sg. The perfect form reduplicates normally here (γεγέννηται) and the passive stem has no kappa. The eta in this form (γεγέννηται) is the alpha contract vowel (γεννάω) lengthened. Cf. *Primer* §14.2 for the basic πεπόρευμαι pattern.

[13]βλέπω/ὁράω 2A A Impv 2 pl. The present imperative (βλέπετε) frequently has a cautionary tone: "watch out for," "keep an eye on" (e.g., Phil. 3:2). The sense of this aorist in 1 John 3:1 is more contemplative: "take a look at. . .", "consider for a moment. . . ."

[14]Result: "Consider the sort of love the Father has bestowed upon us *that, as a result,* we might be called. . . ." See note 2:28d above.

[15]γινώσκω 2A A I 3 sg; see *Primer* §9.2.

[16]εἰμί F D I 1 pl; cf. *Primer* §10.2.

p. 566). Also, the Greek idiom is like English, which expresses reference by the preposition "to" ("we will be similar *to* him"; or the older style, "like *unto* him").

1 John 3:3

3:3a. Parse ἐλπίδα.[17]

3:3b. The preposition ἐπί is one of Greek's most flexible prepositions. Glosses include: *in, on, upon, among, before, because of, about,* and *by.* In v. 3, ἐπ᾽ αὐτῷ conveys the same "place where" idea as ἐν αὐτῷ, "in him," as found in 2:27–28 above On this analysis, αὐτῷ refers to the Christian and acts adverbially on the participle (πᾶς ὁ ἔχων . . . ἐπ᾽ αὐτῷ, "everyone who has within himself"). It is possible to analyze ἐπ᾽ αὐτῷ as adjectival, modifying ἐλπίδα: "this hope which is (placed) in him," in which case αὐτῷ would refer to Jesus. However, the adjectival meaning, though remotely possible, would require the prepositional phrase to stand next to an article; either: τὴν ἐλπίδα ταύτην **τὴν** ἐπ᾽ αὐτῷ, or τὴν **ἐπ᾽ αὐτῷ** ἐλπίδα ταύτην.

3:3c. What kind of pronoun is ἑαυτόν? Cf. *Primer* §§16.3, 7; *Sketch* §68.

3:3d. Like αὐτός, sometimes the nominative demonstrative pronoun is used as the subject of a predicate sentence without any emphasis. Here we have καθὼς **ἐκεῖνος** ἁγνός ἐστιν, "Just as *he* is holy," with no real stress on ἐκεῖνος.

---

[17]ἐλπίς f a sg.

7

Pronouns

REVIEW: *Primer,* Lessons 16–17, 24
READ: *Syntax Sketch* §66–71
STUDY: 1 John 3:4–10

Vocabulary

ἀγοράζω, I am buying (cf. ἀγορά)

ἄνεμος, ὁ, wind (*animate*)

ἀνομία, ἡ, lawlessness (cf. νόμος)

ἀρνίον, τό, lamb, sheep

γνῶσις, –εως, ἡ, knowledge (*Gnostic*)

διάκονος, ὁ, ἡ, servant; deacon (masc. or fem.) (*deacon*)

διδαχή, ἡ, teaching (*didactic*)

ἐγγύς, near (cf. ἐγγίζω)

ἐλεέω, I have mercy on

ἐλπίζω, I hope (cf. ἐλπίς)

ἔξεστι, it is lawful, allowed (impersonal)

ἐπικαλέω, I am calling; I am appealing (middle)

ἐπιτιμάω, I am rebuking, warning

ἴδε, look, behold (originally a second aorist imperative from βλέπω)

ἱερεύς, –έως, ὁ, priest (*hierarchy*)

μάχαιρα, ἡ, knife; sword

ὁμοίως, likewise, similarly

πλῆθος, –ους, τό, crowd; quantity (*plethora*)

πλήν, only, however

ποτήριον, τό, cup (*pot*)

συνείδησις, –εως, ἡ, conscience

συνέρχομαι, I am coming together

φανερός, –ά, –όν, clear, evident (cf. φανερόω)

φυλάσσω, I am guarding (cf. φυλακή)

φυλή, ἡ, tribe, people (*phylum*)

Overview

Pronouns in Greek are often transparent to English speakers, because they often have the same function as in English. For instance, we need no subtle grammatical description to understand the reciprocal pronoun, ἀλλήλους, as here: ἀγαπῶμεν **ἀλλήλους,** "Let us love *one another.*" On the other hand, there are a few unusual features to Greek pronouns like changes in meaning with αὐτός indicated by word position, which are covered in the *Syntax Sketch.* I will point out all the pronouns in this lesson's 1 John passage, not because they are all exegetically interesting, but merely to show you how transparent most Greek pronouns are. It will also show you how frequently pronouns occur (twelve times in these seven verses in 1 John).

I have also appended an Excursus to this lesson on the significance of the present tense form of ἁμαρτάνειν in v. 9. We are not covering "tense" or "aspect" in this book, but this is one of those times when the issue has intruded itself. There is growing scholarly interest and literature in Greek verbal aspect. A thorough acquaintance with this subject will both yield exegetical rewards and help you to avoid pitfalls in this area, particularly problems of oversimplification and of over-interpretation of the "tense forms." The Excursus, although very brief, represents a model of how to approach the issue of tense form analysis.

Reading Notes

1 John 3:4

3:4a. πᾶς ὁ ποιῶν is a fairly common construction found several other times in this passage and in many others (cf. BDF §413[2]). The present tense form is preferred with this use of the substantive participle (ποιῶν[1]), fitting in with the "customary" idea: "practicing sin" is a customary or characteristic action of the person John has in mind. The πᾶς + substantive participle construction is the virtual equivalent of the protasis of an indefinite conditional statement: ἐάν τις ποιεῖ τὴν ἁμαρτίαν, "If someone practices sin," or of an indefinite relative clause: ὃς ἂν ποιῇ τὴν ἁμαρτίαν, "Whoever practices sin."

3:4b. John probably shows his Semitic heritage or at least his colloquial style by using καί so frequently. Hebrew and Aramaic have only a bare handful of conjunctions (ו was put to just about any use).[2] In v. 4 the first καί has the common adverbial meaning *also*: "Everyone who practices sin is *also* practicing lawlessness." The second καί in this verse explains some preceding word or phrase and can be translated: "*indeed*," or "*as a matter of fact* sin is lawlessness." While this is acceptable Greek, γάρ or other word(s) would be more common in other Greek writers than καί here.

3:4c. Explain the significance of the articles with ἡ ἁμαρτία and ἡ ἀνομία (*Sketch* §6).

1 John 3:5

3:5a. οἴδατε ὅτι is indirect discourse with ὅτι + indicative verb. Remember, the other construction used for indirect discourse has no ὅτι but a simple infinitive (cf. Wallace, pp. 603–5; Young, p. 174; BDF §396; *Sketch* §94).

3:5b. ἐκεῖνος is a "far demonstrative" pronoun. It was chosen here to point to a subject (Jesus) who is "farther away" than the immediate context. If John had used οὗτος instead, the referent would be πᾶς ὁ ποιῶν τὴν ἁμαρτίαν in v. 4! And to have used αὐτός would have been the same as using οὗτος but with some sort of emphasis "he has himself appeared." Hence, ἐκεῖνος is a helpful pronoun to point to someone else than the immediately preceding subject. The translation "that one" or "that man" does not do it justice here in English.

3:5c. Does the article with τὰς ἁμαρτίας mean: (1) "sins" (NASB); or (2) "our sins" (KJV; NIV)? (Note the variant reading attested by a variety of ancient Greek manuscripts: τὰς ἁμαρτίας ἡμῶν. This indicates at least how ancient Greek scribes interpreted the article.)

---

[1] ποιέω P A Ptc m n sg.

[2] "Another common feature is the practice, drawn fr[om] Hebrew or fr[om] the speech of everyday life, of using κ[αί] as a connective where more discriminating usage would call for other particles" BAGD, p. 392, §2.b.

3:5d. Parse ἄρῃ.[3]

3:5e. Here the idea of a "once for all" aorist could be imposed on ἄρῃ, but it must be resisted. The fact that Christ did away with our sins once for all is a truth to be cherished, but it is communicated by the *statements* of Scripture, *not* by the aorist aspect of the subjunctive alone. The aorist subjunctive expresses a simple truth: "He appeared in order to *eliminate* our sins." This is what I mean by "simple" action, the event is presented as a fact without further elaboration; grammarians generally call this the "constative" aorist (e.g., Young, 122–23).

3:5f. Why did John switch to the anarthrous ἁμαρτία here when he had used the article with this noun earlier? Is this following Colwell's canon? Is there stress on this word?

> "Perhaps no feature of the biblical languages is the source of more confusion and fanciful interpretation than the verbal 'tenses.' Beginning Greek students, upon being confronted with the term *aorist* (which is normally not used in English grammar), tend to inject quasi-mysterious associations into it. . . . The aorist was normally used to refer to an action as a whole, a complete event; thus it was the tense chosen when the writer did *not* want to say something special about the action." Moisés Silva

3:5g. αὐτός in the phrase ἐν αὐτῷ is a normal third person personal pronoun "in him." We commented above that αὐτός at the beginning of v. 5 would have pointed to the wrong antecedent, so John used ἐκεῖνος there (see note 3:5b above). Here, though, ἐκεῖνος (referring to Jesus) is the more prominent subject of the statement, so John used αὐτός to point back to him. To have said ἐν ἐκείνῳ in v. 5b would have "jumped over" Jesus to point to "everyone who practices sin"! Again, there is nothing unusual or difficult about the pronoun use here; I simply point out these common features so that you will see how pronouns work in Greek.

1 John 3:6

3:6a. For πᾶς + the present substantive participles in v. 6 and below, see note 3:4a above.

3:6b. For the personal pronoun in the phrase ἐν αὐτῷ see note 3:5g above.

3:6c. Compare these translations for ἁμαρτάνει: "No one who abides in him *sins*" (NASB); "No one who lives in him *keeps on sinning*" (NIV). What is the difference between the meaning of the translations? Part of the answer lies in seeing that ἁμαρτάνω for John is evidently synonymous with the phrase ποιῶ τὴν ἁμαρτίαν, "I am practicing sin," found in vv. 4, 8, and 9. The translation "sins" is a general truth ("gnomic" in Young, pp. 110–11; cf. Wallace, pp. pp. 523–25); and "keeps on sinning" expresses the action as a custom, characteristic action, or process (Wallace, pp. 521–23; Young, pp. 108–9). At this point Greek grammar and theology must interact intimately if the proper interpretation is to emerge.

3:6d. For the perfect tense forms in v. 6 (ἑώρακεν and ἔγνωκεν) see note 1:1f above.

3:6e. The two uses of the personal pronoun αὐτόν in v. 6b are simple and worth little more comment than to note how much like English they are here.

---

[3]αἴρω A A S 3 sg. This is a liquid verb; notice the stem change signifying the aorist subjunctive form; see *Primer* §§18.2–3 and §22.5 (the present subjunctive is αἴρῃ).

1 John 3:7

3:7a. Parse μηδείς.[4] This is another pronoun. Why did John choose μηδείς rather than οὐδείς?

3:7b. The formal idea of the third person imperative (πλανάτω[5]) is: The speaker turns to someone and tells him to allow or to forbid another party to do something. So there are three parties: the speaker, the recipient of the imperative who is to allow or to forbid something, and a third party (expressed in the nominative) who is allowed or forbidden to do something. (In some cases parties #2 and #3 may be the same: "Don't let *anyone* deceive *himself*.") Somehow it is in the first person's power to allow, to permit, or to have that action done. Here, the nominative (μηδείς) is the subject and the imperative is given to "you": "Let no one deceive you."

3:7c. Parse ὑμᾶς.[6] This, again, is another simple personal pronoun.

3:7d. We find the demonstrative pronoun ἐκεῖνος again with the same function as we discussed in note 3:5b above.

1 John 3:8

3:8a. Which is the better translation for ὁ ποιῶν τὴν ἁμαρτίαν: "The person who commits sin" or "The person who practices sin" or "The person who practiced sin"? Why? Back up your answer with other examples from 1 John.

3:8b. See note 2:7i above for ἀπ' ἀρχῆς.

3:8c. ἁμαρτάνει is a good example of the present tense form expressing a general or timeless truth. This use of the present tense form is called the "gnomic" or "omnitemporal" present (cf. Wallace, pp. 523–25; Young, pp. 110–11).

3:8d. Parse τοῦτο.[7]

3:8e. There is redundancy with εἰς τοῦτο . . . ἵνα, "for the following reason . . . namely, in order to . . ." (for a similar construction see note 3:1e above). This serves to focus upon the purpose clause. The referent of the "near demonstrative" pronoun τοῦτο is the following ἵνα clause; when a pronoun refers to something which follows it in word order, the referent is called a "postcedent" rather than an "antecedent." And τοῦτο is neuter singular because it refers to a *clause* (the ἵνα clause) rather than to a person or noun.

3:8f. λύω should not be translated "loose" here. Look this word up in BAGD for its meaning.

3:8g. What is the genitive relation in the phrase τὰ ἔργα τοῦ διαβόλου?

---

[4]μηδείς, μηδεμία, μηδέν m n sg; see *Primer* §§30.1–2.

[5]πλανάω P A Impv 3 sg; alpha contract verb cf. *Primer* §§23.2, 4.

[6]σύ 2 a pl.

[7]οὗτος, αὕτη, τοῦτο n a sg; cf. *Primer* §17.2.

1 John 3:9

3:9a. Parse γεγεννημένος.[8]

3:9b. We have seen the following substantive participles in this passage.

3:4	πᾶς **ὁ ποιῶν** τὴν ἁμαρτίαν
3:6	ὁ ἐν αὐτῷ **μένων**
3:6	πᾶς **ὁ ἁμαρτάνων**
3:7	**ὁ ποιῶν** τὴν δικαιοσύνην
3:8	**ὁ ποιῶν** τὴν ἁμαρτίαν
3:10	πᾶς ὁ μὴ **ποιῶν** δικαιοσύνην
3:10	ὁ μὴ **ἀγαπῶν** τὸν ἀδελφὸν αὐτοῦ

They are all present "tense" forms, but with ὁ γεγεννημένος we have the perfect. Why did John switch to the perfect here? Contrast the perfect with ὁ γεννώμενος (present) and ὁ γεννηθείς (aorist) (cf. 1 John 5:18).

3:9c. Case forms generally communicate the same relationships between words as expressed through prepositions. Thus we can describe the meaning of ἐκ in the phrase ἐκ τοῦ θεοῦ with the same terms used to describe the genitive relation. Is the meaning here "personal relation," "agency," "source," or some other relation we studied under the genitive case?

3:9d. In v. 9 we have two uses of the third person personal pronoun αὐτός (αὐτοῦ and ἐν αὐτῷ) next to each other with different referents: "*His* [God's] seed remains in *him* [the believer]." This understanding is clear from the flow of the text, but shows the ambiguity possible with personal pronouns.

3:9e. See the Excursus below for my analysis of ἁμαρτάνειν.

1 John 3:10

3:10a. To what does the near demonstrative pronoun ἐν **τούτῳ** refer? At first glance, we could parse τούτῳ as masculine dative singular and take it to refer to the *person* who has been born "from God": "In *this person* it is evident that. . . ." However, as the sentence proceeds, we see that this is not a possible reading. Hence we must revise our parsing to *neuter* dative singular and see the referent as the *situation* expressed in v. 9: "In this manner [the enduring Christian testimony of the person who has truly been born of God], the children of God . . . are manifest. . . .'"

3:10b. A *neuter plural* noun acting as the subject of a verb may take a *singular* verb rather than an expected plural verb. Hence, although τέκνα is the plural subject of the verb in φανερά ἐστιν τὰ **τέκνα**, because this noun is *neuter* plural, the verb is expressed in its singular form (ἐστιν). This unusual rule of Greek usage is sometimes called τὰ ζῷα τρέχει, "The animals run," which is merely an example of the rule; see BDF §133.

3:10c. What is the genitive relation in the phrases τὰ τέκνα τοῦ θεοῦ and τὰ τέκνα τοῦ διαβόλου?

---

[8]γεννάω Pf P Ptc m n sg.

3:10d. There are two possible interpretations of the statement, καὶ ὁ μὴ ἀγαπῶν τὸν ἀδελφὸν αὐτοῦ. First, it may be an additional idea acting in parallel with the first clause: "Everyone who does not practice righteousness is not from God, neither is the one who does not love his brother" or "likewise, the one who does not love his brother." The failure to practice righteousness and the failure to love one's brother are merely two parallel ideas. Secondly, and more attractive here, καί can introduce an "epexegetical"[9] clause (cf. BDF §442[9]). This means that ὁ μὴ ἀγαπῶν clarifies what ὁ μὴ ποιῶν δικαιοσύνην means. It is like apposition: "Everyone who does not practice righteousness, *that is, the one who does not love his brother,* is not from God."

3:10e. The personal pronoun in τὸν ἀδελφὸν **αὐτοῦ** refers back to the subject of the statement (ὁ μὴ ἀγαπῶν). This situation calls for a *reflexive* pronoun: τὸν ἀδελφὸν **ἑαυτοῦ**. Greeks often employed the simple third person pronoun in place of the reflexive pronoun as John did here (*Sketch* §68). John could also have used the adjective ἴδιος (τὸν ἴδιον ἀδελφόν) with the same meaning (see, for instance, John 1:11). The selection of these different forms is merely a matter of personal style rather than a difference in meaning.

EXCURSUS: *"The Present Infinitive and Perfectionism"*

First John 3:9 has historically been the *locus classicus* for the notion that genuine Christians experience sinless perfection in this life.[10] Our versions illustrate different interpretations of the key segment of this verse (πᾶς ὁ γεγεννημένος ἐκ τοῦ θεοῦ ἁμαρτίαν οὐ ποιεῖ . . . οὐ δύναται ἁμαρτάνειν):

◊   "No one born of God *commits sin . . . he cannot sin*" (RSV).
◊   "No one who is born of God *will continue to sin . . . he cannot go on sinning*" (NIV).
◊   "No one who is born of God *practices sin . . . he cannot sin*" (NASB).

The RSV allows the perfectionist interpretation, and the NIV clearly does not. The NASB is ambiguous. The issue revolves around whether the present infinitive ἁμαρτάνειν in the phrase οὐ δύναται ἁμαρτάνειν signifies characteristic action, *"go on sinning"* in the NIV, or whether it signifies the simple occurrence of the action, "[commit] *sin*." If the latter, then it appears that true Christians can and should obtain sinless perfection in this life.

In questions of this sort, Greek grammar can be stretched beyond legitimate limits. And as always, the issue should be decided by a thorough study of the passage and of other relevant Scriptures. However, in this case, study of *verbal aspect*[11] does help clear up the issue. In my opinion, the fact that John chose to use the present infinitive, ἁμαρτάνειν rather than the aorist ἁμαρτεῖν, shows that he was thinking about "sinning" in v. 9 as a *characteristic action*. Hence, John does not teach "perfectionism"—that Christians can experience sinlessness in this life. Rather,

---

[9]The term "epexegetical" means that something elucidates or expands upon a previous idea.

[10]Scholarly exposition has rarely read 1 John 3:9 this way, but recent commentators have given it more credence. Stephen Smalley writes: "While the New Testament seems to give no approval to a doctrine of 'sinless perfection' this side of heaven, the writer [John] does appear to be saying (uniquely) that the indwelling of God's σπέρμα ("nature") excludes sin *entirely,*" Smalley, p. 175 (the emphasis is Smalley's). See Wallace, pp. 524–25 for discussion along similar lines.

[11]"Verbal aspect" is the term used to refer to the fact that a Greek verb often conveys not temporal information (past, present, or future), but the author's "description" of the verbal event's occurrence (iterative, attempted, simple, incomplete, etc.). "Aspect" is the standard term to describe this description. Review *Primer* §25.7 for verbal aspect and infinitives.

when he says οὐ δύναται ἁμαρτάνειν he teaches that the genuine Christian cannot be characterized by a life of unrepentant sin. To support this interpretation of ἁμαρτάνειν in v. 9, I will discuss three issues: (1) the immediate context; (2) the lexical significance of ἁμαρτάνω and its influence upon tense form choice of the infinitive; and, (3) the influence of δύναμαι upon the tense form of its complementary infinitive, since ἁμαρτάνειν is the complement of this verb in v. 9.

CONTEXT. My interpretation of the clause in question does fit the context. John expresses his concern for characteristic action in various ways: with μένω (a favorite verb in John's writings), "Everyone who *remains* in him does not (characteristically) commit sin" (3:6). Similarly ποιέω is used to focus upon the characteristic practice of sin (in contrast to the committing of sin itself): "He [the true Christian] does not *practice* sin (as a characteristic feature of his life)" (3:9a; cf. 1:6, "is not practicing truth"), and, in contrast, the metaphor "walking in the darkness" (1:6; cf. "walking in the light" in 1:7) communicates a lifestyle dominated by sin. John could just as well have said in v. 9b: οὐ δύναται ἐν τῷ σκότει περιπατεῖν, "[the person born of God] cannot be walking in the darkness." The context does not support perfectionism. Rather, John is teaching that the cruel dominion of sin has been broken for believers (see especially Paul's similar teaching in Romans 6).

LEXICAL MEANING. The question one should ask when dealing with Greek tense form usage for a particular verb is whether that verb is lexically limited or suited to a particular present or aorist form, especially in the dependent (i.e., non-indicative) moods. For example, εἶναι does not have an aorist form—how could it? "To be," "to exist," is a state or a statement of equivalence in a predication; these meanings do not inherently fit the aorist.[12] Likewise, ἀγαπάω, ἔχω, ζάω, περιπατέω are generally found in present tense forms in the dependent moods, because these words denote an action or state which by their nature are progressive, habitual, static, etc.

How this intrinsic character of an event may affect exegesis is best shown by example. The verb, ἀγαπάω, occurs in 1 John 4:20 in a construction parallel to 3:9: "For anyone who does not love his brother, whom he has seen, *cannot love God* (οὐ δύναται ἀγαπᾶν), whom he has not seen" (NIV). Here the NIV chose not to translate the infinitive ἀγαπᾶν as "he cannot *go on loving*," making the present infinitive refer to continuous, habitual action. That is because ἀγαπάω is lexically influenced—it was conceived by Greek writers as most appropriately expressed in the present tense because "loving" itself is a static relationship, rather than an action that occurs over a limited span of time, as in contrast, πίπτω "I fall," ἐγείρω "I raise," or ἐξέρχομαι "I leave." As evidence, ἀγαπάω occurs 8 times in the present infinitive, never in the aorist in the NT; 15 times in the present subjunctive and only once in the aorist subjunctive (Matt. 5:46; perhaps meaning "express love [simply]").[13] The implication is that John would not be expected to use an aorist infinitive of ἀγαπάω in 1 John 4:20. If he had, the nuance would probably be inceptive: "For anyone who does not love his brother . . . cannot *begin to love* God" (as found in the reading of one minuscule manuscript, 33).

But is ἁμαρτάνω a verb like ἀγαπάω? No. The infinitive of ἁμαρτάνω does not occur elsewhere in the New Testament, but its occurrences in the subjunctive mood (which is closest in usage to the infinitive among dependent moods) is only in the aorist (6 times, including twice in 1 John 2:1) but never in the present aspect. If the action designated by ἁμαρτάνω was regarded by the NT authors as a process or state, they would have normally expressed this verb in the *present* subjunctive much as they did with ἀγαπάω. Hence, the present infinitive, ἁμαρτάνειν, in 1 John 3:9 was not influenced by lexical meaning.

---

[12]Sometimes the second aorist of γίνομαι was called into service as the virtual aorist of εἰμί. Even then, γίνομαι is "inceptive" rather than a true constative aorist of εἰμί, since "become" communicates lexically the entrance into being something or starting to exist.

[13]For the LXX, ἀγαπάω occurs 19 times as a present infinitive versus 6 times as aorist (some of the latter were determined by the constructions in which the infinitive occurs).

The Construction. The third point to analyze is whether δύναμαι influences the tense form of its complementary infinitive. This is the case with μέλλω and ἄρχομαι, which, by the nature of their meaning, are most appropriately followed by a *present* infinitive designating a process, etc.[14] In the case of δύναμαι, the NT evidence is clear: δύναμαι is completed by the present infinitive 48 times, compared to 126 occurrences with the aorist infinitive. If these statistics were reversed, one could make the case that ἁμαρτάνω in 1 John 3:9 was expressed as a present infinitive because it completed a verb which required the present infinitive—as, for example, ἄρχεται ἁμαρτάνειν, "he is beginning (the process of) sinning." Instead, we see that because δύναμαι is normally followed by an aorist infinitive, John consciously chose the present infinitive form ἁμαρτάνειν because he wished to convey a special nuance. That nuance is the "characteristic" nature of the action, a lifestyle of sinning. If John *had* wished to express perfectionism, the aorist infinitive of ἁμαρτάνω would have been employed: οὐ δύναται **ἁμαρτεῖν**, "he cannot commit sin (at any point)."

In conclusion then, the phrase οὐ δύναται ἁμαρτάνειν in 1 John 3:9 expresses the fact that the Christian is prevented by the new birth and the abiding presence of God from falling into *persistent sin*. In the context, John uses the phrase ὁ ποιῶν τὴν ἁμαρτίαν and ἁμαρτίαν ποιεῖ with the same sense.[15] The verb ποιέω communicates the notion of characteristic practice lexically. The present form of the infinitive in the phrase οὐ δύναται **ἁμαρτάνειν** is in essence a shorthand version of the ποιέω ἁμαρτίαν phrase, so that it is the equivalent of οὐ δύναται ἁμαρτίαν ποιεῖν, and is thus more accurately rendered by the NIV's "he cannot *go on sinning*," or, more idiomatically, "he cannot *live in sin*."[16]

---

[14]The statistics for the NT are: μέλλω + present infinitive 84 times, μέλλω + aorist infinitive 7 times; ἄρχομαι + present infinitive 87 times, ἄρχομαι + aorist infinitive 0 times.

[15]Cf. J. P. Louw, "Verbal Aspect in the First Letter of John," *Neotestamentica* 9 (1975): 102.

[16]Smalley and Wallace (see footnote 10 above), building on earlier scholarship, reject the "characteristic" interpretation of ἁμαρτάνειν I have defended here. They say this interpretation is "too subtle"; however, it is based upon solid verbal aspect analysis (and one could say that Wallace's "eschatological" interpretation is even more subtle) and it alone fits the context and universal biblical teaching. Secondly, they point to the present adverbial participle ἁμαρτάνοντα in 1 John 5:16 as not having such a "characteristic" action force, therefore ἁμαρτάνειν cannot. But their argument here fails to recognize an essential point in verbal aspect study: the function and force of tense forms varies with the different moods. An author chooses the tense form of a participle and the tense form of a complementary infinitive for different reasons. The adverbial participle ἁμαρτάνοντα in 1 John 5:16 was used in its present tense form to express action contemporary with the main verb; this meaning is not possible for the present infinitive ἁμαρτάνειν when it complements δύναμαι. To bring in ἁμαρτάνοντα in this connection is illegitimate and irrelevant to 1 John 3:9. See my "Introduction to Greek Tense Form Choice" (unpublished manuscript, Westminster Theological Seminary in California, 1999); cf. Moisés Silva, *Explorations in Exegetical Method: Galatians As a Test Case* (Grand Rapids: Baker, 1996), 78–79 for comments on this approach.

8

Adjectives

REVIEW: *Primer,* Lessons 10, 29
READ: *Syntax Sketch* §72–76
STUDY: 1 John 3:11–18

Vocabulary

ἁγιάζω, I am sanctifying, consecrating (cf. ἅγιος)
ἀδικέω, I am doing wrong, harming
ἀνθρωποκτόνος, ὁ, murderer
γαμέω, I am marrying (mono*gamy*)
ἡγέομαι, I am leading, ruling; I am thinking
θυγάτηρ, θυγατρός, ἡ, daughter (*daughter*)
θυσία, ἡ, sacrifice, offering
ἰσχύω, I am able; I am strong (cf. ἰσχυρός)
κλείω, I am shutting
μεταβαίνω, I am passing over, transferring
μισθός, ὁ, wages, reward
μυστήριον, τό, mystery (*mystery*)
νικάω, I am conquering (*Nich*olas)
παράκλησις, -εως, ἡ, comfort, consolation (cf. παράκλητος)
παρέρχομαι, I am passing by; I am neglecting
πάσχα, τό, Passover (*Paschal* lamb)
πόθεν, from where?
ποτέ, once, formerly, ever
προσκαλέω, I am summoning, calling (middle only)
σκανδαλίζω, I am making (someone) stumble (*scandal*)
σπλάγχνον, τό, compassion, feelings
σφάζω, I am slaying
φεύγω, I am fleeing, escaping
φίλος, ὁ, ἡ, friend (masc. or fem.); friendly (as adj.) (*phil*osophy)
χάριν + gen., because of, for the sake of (often occurs *after* its object)

Overview

Adjectives are the words which provide color to statements. They describe the traits of objects as either part of a descriptive phrase (attributive use) or as the main part of a statement (predicate use). And you will recall that neuter accusative adjectives may serve as adverbs in some places (review *Sketch* §32).

You are reviewing the main adjective forms in the *Primer* assignment, but an unusual characteristic of certain adjectives justifies a special note. Most compound adjectives have only two gender forms, a shared masculine and feminine form and a neuter form, even if they are constructed from adjectives which have the uncompounded three gender configurations. For instance, uncompounded πιστός, πιστή, πιστόν ("faithful," "believing") has the standard three gender forms, but compound ἄπιστος, ἄπιστον ("unbelieving") has only two forms; ἄπιστος performs double duty for both the masculine and feminine.[1]

Reading Notes

1 John 3:11

3:11a. Recall that the relative pronoun (ἥν[2]) does not have to agree with its antecedent (ἀγγελία) in its case, because the two words have different functions in their respective clauses (*Primer* §24.5; *Sketch* §69). ἥν is the direct object of ἠκούσατε in v. 11; it could have been expressed as a genitive (ἧς) since ἀκούω may take either a genitive or an accusative object.

3:11b. The aorist (ἠκούσατε) may seem unusual with the prepositional phrase ἀπ' ἀρχῆς if the verb is interpreted as denoting a "one-time action": "Which *you heard* (once) from the beginning." This is a case where the Greek aorist must be understood as referring to an act "simply" or to a group of discrete actions which occur over a length of time. The aorist in the case of the latter, simply regards the actions as a whole and summarizes them. For example: "I *taught* many times in your synagogues"; "He *healed* many people during that period." Both would be Greek aorists referring to many discrete actions viewed as a whole.[3] An imperfect verb in 1 John 3:11 (ἠκούετε) would have communicated the iterative idea more expressly: "Which *you used to hear* from the beginning"; "Which you *have heard from time to time* from the beginning." Instead, the aorist communicates the *fact* of hearing: "you did hear it," rather than the repeated nature of the event. The Greek aorist is often rendered by an English perfect in this usage ("You *have heard* from the beginning"). See Burton §46, and §§52–54 for a helpful comparison of English and Greek usage.

3:11c. In the expression ἵνα ἀγαπῶμεν, it is remotely possible to read ἵνα as introducing a purpose clause answering the question, "Why is it that this message was given from the beginning?" More likely, though, the ἵνα clause introduces a "content clause" synonymous with ὅτι "that." The clause gives the "content" of "this": "This is the message . . . (namely) *that* we love" equivalent to: "*That* we love one another is the message which you have heard from the beginning." This use of ἵνα is found mostly in John; cf. BDF §394.

3:11d. ἀλλήλους, remember, is called a reciprocal pronoun; see *Primer* §24.7; cf. BAGD.

1 John 3:12

3:12a. Parse ἔσφαξεν.[4]

3:12b. The aorist itself does not denote a one-time action, as noted above. This does not mean that it *cannot* be referring to an action which has one occurrence such as ἔσφαξεν in v. 12 (Cain only

---

[1] ἄπιστος, –ον illustrates a common way to form a compound in Greek with the so-called "alpha privative." A simple alpha (α) prefixed to an adjective makes it negative like the "un-" prefix in English: faithful, *un*faithful; πιστός, ἄπιστος. Adjectives with the *alpha privative* usually have only two forms.

[2] ὅς, ἥτις, ὅ f a sg.

[3] I prefer to call this the "simple" use of the aorist; however, you will find many other terms for it in the grammars including "constative," and "complexive"; see Wallace, pp. 557–58; Young, 122–23.

[4] σφάζω A A I 3 sg. Usually, the aorist stem merely drops the zeta (ζ) of the present stem when adding the sigma (βαπτίζω, ἐβάπτισα). Here, though, the stem changes to xi (ξ); see also κράζω, ἔκραξα.

murdered Abel once). The aorist indicative is flexible, and the meaning of any verb expressed in the aorist or any other "tense" can only be known from the meaning of the verb, its context, and the perceived reference of the statement as a whole.

How does σφάζω differ in meaning from, for instance, ἀποκτείνω? Check BAGD.

3:12c. The irregular preposition χάριν takes an object in the genitive case (τίνος[5]): "Because of what?" meaning, "Why?" here. This is the equivalent of τί. And, as noted in the vocabulary section, χάριν often comes *after* its object: τούτου **χάριν**, "for this reason" (Titus 1:5).

3:12d. Parse πονηρά.[6]

3:12e. The two adjectives πονηρά and δίκαια have the same function in their respective, parallel statements: they are both predicate adjectives; see *Primer* §10.5. If these were attributive adjectives, they would have been preceded by an article; e.g., **τὰ πονηρὰ** ἔργα αὐτοῦ, or even, τὰ ἔργα αὐτοῦ **τὰ πονηρά**. Remember to check the position of any adjective in relation to an article (if present) in order to determine its function.[7]

3:12f. Why did John use a singular verb, ἦν,[8] when its subject (ἔργα[9]) is plural? Answer: τὰ ζῷα τρέχει! (Cf. note 3:10b above.)

3:12g. Rather than repeating the noun ἔργα in the second clause, John simply uses the article as a rough and ready pronoun: **τὰ** (ἔργα) τοῦ ἀδελφοῦ, "the (works) of his brother" = "those of his brother" (*Sketch* §9). There is also ellipsis of the verb ἦν in this second statement.

1 John 3:13

3:13a. In the expression μὴ θαυμάζετε[10] the present imperative is used with the negative particle μή. Remember that the aorist imperative was not normally used with μή for prohibitions (μὴ θαυμάσατε); rather, the aorist subjunctive was used (μὴ θαυμάσητε); cf. *Primer* §23.7 (the "prohibitory subjunctive").

John used the *present* imperative in v. 13 rather than the *aorist* subjunctive because of the inherent character of θαυμάζω; it refers to a condition of mind which continues without any clear termination point (atelic). The translation, "Don't *be surprised*" brings out the nature of this event and the significance of the present "tense" form of the imperative here.[11] Some grammarians assume that prohibitions with the present tense form usually reflect the author's assumption that the action is already happening; i.e., "*Stop* being surprised (as you obviously are now)."[12] While this

---

[5]τίς, τί n g sg; the interrogative pronoun; see *Primer* §§17.2, 5.

[6]πονηρός, ά, όν, n n pl.

[7]It goes without saying that the article must agree in gender, case, and number in order to influence the adjective's meaning.

[8]εἰμί Impf A I 3 sg.

[9]ἔργον n n pl.

[10]θαυμάζω P A Impv 2 pl.

[11]I put "tense" in quotation marks because this term refers to the *time* of an event's occurrence, whereas all imperatives are necessarily *future*. This is particularly clear with the aorist imperative; this is not *past* time!

[12]Nigel Turner in particular presents this viewpoint in MHT 3: 75–76.

is a possible nuance in some cases, it requires that we can discern that the action has already begun (e.g., μὴ κλαίετε, "Stop weeping" Luke 8:52). But we cannot make that assumption in 1 John 3:13.

3:13b. ἀδελφοί is vocative plural, which looks like the nominative plural (*Sketch* §26).

1 John 3:14

3:14a. Why was ἡμεῖς used with οἴδαμεν? Is it needed? What is its significance here?

3:14b. Parse μεταβεβήκαμεν.[13]

3:14c. Check BAGD for the meaning of μεταβαίνω (p. 510, §2.a.). Note especially John 5:24 too. What is the significance of the perfect tense here?

3:14d. The common conjunction ὅτι often introduces the reason or rationale that a certain event takes place: Cain murdered Abel, *because* his deeds were wicked. The second ὅτι in v. 14, though, does not introduce the reason why Christians have been translated from death into life; it specifies the *evidence* by which we know (οἴδαμεν) this to be true. If you think about it for a moment, there is some causation here, but it flows backwards. There is a vital theological point at stake here, so make sure you understand it! (See the accompanying box for further discussion.)

3:14e. In the expression τοὺς ἀδελφούς, should the article be rendered "the" or "our" here? Why?

> We may use "because" in the same situation as found in I John 3:14. Consider these two examples: "The window is wide open, *because* a thief broke in." Here there is a cause and effect relation between the two clauses: the window is open because the thief opened it; "because" marks the causal clause. Now let's move "because" to the other clause (and reverse the clause order only for the sake of English style): "A thief broke in, *because* the window is wide open." In this second statement, the underlying causation remains the same (the window is open because a thief opened it and broke in), but the speaker is identifying the *evidence* used to deduce the invasion of a thief with the "because" marker. (Having a window open did not *cause* a thief to break in.) We can clarify by saying: "*We know that* a thief broke in, *because* the window is wide open." John does adds this clarifying point in I John 3:14 when he says ἡμεῖς οἴδαμεν ὅτι. For other examples of this same idiom in the New Testament (but without "we know that"), see Matt. 26:73; Luke 7:47; John 5:18; and Acts 2:15.

1 John 3:15

3:15a. Parse πᾶς.[14]

3:15b. The adjective πᾶς, πᾶσα, πᾶν is peculiar in that it is placed in the *predicate* position, even though it is *attributive* in function. It may also occur in the attributive position in rare cases with a slightly different meaning: τὸν **πάντα** χρόνον, "the *whole* time" or "the *entire* time" (Acts 20:18). It is easier to see the difference in this example: **πᾶς** ὁ ἄνθρωπος, "*every* man," versus ὁ **πᾶς** ἄνθρωπος, "the *entire* man."

---

[13]μεταβαίνω Pf A I 1 pl.

[14]πᾶς, πᾶσα, πᾶν m n sg.

3:15c. As we have seen several times before, πᾶς ὁ μισῶν employs a present substantive participle denoting "characteristic" action.[15]

3:15d. πᾶς ἀνθρωποκτόνος οὐκ ἔχει ζωήν is a peculiarly Semitic form of speech, "every murderer does not have life." In Greek (and English), the *noun* would normally be negative: **οὐδεὶς** ἀνθρωποκτόνος ἔχει ζωήν, "No murderer has life"; see BDF §302.

3:15e. Since ἐν αὐτῷ refers back to the subject of the verb, this personal pronoun functions as a reflexive pronoun, "in *himself*" (*Sketch* §68). John could have said, ἐν ἑαυτῷ (cf. *Primer* §§16.3, 7).

3:15f. Parse αἰώνιον.[16]

3:15g. αἰώνιον is an attributive adjective modifying ζωήν, yet the adjective does not have an article preceding it, because the noun is anarthrous. You will find the structure ζωὴν αἰώνιον and **τὴν** ζωὴν **τὴν** αἰώνιον but not ζωὴν **τὴν** αἰώνιον.[17]

3:15h. Parse μένουσαν.[18]

3:15i. μένουσαν is an attributive participle (agreeing with ζωήν): "life eternal *which remains* in him." You can see with this example that an attributive participle is essentially an adjective, since both the participle μένουσαν and the adjective αἰώνιον modify the same noun ζωήν in parallel.

1 John 3:16

3:16a. ἐν τούτῳ . . . ὅτι is the same "content clause" idea encountered in v. 11 except that ἵνα was used there instead of ὅτι as here in v. 16; see BDF §394.

3:16b. Parse ἐγνώκαμεν.[19]

3:16c. τίθηναι[20] ψυχήν is an idiomatic expression meaning "to lay down one's life," "to voluntarily die" (see *Louw and Nida* §23.113). Because the phrase is idiomatic, would it be correct to regard ψυχή as "literally" meaning "soul"? John clearly alludes here to John 15:13.

3:16d. Is ἡμεῖς required with ὀφείλομεν? What is its significance in v. 16?

3:16e. Should we render τὰς ψυχὰς as "*the* lives," "*our* lives," or some other way? Why?

3:16f. Parse θεῖναι.[21]

---

[15]μισῶν—μισέω P A Ptc m n sg.

[16]αἰώνιος, –ον f a sg. Some adjectives like this one share one form in the masculine and the feminine.

[17]There is an exception to this principle—isn't there always?!—if the anarthrous noun is definite for some reason; e.g., as the object of a preposition (ἐν ζωῇ τῇ αἰωνίῳ) or a proper name (Ἰωάννης ὁ ἀγαθός).

[18]μένω P A Ptc f a sg.

[19]γινώσκω Pf A I 1 pl.

[20]Occurring first as ἔθηκεν in v. 16; parsed as: τίθημι A A I 3 sg; cf. *Primer* §§26.2, 5.

[21]τίθημι A A Inf; cf. *Primer* Lesson 26 for parsing tips.

3:16g. θεῖναι is a complementary infinitive with ὀφείλομεν; cf. *Primer* §§25.5–6.

1 John 3:17

3:17a. The indefinite relative clause ὃς δ' ἂν ἔχῃ functions much like a conditional clause; i.e., ἐάν τις ἔχῃ, "If someone has . . ."; cf. BDF §380.

3:17b. Parse ἔχῃ,[22] θεωρῇ,[23] and κλείσῃ.[24]

3:17c. Check BAGD for the meaning of βίος here. Is this meaning found outside the NT also?

3:17d. The string of subjunctive verbs implies a repetition of the indefinite relative pronoun: ὃς ἂν ἔχῃ . . . καὶ (ὃς ἂν) θεωρῇ . . . καὶ (ὃς ἂν) κλείσῃ. Note the tense forms of these three subjunctives (two present forms and one aorist). The reason for the variation is probably related to the inherent meaning of each verb here.

3:17e. ἔχοντα has an adverbial use indicating a state contemporaneous with the main verb. Even though the translation "while having" is clumsy, it is accurate. The subject beholds the brother *while* he has the need.

3:17f. The NASB has this marginal note for σπλάγχνα: "Lit., inward parts." However, this notion of "literalness" is mistaken and unhelpful. The word simply has a transferred meaning from "intestines" (where emotional responses are physically felt) to "compassion." Compare English idioms: "Have a *heart* will you!"; "She's a real *brain*"; "He's got *guts*." Knowing the "literal" referent of these English words gives one no real insight into their meanings in these statements. Remember than in every case, translations are nothing more than good commentaries.

3:17g. What use of the genitive is θεοῦ in the phrase ἡ ἀγάπη τοῦ θεοῦ? What is the significance of the various options for the interpretation of the verse?

1 John 3:18

3:18a. The use of μή clarifies that ἀγαπῶμεν[25] is (hortatory) subjunctive, whereas οὐ ἀγαπῶμεν would be indicative.

3:18b. How is the dative case used in the expression λόγῳ μηδὲ τῇ γλώσσῃ here? Note that one word is anarthrous and the another is articular. Why? (Cf. *Syntax* §§58 and 61.) What does ἐν ἔργῳ καὶ ἀληθείᾳ mean and how does it differ from the previous dative phrase?

---

[22]ἔχω P A S 3 sg.

[23]θεωρέω P A S 3 sg.

[24]κλείω A A S 3 sg.

[25]ἀγαπάω P A S 1 pl.

9

Participles

Vocabulary

ἀδελφή, ἡ, sister (cf. ἀδελφός)
ἀρεστός, –ή –όν, pleasing
ἀσθενής, –ές, weak, helpless (cf. ἀσθενέω)
βαστάζω, I am bearing, carrying; I am enduring
δοκιμάζω, I am testing, proving; I am tempting
ἐκχέω, I am pouring out, shedding
ἔλεος, –ους, τό, mercy, compassion (cf. ἐλεέω)
ἐνδύω, I am dressing; I am putting on (middle)
ἕνεκα + gen., because of, on account of
ἐπεί, since, for
ἥκω, I have come; I am present
καθαρός, –ά, –όν, clean (*cathartic*; cf. καθαρίζω)
καταγινώσκω, I am condemning, blaming
καταργέω, I am abolishing, nullifying
κρίμα, κρίματος, τό, judgment (*criminal*; cf. κρίνω)
κώμη, ἡ, village
πλάνη, ἡ, deception; error (*planet*; cf. πλανάω)
πλούσιος, –α, –ον, rich, wealthy (*Pluto* [Greek god of wealth])
πόσος, –η, –ον, how many (?); how great (?) (sometimes interrogative)
προφητεύω, I am prophesying (*prophet*)
σός, σή, σόν, your (pronominal adjective like ἐμός)
σταυρός, ὁ, cross
τελέω, I am completing, fulfilling (*telic*; cf. τελειόω)
ψευδοπροφήτης, –ου, ὁ, false prophet
χώρα, ἡ, field, rural area, countryside

Overview

John's use of participles in this Epistle is very simple. There are quite a few substantive uses, and a sprinkling of attributive and adverbial participles.[1] There are no genitive absolutes and very few of the minor uses covered in the *Syntax Sketch*. This means that you will need to study the examples given in the *Syntax Sketch* carefully, and it would be a good idea to consult one of the reference grammars on participles for more examples and fuller discussions. Beyond that, you have already learned the main uses of the Greek participle in the *Primer* which you are assigned to review carefully.

---

[1]My informal count for 1 John is 49 substantive participles, four adverbial (2:4, 9; 3:17; 5:16), two attributive (3:15; 5:4), two periphrastic uses (1:4; 4:12), and one in indirect discourse (4:2).

Reading Notes

1 John 3:19

3:19a. Many commentators take the expression ἐν τούτῳ in v. 19 to refer back to vv. 10–18; it may be paraphrased, "In the preceding manner we will know." Another, less attractive option, is to read τούτῳ as looking forward to the first ὅτι in v. 20: "By the following fact we will know . . . namely that . . . ." See note 3:20a below for discussion of ὅτι in v. 20.

3:19b. Parse γνωσόμεθα.[2]

3:19c. ἔμπροσθεν is an "improper" preposition. "The so-called improper prepositions are those that do not combine with verb roots to form compound words. The designation 'improper' is misleading, since they are prepositions in the fullest sense of the word" (Young, 103).

3:19d. Parse πείσομεν.[3]

3:19e. Is the article expected or unusual in the phrase, τὴν καρδίαν ἡμῶν? Also, could John have written τὴν καρδίαν with the same meaning?

1 John 3:20

3:20a. The meaning of both uses of ὅτι is difficult in v. 20. The following are the options: (1) The first ὅτι is the content of our persuasion (πείσομεν . . . ὅτι from v. 19). But this makes the second ὅτι meaningless. In some manuscripts the second ὅτι is missing for this reason; however, it is generally thought that the second ὅτι is original, but that the scribes dropped it to solve a problem. (2) The first ὅτι may explain the grounds of our persuasion ("for," "because"); the second ὅτι must be dropped again ("*For* if our heart condemn us, God is greater than our heart" KJV; cf. NKJV). (3) ὅτι may be taken not as the conjunction ("that" or "because"), but as the neuter indefinite relative pronoun ὅ τι (recall that John would originally have written: ΟΤΙΕΑΝΚΑΤΑΓΙΝΩΣΚΗ. . .).[4] ὅ τι would be parsed as accusative and interpreted as the accusative of respect (*Sketch* §31): "We persuade ourselves *with regard to whatever* our heart condemns us." This allows the second ὅτι clause to be taken as an explanation of the basis of our assurance. Thus we find the following in our versions: "(We) shall assure our hearts before Him, *in whatever* (ὅ τι ἐάν) our heart condemns us; *for* (ὅτι) God is greater than our heart" (NASB); "(W)e set our heart at rest in his presence *whenever* (ὅ τι ἐάν) our hearts condemn us. *For* (ὅτι) God is greater than our hearts" (NIV; cf. NRSV). Most commentators, myself included, opt for this third solution (see, for instance, Smalley, pp. 200–202).

---

[2]γινώσκω F D I 1 pl. For some inexplicable reason, γινώσκω switches to deponent γνώσομαι in the future; the principal parts are given in *Primer*, p. 226.

[3]πείθω F A I 1 pl. Understandably, the theta of the present stem drops when the sigma of the future (simple) stem is added; πείθσω is hard to pronounce (see *Primer* §7.4). Cf. *Primer*, p. 229 for the principal parts of πείθω.

[4]ὅ τι ἄν is found in John 2:5; 14:13; and 15:16 (cf. 8:25). ὅ ἐάν is found in 1 John 3:22; 5:15; and 3 John 5. All have the meaning "whatever." The forms ὅ τι may also be joined in one word like ὅστις, ἥτις, οἵτινες, αἵτινες, κτλ. See *Primer* §§24.2, 4, 6.

3:20b. Parse καταγινώσκῃ.[5]

3:20c. Notice the word order of ἡμῶν ἡ καρδία. The normal word order is article, noun, possessive pronoun (ἡ καρδία ἡμῶν; see v. 19 and later in v. 20); cf. BDF §473(1). Perhaps there is some slight emphasis on ἡμῶν to contrast our hearts with God.

3:20d. Identify the use of the genitive καρδίας. Keep in mind that there is a comparative adjective in the vicinity (*Sketch* §47).

"Even if our conscience makes us fainthearted and presents God as angry, still 'God is greater than our heart.' Conscience is one drop; the reconciled God is a sea of comfort. The fear of conscience, or despair, must be overcome, even though this is difficult. It is a great and exceedingly sweet promise that if our heart blames us, 'God is greater than our heart' and 'knows everything.'" Martin Luther

1 John 3:21

3:21a. There are some textual questions surrounding ἡμῶν here. Check the critical apparatus of your Greek editions and the commentaries.

3:20b. Recall that the expression ἐάν . . . καταγινώσκῃ in v. 21 forms the protasis of a future condition (*Primer* §22.6) and παρρησίαν ἔχομεν. . . forms the apodosis. Traditionally, this conditional construction has been called the "third class" condition—a label with little meaning and difficult to remember. One will also want to move beyond the form of conditions to analyze their various functions. Fortunately more recent grammars provide very helpful discussions of conditional statements on this level; see Young, pp. 226–30 and Wallace, pp. 679–712.

1 John 3:22

3:22a. Indefinite relative clauses use a relative pronoun, ἄν or ἐάν, and a subjunctive mood verb (*Primer* §24.6). In v. 22, ὃ ἐάν is used as the indefinite relative pronoun: "*whatever* we may request." See note 3:20a above for ὅ τι ἐάν with the same meaning.

3:22b. What is the use of the adjective ἀρεστά? This is not a hard or trick question, just an opportunity for review! See *Primer* §10.5.

1 John 3:23

3:23a. Parse αὕτη.[6]

3:23b. The αὕτη . . . ἵνα construction is slightly ambiguous. In the first place, we might take ἵνα as a purpose clause. But to read it as purpose, we must read in an extra idea: "This is his commandment [which he gave to us] *in order that we might believe. . . and that we love. . . .*" While this is possible and makes good sense—it does not make good sense unless we read in something—the ἵνα clause could also be functioning here as a *content* clause, expressing the content of the command. As a content clause, translate: "This is his commandment, *namely that* we believe. . . and (*that*) we love. . . ." The difference in meaning between these options is quite real and important

---

[5]καταγινώσκω P A S 3 sg.

[6]οὗτος, αὕτη, τοῦτο f n sg. This is the *demonstrative* pronoun not the feminine personal pronoun αὐτή which has smooth breathing and the accent on the last syllable (the "ultima"); cf. *Primer* §17.3.

when you consider it. I prefer this second interpretation, and we have seen virtually the same construction already in 1 John (cf. note 3:11c above).

3:23c. John uses different forms of the subjunctive with aorist πιστεύσωμεν[7] and present ἀγαπῶμεν.[8] This is significant, because these two verb forms are in the same construction in the same statement. In other words, there was some reason for the "tense" form variation. We are not treating verbs in detail in this *Reader*, so let me simply give my opinion that πιστεύσωμεν has an inceptive (or "ingressive") force to it, signifying the entrance into the state of belief. The rendering, "that *we might come to believe*" would bring this out. The present tense form with ἀγαπῶμεν is normal and expected with this verb with this meaning and therefore has no special nuance: "that *we might love* one another" is an adequate translation.

3:23d. Account for the use of the dative ὀνόματι in v. 23. Is this the dative of location (*Sketch* §63), or the dative of direct object (*Sketch* §65)? If the latter, does "I believe the name" mean something different from "I believe *in* the name" (πιστεύω εἰς τὸ ὄνομα)?

3:23e. Why did John express Ἰησοῦ Χριστοῦ in the genitive case?

1 John 3:24

3:24a. See John 14:15–17 and John 15 for the inspiration of this verse.

3:24b. Parse τηρῶν.[9]

3:24c. τηρῶν is a substantive participle—one of many we have already seen in 1 John. The translation of this type of participle is quite straightforward when you follow the procedure recommended in the *Primer* §20.7, which you should review now if needed.

3:24d. We can paraphrase ἐν τούτῳ γινώσκομεν ὅτι as "because of what precedes, we may be assured that." The keeping of Christ's commandments is evidence of his indwelling presence and power in the life of the believer. Sometimes ἐν τούτῳ points forward to the basis of John's statement, and sometimes it points backward. Only context can settle the question.

3:24e. Parse οὗ.[10]

3:24f. The relative pronoun οὗ would normally be expressed in the accusative case as the direct object of ἔδωκεν (ὃ ἡμῖν ἔδωκεν), but it has been attracted into the case of its antecedent πνεύματος. See Wallace, pp. 338–39; Young, pp. 76–77.

3:24g. μένει ἐν ἡμῖν ἐκ τοῦ πνεύματος οὗ ἡμῖν ἔδωκεν is a bit difficult to fathom at first, partly because ἐκ expresses agency here. John states that Christ dwells in believers *through the agency of* his Spirit: "He remains in us *by* his Spirit whom he granted to us." Cf. Young, p. 95; BAGD p. 235, §3e; BDF §212 (though none gives a very full explanation of this verse).

---

[7]πιστεύω A A S 1 pl.

[8]ἀγαπάω P A S 1 pl.

[9]τηρέω P A Ptc m n sg.

[10]ὅς, ἥτις, ὅ n g sg; the relative pronoun is neuter in agreement with πνεῦμα.

1 John 4:1

4:1a. Explain the use of the dative case of πνεύματι (*Sketch* §65).

4:1b. There is an ellipsis of thought in the second part of v. 1. Supply something like this: "But test the spirits *to discover* whether they are from God *or not*." εἰ can be translated by English "whether," which is a form of conditional "if" used when there is an alternative condition expressed or implied (as here in v. 1).

4:1c. Parse ἐξεληλύθασιν.[11]

1 John 4:2

4:2a. John uses the phrase ἐν τούτῳ frequently. Here it points forward: "You know the Spirit of God *in the following manner:* every spirit. . . ."

4:2b. Differentiate the meaning of ὁμολογέω as "confess" and as "profess." I have seen this term used in a Greek inscription for the action of an official herald (κῆρυξ) who was charged with going to the home city of a certain man and to "publicly declare" (ὁμολογέω) a laudatory message in honor of the man. Cf. BAGD, p. 568.

4:2c. Parse ἐληλυθότα.[12]

4:2d. Ἰησοῦν Χριστόν and its adverbial participle ἐληλυθότα are in the accusative case because this statement is indirect discourse as the object of ὁμολογεῖ: ". . . which professes *that* Jesus Christ has come in the flesh"; see *Sketch* §81; cf. Wallace, pp. 645–46. In the case of indirect discourse, the participle retains the tense form which would have been used in a direct quotation; hence, the perfect participle represents a perfect indicative verb in the original statement: Ἰησοῦς Χριστὸς ἐν σαρκὶ **ἐλήλυθεν**, "Jesus Christ *has come* in the flesh."

1 John 4:3

4:3a. The statement opening v. 3 is an alternative to the last statement of v. 2. John connects them with the simple καί, although a contrastive μέν . . . δέ series would have been used in more literary Greek style: πᾶν **μέν** πνεῦμα ὃ ὁμολογεῖ . . . πᾶν **δὲ** πνεῦμα ὃ μὴ ὁμολογεῖ, "*On the one hand*, every spirit which professes . . . *on the other hand*, every spirit which does not profess." Cf. Young, p. 183 for μέν . . . δέ and p. 189 for contrastive καί.

4:3b. The use of the article τόν with Ἰησοῦν in v. 3 is the only time John uses the article with Ἰησοῦς in this Epistle (which occurs twelve times overall). As in many places where the article is used with proper names, this article points to a "previous reference" of the name (*Sketch* §§3 and 7). The significance of this interpretation here, is that the article serves to refer the reader to the whole expression Ἰησοῦν Χριστὸν ἐν σαρκὶ ἐληλυθότα in v. 2. We can thus translate v. 3a as: "And every spirit which does not profess *this Jesus [who has come in the flesh]* is not from God." The article of previous reference makes this whole predication implicit. This was obviously the interpretation

---

[11]ἐξέρχομαι Pf A I 3 pl.

[12]ἔρχομαι Pf A Ptc m a sg; cf. *Primer* §19.3.

adopted by Greek scribes, many of whom wrote out ἐν σαρκὶ ἐληλυθότα in v. 3 to make this meaning explicit.

4:3c. The article in the phrase τὸ τοῦ ἀντιχρίστου is pronominal and stands for τὸ (πνεῦμα) τοῦ ἀντιχρίστου (*Sketch* §14). Why is ἀντιχρίστου articular?

4:3d. What is the subject of ἐστίν (which is now in the world)—the πνεῦμα understood after τὸ or ἀντιχρίστου? It is most likely the understood πνεῦμα, since it is the primary subject of discussion to this point.

4:3e. Do not let the significance of ἤδη escape your notice. John expresses the notion that there is a proleptic fulfillment of the Antichrist prophecy in his day (and ours by implication) "*even now.*"

1 John 4:4

4:4a. Recall that a nominative pronoun like ὑμεῖς is not necessarily emphatic in a predicate statement (with ἐστε in v. 4).

4:4b. Parse νενικήκατε[13] and explain the force of its tense form.

4:4c. We expect John to have said νενικήκατε **αὐτό** (neuter singular): "every spirit . . . the (spirit) of the Antichrist . . . and you have conquered *it* (the spirit of the Antichrist)." Even if the reference were plural, we expect neuter αὐτά, but John wrote αὐτούς instead. The only explanation is that there are ἀντίχριστοι πολλοί (1 John 2:18).

4:4d. In 1 John 3:20, John had used the genitive of comparison (μείζων . . . **τῆς καρδίας** ἡμῶν) (see note 3:20d above). In v. 4, however, John uses ἤ, "than," with μείζων. There is no difference in meaning between these two constructions. Both specify the item used for comparison.

4:4e. Explain the use of ὁ in the phrases ὁ ἐν ὑμῖν and ὁ ἐν τοῦ κόσμου (*Sketch* §9).

1 John 4:5

4:5a. The antecedent of αὐτοί is the same as of αὐτούς in v. 4. See note 4:4c above.

4:5b. Explain the use of the genitive αὐτῶν (*Sketch* §51).

1 John 4:6

4:6a. Parse and explain the use of the participle γινώσκων.[14]

4:6b. Explain the meaning of the genitives ἀληθείας and πλάνης (*Sketch* §42).

---

[13]νικάω Pf A I 2 pl; cf. *Primer* §14.6.

[14]γινώσκω P A Ptc m n sg.

10

Infinitives

REVIEW: *Primer,* Lessons 18, 25
READ: *Syntax Sketch,* §§84–95
STUDY: 1 John 4:7–21

Vocabulary

ἀναβλέπω, I am receiving sight; I am looking up
γέ, indeed
γνωρίζω, I am making known (cf. γινώσκω)
δέκα, ten (*deca*gon)
δένδρον, τό, tree (rhodo*dendron*)
δουλεύω, I am enslaved; I am serving (cf. δοῦλος)
ἑορτή, ἡ, feast
ἰάομαι, I am healing (ped*iatrics*)
κελεύω, I am commanding
κόλασις, –εως, ἡ, penalty, punishment
λευκός, –ή, –όν, white (*leuke*mia)
λυπέω I am grieving, hurting
μανθάνω, I am learning (*mathematics*)
μήποτε, lest, otherwise; perhaps
μονογενής, –ές, only-begotten, unique
νεφέλη, ἡ, cloud (10)
ὀμνύω, I swear an oath
πνευματικός, –ή, –όν, spiritual (cf. πνεῦμα)
πώποτε, ever, at any time
στρατιώτης, –ου, ὁ, soldier (*strategy*)
συνίημι, I understand
σωτήρ, –ῆρος, ὁ, savior, benefactor (*savior*)
τέλειος, –α, –ον, complete, perfect (*telic*; cf. τελέω)
φρονέω, I am thinking
χήρα, ἡ, widow

Overview

The discussion of the Greek infinitive in the *Syntax Sketch* may be a bit intimidating at first. Perhaps it will soften the blow to review the discussion of infinitives in the *Primer* first (§§25.5–6). It may also help to know that the most common use of the infinitive in the New Testament is as a complement to another verb, which is frequently found in English also: ὀφείλομεν τὰς ψυχὰς **θεῖναι**, "We ought *to lay down* our lives" (1 John 3:16). When an English verb requires an infinitive complement, the Greek equivalent normally does also, identified in English by "to": I ought *to* (ὀφείλω), I am able *to* (δύναμαι), I want *to* (θέλω), etc. (cf. *Primer* §§25.1, 6).

One further obstacle for our study of the infinitives in this lesson is that there are so few in 1 John for practice (and none at all in 1 John 5). Look at the examples in the *Syntax Sketch* carefully and review those found in 1 John already (e.g., 1 John 2:6, 9; 3:9, 16).

Reading Notes

1 John 4:7

4:7a. What is the use of the subjunctive for ἀγαπῶμεν[1] in v. 7? Cf. *Primer* §23.7.

4:7b. Notice the article with the abstract noun ἡ ἀγάπη. The same noun is anarthrous in the next verse because of a "canon" of article usage (see note 4:8c below).

4:7c. We have seen substantive participles like πᾶς ὁ ἀγαπῶν ("everyone who loves") many times already in 1 John.

1 John 4:8

4:8a. The substantive participle ὁ μὴ ἀγαπῶν is negatived by μή rather than οὐ as is normal for Koine Greek. Also notice the common word order: article, negative particle, participle. The article and participle act as a "sandwich" for μή, so that we can only take it with the participle. Let us take, for instance, this statement: μὴ ὁ ἀκούσας τὸν λόγον ζητείτω τὸν κύριον. It is not clear whether μή acts as a negative for the participle, ἀκούων, or the imperative, ζητείτω.[2] We could render: "Let the one who has heard the word *not seek* the Lord" if μή goes with ζητείτω! The word order: ὁ μὴ ἀκούσας solves any ambiguities: "Let the one *who has not heard* the word seek the Lord." The "sandwich" word order is popular in Greek, and one often finds any number of modifiers of an attributive or substantive participle sandwiched between its article and the participle itself; e.g., ὁ κατὰ τὸ πολὺ αὐτοῦ ἔλεος **ἀναγεννήσας**, "Who according to His great mercy has caused us to be born again" (1 Pet. 1:3), or οἱ περὶ τῆς εἰς ὑμᾶς χάριτος **προφητεύσαντες**, "Who prophesied concerning the grace unto you" (1 Pet. 1:10).

4:8b. One benefit of Greek is that it forces you to slow down when reading a New Testament passage. We tend to read our first language too fast to notice many little points which are sometimes important. For example, in v. 7 John said πᾶς ὁ ἀγαπῶν . . . **γινώσκει** τὸν θεόν. In v. 8, though, he says, ὁ μὴ ἀγαπῶν οὐκ **ἔγνω** τὸν θεόν. Account for the shift in verb tenses. There is an important reason.

4:8c. What is the stylistic rule called when a definite noun used as a predicate is anarthrous when placed before the copulative verb? (*Sketch* §17). Is ὁ θεὸς ἀγάπη ἐστίν in v. 8 (and in v. 16 below) an example of this canon? Notice that ἀγάπη is articular in vv. 7 and 10 (the latter is also a predication).

1 John 4:9

4:9a. What is the genitive relation in the phrase ἡ ἀγάπη τοῦ θεοῦ?

4:9b. The prepositional phrase ἐν ἡμῖν is the equivalent of a dative of respect: "in our case"; so BDF §220(1); cf. *Sketch* §56.

---

[1] ἀγαπάω P A S 1 pl.

[2] See Heb. 11:3 and commentaries for such an ambiguity.

4:9c. ζήσωμεν[3] may be an inceptive (ingressive) aorist. If so, we could translate: "that we may come to live through him"; cf. Wallace, pp. 558–59; Young, p. 123.

1 John 4:10

4:10a. Is either ἡμεῖς or αὐτός required in the sentence? Why were they expressed?

4:10b. What is the use of the accusative case for υἱόν and ἱλασμόν? (*Sketch* §30).

1 John 4:11

4:11a. Notice that οὕτως does not mean "how much," but "thus" or "in this fashion." It is not the quantity, but the quality of God's love which is cause for such marvel by John. The same point may be made about the famous John 3:16 passage where οὕτως is also found.

4:11b. Parse ἀγαπᾶν.[4]

4:11c. Explain the use of ἀγαπᾶν in the sentence. This is the first of two infinitives in this passage (cf. v. 20).

1 John 4:12

4:12a. Parse τεθέαται.[5]

4:12b. τετελειωμένη ἐστίν is a periphrastic construction equivalent to τετελείωται found in vv. 17–18 below; cf. *Primer* §21.6; Wallace, pp. 647–49.

1 John 4:13

4:13a. The demonstrative pronoun τούτῳ in v. 13 refers to the following ὅτι clause: ἐν τούτῳ γινώσκομεν . . . ὅτι, "In the following manner we know . . . (namely) that."

4:13b. God's Spirit granted to us is "the guarantee of our inheritance" (Eph. 1:14; 2 Cor. 1:22; 5:5) who assures the fainthearted saint that God's fatherly kindness is his (Rom. 8:15–16). John's statement in this verse communicates a similar teaching.

1 John 4:14

4:14a. Cf. note 4:12a for the parsing of τεθεάμεθα.

---

[3]ζάω A A S 1 pl.

[4]ἀγαπάω P A Inf. The alpha contract verb infinitive lacks the iota of the present infinitive ending (–ειν); cf. γεννᾶν in *Primer* §25.3.

[5]θεάομαι Pf D I 3 sg. Remember that when a word beginning with theta (θ) reduplicates, it does so with a non-aspirated tau (τ); cf. *Primer* §14.4.

4:14b. May we render τὸν υἱόν as "*his* Son"? Or is "the Son" better? What is the difference?

4:14c. As in v. 10 above, what is the use of the two accusatives υἱόν and σωτῆρα? (Young, 17).

1 John 4:15

4:15a. What is the construction with ὃς ἐάν + subjunctive called? (*Primer* §24.6; Young, 139).

4:15b. In 1 John 1:9, we read ἐὰν ὁμολογῶμεν (present subjunctive) and in 4:15 we find ὃς ἐὰν ὁμολογήσῃ (aorist subjunctive). The difference in tense forms is significant. In 1 John 1:9, the confession of sins is presented as a reiteration of discrete events (Young's *iterative* category, pp. 108–9). John says in effect: "If we make it our practice to confess our sins which we periodically commit. . . ." In 1 John 4:15, however, the aorist ὁμολογήσῃ expresses a simple *profession* of faith in Jesus as God's Son: "Whoever professes that Jesus is the Son of God. . . ." This profession is not presented as a succession of discrete events (though one must live according to that profession as John's epistle makes abundantly plain). The aorist presents the profession as a discrete event or as a simple fact without explication of any reiteration.

4:15c. Who is it that remains in the believer? God the Father (4:15), the Son (2:24), or the Spirit (2:27)? All, of course, and the orthodox doctrine of the Trinity is clearly implied in this aspect of John's teaching (see also Rom. 8:9–11).

1 John 4:16

4:16a. Parse πεπιστεύκαμεν.[6]

4:16b. See note 4:8c for anarthrous ἀγάπη in ὁ θεὸς ἀγάπη ἐστίν.

1 John 4:17

4:17a. Would you classify ἵνα in v. 17 as expressing purpose or result? Why?

> "I know not whether charity could be more magnificently commended to us, than that it should be said, 'Charity is God.' Brief praise, yet mighty praise: brief in utterance, mighty in meaning! How soon it is said, 'Love is God!' This also is short: if you count it, it is one: if you weigh it, how great is it! 'Love is God, and he that dwells,' says he, 'in love, dwells in God, and God dwells in him.' Let God be your house, and be you an house of God."
> Augustine

1 John 4:18

4:18a. The first occurrence of φόβος is anarthrous and the next two are articular. Explain why.

4:18b. Parse φοβούμενος[7] and explain its use in the sentence.

1 John 4:19

4:19a. Note the nominative personal pronouns ἡμεῖς and αὐτός (cf. Young, p. 72).

---

[6]πιστεύω Pf A I 1 pl.

[7]φοβέομαι P D Ptc m n sg. This is one of the few deponent contract verbs; cf. *Primer* §6.4.

1 John 4:20

4:20a. The use of ὅτι in the statement ἐάν τις εἴπῃ ὅτι ἀγαπῶ τὸν θεὸν may take some practice. English speakers expect ὅτι after a verb of speaking to mean "that" and introduce indirect discourse. ὅτι in Greek, though, may also introduce *direct* discourse depending merely upon the form of the statement in the quotation itself. It is obvious that with ἀγαπῶ John is not referring to himself ("If someone says that I, John, love God . . ."), but is representing the statement of the speaker (τις): "If someone says, 'I love God.'" ὅτι may be viewed in this case as the equivalent of Greek quotation marks, since the Greeks used only the most rudimentary marks in their writing system. See Burton §345; Young, p. 190; cf. Zerwick §§416–22 for ὅτι in general. For indirect discourse see especially Burton §§334–56.

4:20b. Parse μισῇ.[8] Note the ellipsis of ἐάν τις before it: ἐάν τις εἴπῃ . . . καὶ (ἐάν τις) . . . μισῇ.

4:20c. Parse ἀγαπᾶν.[9] How is this form used here?

1 John 4:21

4:21a. The ἵνα in v. 21 introduces the content of the commandment: "this commandment . . . (namely) *that* the one who loves. . . ." See the note on 1 John 3:11 for another example; cf. Young, p. 187.

---

[8]μισέω P A S 3 sg. The sigma in this form (μισῇ) is part of this verb's root, not the simple stem sign like λύσῃ.

[9]ἀγαπάω P A Inf. See note 4:11b for the same form.

Prepositions

REVIEW: *Primer*, Lessons 13, 22
READ: *Syntax Sketch*, §§96–102
STUDY: 1 John 5:1–12

*✻ 3rd. Wk. Vocab.
Primer 24–30*

*✻ No 1 Jn. 5 passage
on quiz, only on
final*

Vocabulary

ἀκοή, ἡ, hearing; account (cf. ἀκούω)
ἀμπελών, –ῶνος, ὁ, vineyard
ἀναιρέω, I take away, destroy; take up (middle)
ἄπιστος, –ον, unbelieving (cf. πιστός)
ἀσθένεια, ἡ, weakness, sickness (cf. ἀσθενής)
ἀστήρ, –έρος, ὁ, star (*astronomy*)
αὐξάνω, I increase, grow
βαρύς, βαρεῖα, βαρύ, heavy, burdensome
διότι, therefore; because
εἰκών, –όνος, ἡ, image (*icon*)
ἐλεύθερος, –α, –ον, free
ἐπιστολή, ἡ, letter, epistle (*epistle*)
ζῷον, τό, living being, animal (cf. ζάω; *zoology*)
θυσιαστήριον, τό, altar (θυσία means "sacrifice")
καταλείπω, I leave behind, abandon
κεῖμαι, I lie down; I exist
νική, ἡ, victory (cf. νικάω; *Nicolas*)
νοῦς, νοός, ὁ, mind; thought (*noetic*)
οὗ, where, to which
παῖς, παιδός, ὁ or ἡ, boy or girl, child; slave (cf. παιδίον; *pedagogue*)
πάρειμι, I am present
πίμπλημι, I fill, fulfill; come to pass (passive)
πορνεία, ἡ, fornication, sexual immorality (*porn*ography)
προσέχω, I devote myself to
φιλέω, I love; I kiss (*philo-*; cf. φίλος)

Overview

The *Syntax Sketch* lesson on prepositions gives some overview of these small but vital components of language. I will make some observations on a few of the fourteen which occur in 1 John 5:1–12 as they come up in the passage. Because you have already read so much of 1 John successfully, the reading notes will not comment upon familiar points of grammar we have already learned. Use this opportunity to review those aspects of Greek (like participles!) for which you may need further review.

Reading Notes

1 John 5:1

5:1a. This verse provides four participles for you to practice on! Find them and identify their use in v. 5:1.

5:1b. The ὅτι clause here identifies the content of what is believed. This is a variety of indirect discourse. Here is another way to express the same thing with the infinitive of indirect discourse: πᾶς ὁ πιστεύων Ἰησοῦν εἶναι τὸν Χριστόν (*Sketch* §94). Notice that the subject and predicate of the infinitive are put into the accusative case (*Sketch* §34).

5:1c. To say, "Every believer has been begotten *from* God (ἐκ τοῦ θεοῦ)" is quite another thing than saying "begotten *by* God (ὑπὸ τοῦ θεοῦ)." At least, I hope you see the difference. The first, which is what John says here and elsewhere[1] identifies God as the *source* of the new birth; the second identifies God as the parent. While the latter is certainly true in a spiritual sense (e.g., 1 John 3:1–2), John's point is to focus on God as the originator and source of the believer's new birth.

5:1d. Parse γεννήσαντα[2] and γεγεννημένον.[3]

5:1e. Note that John switches between the aorist participle, γεννήσαντα, and the perfect participle, γεγεννημένον, of the same verb, γεννάω. The difference in meaning between these two forms is impossible to express through English participles. The English relative clause is the easiest way to render a Greek substantive participle. τὸν γεννήσαντα ("he who sires a child") is either a reference to a father in general or to God the Father (the source of every πατρία [Eph. 3:15]) who has "sired" or "borne" the believer. The perfect τὸν γεγεννημένον, on the other hand, refers to the Christian who has experienced the new birth from God, consistent with John's usage in this and in previous passages (e.g., 1 John 3:9).

1 John 5:2

5:2a. We have seen other versions of John's tendency to refer ahead to a statement with a demonstrative pronoun: "*This* is the message . . . (namely) that we love one another" (3:11); "By *this* we know love, (namely) by the fact that he laid down his life for us" (3:16). (See also αὕτη . . . ἵνα in 1 John 5:3.) ἐν τούτῳ . . . ὅταν functions the same way except that ὅταν expresses a temporal notion. Substitute the ὅταν clause for ἐν τούτῳ to obtain the basic idea: "*When* we love God . . . (then) we know that we love the children of God."

5:2b. There is a textual variation between ποιῶμεν and τηρῶμεν, though "*practice* his commandments" and "*keep* his commandments" mean about the same thing. (τηρῶμεν occurs in v. 3 which may account for it slipping into v. 2.)

---

[1] E.g., τὸν γεγεννημένον **ἐξ** αὐτου in 5:1 and πᾶν τὸ γεγεννημένον **ἐκ** τοῦ θεοῦ in 5:4.

[2] γεννάω A A Ptc m a sg.

[3] γεννάω Pf P Ptc m a sg.

1 John 5:3

5:3a. The structure of αὕτη . . . ἵνα is the same use of the demonstrative pronoun addressed above (note 5:2a): *"This is the love of God (namely) that we keep his commandments."* The idea may be paraphrased by dropping αὕτη altogether and replacing it next to the ἵνα clause: *"That we keep his commandments is the love of God."* This paraphrase helps John's statement take on a certain freshness.

5:3b. In 1 John 2:5 we encountered the phrase ἡ ἀγάπη τοῦ θεοῦ (see note 2:5d above; cf. 1 John 4:9). In my opinion, the genitive in v. 2:5 is best taken as a *subjective genitive* (*Sketch* §38): *"God's love for us."* Though an objective genitive is not impossible, it does not fit the context well. The genitive τοῦ θεοῦ in v. 5:3 cannot be taken as a subjective genitive though, can it? What is its use? (*Sketch* §41).

5:3c. The statement beginning with καὶ αἱ ἐντολαὶ is an aside addressing a potential objection to v. 3b. In English we would put this statement in parentheses. John, of course, used no punctuation in his original except possibly one simple dot sometimes used to mark the end of what we would call a paragraph or a larger unit. In that day, one simply picked up the author's intent from context rather than from punctuation. Reading took great skill, and reading aloud was practiced assiduously by school children. In fact, there is an old story about how Julius Caesar received a private communiqué from an ally while in the field with his army; his subordinates were surprised when he read the message silently. Apparently it was the custom to read everything aloud.

1 John 5:4

5:4a. As part of the exegetical process, you must decide on the connection between statements. ὅτι introduces the reason or rationale for a previous assertion (cf. Young, 190). Now the interpreter must decide what the previous assertion is: keeping God's commandments, or the fact that his commandments are not burdensome? What do you think?

5:4b. Parse πᾶν.[4]

5:4c. The reason I asked you to parse πᾶν in the previous note is to help you notice that John switches gender on the participle γεγεννημένον. In v. 5:1 the same participle is masculine (notice the masculine accusative article τόν) and here it is neuter (notice πᾶν τό): *"every*thing *born of God."* The use of the neuter gender with a personal reference is sometimes found elsewhere (cf. note 1:1a).

> "St John chooses the abstract form [πᾶν] . . . in order to convey an universal truth. The thought is not so much of the believer in his unity, nor of the Church, but of each element included in the individual life and in the life of society." Brooke Foss Westcott

5:4d. Parse νικήσασα.[5]

5:4e. πίστις is in apposition with αὕτη. Supply English "namely" to identify apposition: *"This is the victory which has conquered the world, namely our faith."* Or we could substitute πίστις for αὕτη since this demonstrative pronoun, like the constructions discussed above with ὅτι or ἵνα clauses, points ahead to its postcedent πίστις: *"Our faith* is the victory."

---

[4]πᾶς, πᾶσα, πᾶν, n n sg.

[5]νικάω A A Ptc f n sg; cf. *Primer* §19.2 (p. 98).

5:4f. Explain the use of the article with κόσμον. (The answer is not profound, but remember that one must become accustomed to the *usual* features of Greek in order to know more readily when something is unusual for reasons of stress, emphasis, style, etc.)

1 John 5:5

5:5a. Rhetorical questions like the one which makes up v. 5 "often function like statements, but with the added advantage of evoking the listener to ponder the implications of what was said" (Young, 221).

5:5b. Notice that "Colwell's canon" is observed here: ὁ υἱός, the predicate noun, because it follows the copulative verb (ἐστιν), is articular (*Sketch* §17). If the noun precedes the copulative, we would expect it to be anarthrous even though definite: Ἰησοῦς υἱὸς θεοῦ ἐστιν would mean the same thing, though perhaps with slightly different stress or focus.[6]

1 John 5:6

5:6a. What does οὗτος refer to? (Cf. note 5:4e for the same syntactical structure.)

5:6b. Note the meaning of the preposition διά in the phrase δι' ὕδατος καὶ αἵματος. This is a metaphorical use of διά applying the idea of travelling *through* some object or location, to a temporal event. English commonly uses "through" the same way: "She came *through* labor fine!" "He just went *through* a divorce." To take this tack here in v. 5:6 requires that one takes "water" and "blood" as metaphors for some experience of Jesus. See Smalley (pp. 277–79) for an interesting and helpful discussion that the "water and blood" here refer to Jesus' baptism at the inauguration of his earthly ministry and to his death on the cross.

5:6c. In my opinion, when determining the meaning of the present, aorist, or perfect tenses in non-indicative mood verb forms, one must distinguish the usage in the different moods. It is simply too inaccurate, even misleading, to say, "The aorist verb form is used to mean. . . ." What is more, even within a particular mood like the participle,[7] the usage may vary. So, I treat adverbial participle tense-form usage separately from substantive participle tense-forms. The function of the participle is significantly different grammatically, and the tense-form choice correspondingly rests upon different principles.

More to the point of v. 6, an aorist substantive participle like ἐλθών here, typically refers to a simple event which was in the past either from the author's time frame or from the time frame of the sentence's central statement. It is not that the aorist participle *must* refer to a past event; the lack of an augment shows that the form itself was not originally seen as inherently past. Rather, this form and participle function was often merely put to this use by convention. In contrast, the present form of the substantive participle often—though not always—refers to a general action which is

---

[6]Young (p. 65) lists this statement in v. 5 (and the similar predication in v. 1) as an exception to Colwell's formulation. The subject of a predication usually has an article, but here Ἰησοῦς is anarthrous. This is probably caused by John's style. The name Ἰησοῦς is only articular in 1 John 4:3, and there it has the special significance of previous reference pointing to all the information about Jesus' incarnation in v. 2: "that Jesus (who has come in flesh)."

[7]Grammarians and linguists will point out that the participle is technically not a "mood" of the verb. Quite right, of course, but we must call it something.

characteristic of the referent: ὁ πιστεύων, "the one who [typically] believes," "the believer"; ὁ ἀγαπῶν, "the one who practices love" (versus the one who hates) (1 John 5:1).

With this in mind, ὁ ἐλθών refers to an arrival of Jesus: "he who came through the water and blood." This is not a characteristic action, but a simple, historical event.

5:6d. What was said in the previous note about present substantive participles may hold true for τὸ μαρτυροῦν and it may not. "The Spirit is *the one who generally bears testimony*" is a possible paraphrase, or the present tense may here signify that the action is underway: "The Spirit is *the one (currently) bearing witness*."

1 John 5:7

5:7a. This verse contains a well-known variant reading known as the *Comma Johanneum*: μαρτυροῦντες ἐν τῷ οὐρανῷ, ὁ πατὴρ ὁ λόγος καὶ τὸ ἅγιον πνεῦμα, καὶ οὗτοι οἱ τρεῖς ἕν εἰσιν, κτλ. (cf. KJV). That it is not original seems to be quite certain from careful textual criticism, though there are people who still question the motives of scholars who hold to this position because it bears on the doctrine of the Trinity. However, this doctrine is amply expressed elsewhere in Scripture, so that we really have no need to resort to questionable variants.

> The first edition of Erasmus' Greek New Testament in the early sixteenth century (1516) lacked the *Comma Johanneum*. Erasmus received quite a bit of flack over its omission, but he explained that these words do not appear in any Greek manuscript he had seen; however, he did promise to include it in a later edition of his text if a Greek manuscript were found to contain it. A few years later, lo and behold, a Greek manuscript was presented to him which had the disputed reading. Erasmus dutifully included the *Comma* in his third edition of 1522, though he himself and most subsequent text critics believe that this Greek manuscript was composed by a contemporary Franciscan friar at Oxford expressly for this one purpose! This was not the first or last bit of skullduggery connected with the Greek text of the New Testament!

1 John 5:8

5:8a. The first three nouns in v. 5:8 are in apposition with the participle μαρτυροῦντες found in v. 5:7.

5:8b. The expression εἰς τὸ ἕν is a rather unusual use of this preposition to indicate the predicate nominative under Semitic influence. In English, εἰς is not translated: "The three are one." The few other New Testament examples of this use of εἰς with εἰμί all occur in LXX quotations (BAGD, p. 230, §8aβ).

1 John 5:9

5:9a. There is no particular problem understanding the grammar of v. 9; the difficulty lies in deciding what αὕτη refers to. Does it refer back to the witnesses invoked in vv. 6-8? to the immediately preceding statement about the superiority of God's testimony (v. 9a)? or to the following ὅτι clause? For extensive and interesting discussion see Smalley, pp. 283–85.

1 John 5:10

5:10a. The preposition εἰς in the phrase ὁ πιστεύων εἰς τὸν υἱόν is an important indicator for the meaning of the verb πιστεύω. If there were no preposition, ὁ πιστεύων τῷ υἱῷ, the meaning is "the one who believes the Son" *viz.* the person believes the word of the Son to be true. This verb, πιστεύω, however, takes on the meaning "to place one's trust in" when accompanied by εἰς (as here in v. 5:10), ἐπί, or even ἐν. The difference in meaning is profound, and the little preposition is the contextual feature which clarifies the meaning (cf. BAGD p. 661, §2aβ–ε under πιστεύω).

5:10b. What is the use of the accusative in the phrase ψεύστην πεποίηκεν αὐτόν? (*Sketch* §30; cf. 1 John 1:10 and note 1:10d above). Paraphrase this sentence.

1 John 5:11

5:11a. We are faced again with deciding what αὕτη refers to. Does it point to ὅτι as a content clause? If so, we must read μαρτυρία not as an act of bearing witness, but the content of that witness, the testimony itself. I paraphrase: "And this is the fact to which God has borne witness, namely, that God has given eternal life to us and that this life is in his Son." μαρτυρία, like the nouns "hope" (ἐλπίς) or "trust" (πίστις) can refer either to an action: "the act of bearing witness, testifying" or to the content or subject matter of the action: "that matter about which testimony is borne." For ἐλπίς the difference can be expressed as: "the act of hoping" and "that thing for which one hopes"; for πίστις "putting one's trust in something," "the act of belief," and "the thing in which one trusts or believes."

5:11b. How would you analyze the meaning of the preposition ἐν in the phrase ἐν τῷ υἱῷ?

1 John 5:12

5:12a. It is difficult to think of a clearer statement regarding the exclusive claims of the Gospel of Christ as the only way of salvation for sinners—unless one points to John's comparable statement in John 3:36.

5:12b. Notice that ζωὴν αἰώνιον in v. 11 is anarthrous and that both occurrences of ζωή in v. 12 are articular. In v. 11, the concept is introduced: "God has granted us *eternal life*." The next references to ζωή with the article are to the same concept, so that one must include the notion of αἰώνιον in v. 12 also: "has *this eternal life* mentioned previously." That is the effect of an article used for previous reference (*Sketch* §3).

Words and Phrases

REVIEW: *Primer,* Lessons 26–27 27-28
READ: *Syntax Sketch,* §§103–106
STUDY: 1 John 5:13–21

Vocabulary

αἴτημα, –ατος, τό, request (cf. αἰτέω)

ἀντί, instead of, on behalf of (prep. + gen.) (*anti*christ)

γρηγορέω, I am watching, awake (*Gregory*)

δέομαι, I am begging, praying

διάνοια, ἡ, understanding, insight; mind (cf. νοῦς)

ἀγνοέω, I am ignorant, do not know (cf. γινώσκω)

εἴδωλον, τό, idol (*idol*)

ἐκλέγομαι, I am choosing, electing (*elect*)

ἐκλεκτός, –ή, –όν, chosen, elect (cf. ἐκλέγομαι)

καθεύδω, I am sleeping

κατεργάζομαι, I am accomplishing, producing

κατηγορέω, I am accusing

κοιλία, ἡ, stomach; womb

κοπιάω, I am laboring, working hard; bearing

κωλύω, I hinder

μετάνοια, ἡ, repentance (cf. μετανοέω)

μιμνήσκομαι, I remember (*mnemonic*)

νέος, –α, –ον, new, young (*neo*phyte)

πεινάω, I am hungry

πέραν, other side; across (prep. + gen.)

περιβάλλω, I am clothing, dressing

πληγή, ἡ, blow (from hitting); plague (*plague*)

πλοῦτος, ὁ, wealth (*Pluto*; cf. πλούσιος)

σκεῦος, σκεύους, τό, vessel, jar

χαρίζομαι, I am granting; I am forgiving (cf. χάρις)

Overview

As you finish reading 1 John with this lesson, you will find that you can read this final passage with little further syntax help. You have already learned the bulk of Greek syntax for nouns, pronouns, articles, participles, etc. Intermediate syntax books usually have some treatment of other small (but important) words: conjunctions, adverbs, and particles;[1] however, I have chosen to depart from syntax in this last lesson and to introduce word and phrase study principles instead. This is, I hope, a little more interesting. And I think that conjunctions, adverbs, and particles can be studied from the lexicons or grammars when encountered in a passage where they significantly affect exegesis.

---

[1]For instance, Wallace, pp. 666–712; Young, Chapters 12–13.

Reading Notes

1 John 5:13

5:13a. Verse 13 begins without a conjunction. John's style, being somewhat more Semitic than Hellenistic in flavor, employs "asyndeton" (no conjunction) or simply καί with a wide range of meanings (see, e.g., v. 15) much more often than other Greek writers. For example, most Greek speakers and writers would feel that a transitional conjunction like δέ would be called for to begin v. 13: ταῦτα **δὲ** ἔγραψα . . . . Richard Young discusses various reasons for and effects of asyndeton (p. 180), although he could have added that it may be merely a matter of an author's style.

5:13b. Parse ἔγραψα.[2]

5:13c. The aorist in the verb ἔγραψα is called the "epistolary aorist" and represents the action of writing from the recipients' perspective as past (cf. Wallace, pp. 562–63; Young, pp. 124–25).

5:13d. Parse εἰδῆτε.[3]

5:13e. Knowing that τοῖς πιστεύουσιν is in apposition to ὑμῖν clears up any confusion in the flow of thought caused by the flexibility of Greek word order. In this instance, the fact that a Greek word or phrase is placed in the same case form with the word or phrase with which it is in apposition clarifies the statement. One may move things around in English paraphrase: "I wrote these things to you—that is, to those of you who believe in the name of the Son of God—in order that you might know that you have life eternal."

1 John 5:14

5:14a. We have already seen the forward-looking use of the demonstrative pronoun often in 1 John: "*This* is the boldness . . . (namely) *that* if we ask for anything. . . ." Young discusses this use of ὅτι under *Noun Clauses*: "Ὅτι often introduces an appositional clause after a cataphoric demonstrative pronoun" (Young, 190). I prefer the term "content clause" to "noun clause"; the ὅτι clause gives the "content" of αὕτη. Either label describes the same idea. Note that taking ὅτι as a *reason* clause ("because") would not make sense here.

5:14b. Parse τι.[4]

5:14c. As practice in word study, determine the meaning of παρρησία in v. 14. "Boldness" or "confidence" are the two English glosses found most frequently in our translations, yet these two terms have different shades of meaning in English.

5:14d. Recall that some verbs, like ἀκούω, may take direct objects in the genitive case (*Sketch* §51). This explains the genitive ἡμῶν here and in v. 15. What other kinds of verbs take the genitive direct object? There is another example in this passage for you to discover.

---

[2] γράφω A A I 1 sg.

[3] οἶδα A A S 2 pl. This form is easy to confuse with ἴδητε (from βλέπω/ὁράω/εἶδον).

[4] τις, τι n a sg. This form must be taken as accusative here (τι is also the nominative form of the neuter indefinite pronoun [*Primer* §17.2]) because it functions as the direct object of the verb αἰτώμεθα.

1 John 5:15

5:15a. For the use of the genitive in ἡμῶν see note 5:14c.

5:15b. The indefinite relative clause ὃ ἐὰν αἰτώμεθα may seem awkward to us: "He hears us whatever we request." ὃ is taken as the direct object of αἰτώμεθα in this rendering, and the connection between its clause and the preceding seems to require fleshing out. Several English versions treat the clause as a parenthetical idea: "And if we know that he hears us—whatever we ask—we know . . ." (NIV). The awkwardness is easily cleared up, though, by regarding ὃ as performing double duty with both ἀκούει and αἰτώμεθα. Its relationship to ἀκούει is to be taken as an accusative of respect or reference (*Sketch* §31): "He hears us *with regard to whatever* we request."

5:15c. Parse ᾐτήκαμεν.[5]

5:15d. John uses asyndeton again with the second οἴδαμεν clause, though the connection is clear enough: "If we know that . . . (then) we (also) know that. . . ." The second clause with οἴδαμεν is an inference drawn out from the earlier proposition: The fact that God hears our requests (according to his will—v. 14) means necessarily that he will also grant those requests. Perhaps the simple translation of ἀκούει ἡμῶν in v. 15 as "he *hears* us" could be improved by paraphrase to: "he *attends to* our prayers." The idea is not simply that God 'aurally perceives our requests' and no more, but that he acts upon them. To test my interpretation here, perform a quick study of ἀκούω.

1 John 5:16

5:16a. To illustrate the kind of requests authorized for Christians to make of God, John gives this very remarkable example: to ask eternal life for a fellow Christian who has fallen into evil practices. One cannot but wonder at the high privilege God has granted to us: to intercede for one another with such profound effect. He takes us into his own counsel and marvelously uses our feeble love and prayers for one another to confirm and affect his own free salvation. How unsearchable are his ways! But we must get back to Greek grammar.

5:16b. The time relationship between the adverbial participle ἁμαρτάνοντα and its controlling verb, ἴδη, is a very important factor in the interpretation of John's statement. The simple translation strategy given in the *Primer* (§20.5) provides a good starting place for seeing the time relation. Translate ἁμαρτάνοντα with "while": "If anyone sees his brother *while he is committing sin*. . . ." The two actions are contemporaneous and the intercessor is clearly an eyewitness of the offense. To see the importance of this point, imagine that John had used an aorist participle here: ἁμάρτοντα. What would John have communicated to his readers in that case?!

5:16c. When a verb (including a participle) and its direct object are cognate (ἁμαρτάνοντα ἁμαρτίαν), what is the use of the accusative called? (*Sketch* §29).

5:16d. Because ἁμαρτίαν is anarthrous, we might take the first occurrence of μὴ πρὸς θάνατον as an adjectival phrase (versus adverbial phrase) with ἁμαρτίαν: "a sin *which does not lead to death*." However, the negative particle would then be οὐ. (If you don't believe me, see ἁμαρτία **οὐ** πρός θάνατον in v. 17!) The phrase in both its occurrences should be taken as adverbial with the participles ἁμαρτάνοντα and τοῖς ἁμαρτάνουσιν: "committing sin *in a way which does not lead to*

---

[5]αἰτέω Pf A I 1 pl. Some manuscripts have aorist ᾐτήσαμεν.

death." There is not much difference in meaning in this particular example, but there might be in other passages, so this grammatical point was worth mentioning.

5:16e. The phrase ἁμαρτάνοντα ἁμαρτίαν μὴ πρὸς θάνατον is well worth close study. What specifically does John mean?

5:16f. ἔστιν ἁμαρτία posits the existence of something: "There is a sin (which leads to death)." (The conception is: "A death-dealing sin exists.") Because Greek has no equivalent of the English word "there" in the construction "*there* is . . .", one must supply it in translation and understand that εἰμί has this "existential" meaning sometimes.

1 John 5:17

5:17a. The phrase οὐ πρὸς θάνατον is adjectival modifying ἁμαρτία: "a sin *which does not lead to death*"; cf. note 5:16d above.

1 John 5:18

5:18a. In 1 John 3:9, John said πᾶς ὁ γεγεννημένος ἐκ τοῦ θεοῦ ἁμαρτίαν οὐ ποιεῖ. The verb phrase ἁμαρτίαν οὐ ποιεῖ, refers to the practice of sin as a characteristic of one's life. It is possible to read οὐχ ἁμαρτάνει with the same iterative idea in 5:18. Another possible nuance, however, is derived from a Hebrew grammatical source.[6] In a very few places in the Greek New Testament, a present indicative like ἁμαρτάνει[7] may indicate that the subject has permission or the capability to perform the action of the verb: "*I may give* [this authority] to whomever I wish" or "*I can give*" (Luke 4:6). The word rendered "I may give" is the simple form δίδωμι. Likewise in 1 John 5:18, ἁμαρτάνει may conceivably have the same "modal" significance: "everyone born of God *cannot sin*," an idea explicitly found in 1 John 3:9 in the phrase οὐ δύναται ἁμαρτάνειν. This line of analysis is admittedly somewhat tenuous, but there are times when the Semitic influence upon New Testament semantics is patent and important.

> "The more I love to speak of charity, the less willing I am that this epistle should be finished. None is more ardent in the commending of charity. Nothing more sweet is preached to you, nothing more wholesome drunk by you, but only thus if by godly living you confirm in you the gift of God. Be not ungrateful for His so great grace, who, though He had one Only Son, would not that He should be alone a Son; but, that He might have brethren, adopted unto Him those who should with Him possess life eternal."
> Augustine

5:18b. Parse γεννηθείς.[8]

5:18c. The referent of ὁ γεννηθείς in this verse is difficult to identify. Is this the Christian? or Christ? The same question occurred to early copyists, which accounts for the variant reading ἑαυτόν found for αὐτόν in some early manuscripts.[9] ὁ γεννηθείς . . . ἑαυτόν would mean "the one

---

[6]See Paul Joüon and T. Muraoka, *A Grammar of Biblical Hebrew* (Rome: Pontifical Biblical Institute, 1993), §113l–m for the modal nuance of the Hebrew *Yiqtol* form.

[7]ἁμαρτάνω P A I 3 sg.

[8]γεννάω A P Ptc m n sg.

[9]Bruce M. Metzger (*A Textual Commentary on the Greek New Testament* [Stuttgart: United Bible Societies, 1975]) writes: "The Committee understood ὁ γεννηθείς to refer to Christ, and therefore adopted the reading αὐτόν. . . . Copyists who took ὁ γεννηθείς to refer to the Christian believer (although elsewhere John

born from God guards *himself*" and would be a statement about the regenerate Christian's self-discipline in sanctification. The reading ὁ γεννηθείς . . . αὐτόν would mean: "The one born from God—the incarnate Christ—guards *him* (the regenerate believer)." To complicate matters, remember that the simple form of the pronoun αὐτόν may be taken to have the reflexive meaning (= ἑαυτόν), which is allowed in the Greek of our era (*Sketch* §68). I do not bring all this up to confuse you, but to show that careful exegesis must weigh a variety of sometimes complex factors before making interpretive judgments. If you want my opinion, I think it is a statement about Christ's guardianship of the believer; this is the underlying truth of why "everyone who has been born of God" cannot apostatize. Otherwise, John's statement gives no real assurance of infallible protection even from our own deceiving hearts (cf. 1 John 3:19–20).

5:18d. Does the modal nuance posited for ἀμαρτάνει in this verse (see note 5:18a above) elucidate John's meaning for ἅπτεται also? "The evil one *cannot touch* him" or "The evil one *may not touch* him" certainly seems more plausible than a mere statement of fact: "The evil one *does not touch* him."

5:18e. Explain the genitive αὐτοῦ. (See note 5:14d above.)

1 John 5:19

5:19a. Explain the word position of the adjective in the phrase ὁ κόσμος ὅλος. Hint: if this is an attributive adjective, should we not expect a different word order?

5:19b. Does ἐν τῷ πονηρῷ mean "in evil" or "in the evil one's (spell)"? One way to answer this is to ask whether πονηρός used as a substantive noun has an abstract meaning ("evil," "wickedness") or not. A word study on πονηρός in this case is not aiming at determining the meaning of the word itself, but in ascertaining whether this adjective is regularly used to refer to a person or to an abstract quality (or to both!).

1 John 5:20

5:20a. Parse δέδωκεν.[10]

5:20b. One can only discern the intended meaning of ἵνα in v. 20 from the context: "He has granted us understanding ἵνα we might know. . . ." The verb δέδωκεν might take a direct object clause, but that is ruled out here because the direct object is διάνοιαν. Is the ἵνα clause here, then, purpose or result? The only distinguishing trait is whether intention (purpose) is prominent in the statement. Purpose clauses can be characterized as *intended result* and result clauses as *actual result whether intended or not.*

5:20c. The textual variants with τὸν ἀληθινόν are: τὸ ἀληθινόν, τὸν θεὸν τὸν ἀληθινόν, and τὸν ἀληθινὸν θεόν (the latter two are synonymous, of course, and inspired by the last sentence of this verse). The editors of our editions believe that the reading τὸν ἀληθινόν is original and that θεόν entered into the text as scribes added their opinion of what John meant in the margins of their

---

always uses ὁ γεγεννημένος, never ὁ γεννηθείς, of the believer) naturally preferred the reflexive ἑαυτόν" (p. 718).

[10]δίδωμι Pf A I 3 sg.

texts. Such marginal notes often crept into the text itself over time. τὸ ἀληθινόν would mean "the truth," but certainly be the less expected Johannine form than ἡ ἀλήθεια. The neuter article might have arisen again as scribes sought to explain John's meaning to readers of their manuscripts. As normally happens, though, the difference between variant readings causes no serious confusion or erroneous teaching. Either one of these readings yields intelligible statements which fully conform to the teaching of John and of the Bible elsewhere.

5:20d. Who is the antecedent of οὗτος? Jesus, the Son of God? Is this not an unambiguous statement of his deity?

1 John 5:21

5:21a. Parse τεκνία[11] and you will discover why ἑαυτά is expressed as a neuter plural in place of the expected masculine plural (ἑαυτούς) for a second person reflexive pronoun (cf. *Sketch* §68).

5:21b. Parse φυλάξατε.[12]

5:21c. One cannot always easily express the force of Greek aorist imperative forms in English. Our language has no such distinction in imperative forms; we need explanatory words, tone of voice, select vocabulary, etc. to communicate different kinds of imperatives. In part, the Greek form chosen often coincides with the nature of the action to which the verb refers. "Watch out!" is perhaps the best way to translate φυλάξατε here with its sharp tone. Another possible interpretation is that John intends an inceptive nuance: *"Set your guard out* against idols!" The two other aorist imperative forms of φυλάσσω occur in 1 Tim. 6:20 and 2 Tim. 1:14 where the inceptive nuance is also possible (*"set a guard* on the deposit"). The verb φυλάσσω seems to me to be more natural in the present imperative form with the meaning: "keep on your guard" or "keep a watch out for" as found in Luke 12:15 ("Be on the lookout and *keep watch* against greediness"), 2 Tim. 4:15 ("be on the lookout against him"), and 2 Pet. 3:17 ("be on your guard"). This fact seems to confirm that the aorist form was used by authors intending some special nuance like the inceptive idea or a sharp, urgent tone.

5:21d. John's parting exhortation in v. 21 seems abrupt and out of sync with his concerns raised throughout the Epistle.[13] Think about it more carefully. Perhaps it is more central to John's Epistle than may first appear.

Congratulations! You have now read your first New Testament book in Greek. May you read them all now with greater profit!

---

[11]τεκνίον n v pl.

[12]φυλάσσω A A Impv 2 pl.

[13]This verse has even inspired at least one doctoral thesis; cf. Terry Griffith, "'Little Children, Keep Yourselves from Idols' (1 John 5:21)," *Tyndale Bulletin* 48 (1997): 187–90.

Sketch of Greek Word and Phrase Syntax

The Greek Article §§1-20

1. INTRODUCTION. (See Wallace, pp. 206–90; Young, Chap. 4; Porter, Chap. 5.) To focus on the Greek article—that rarely noticed part of speech—carries a twofold danger. On the one hand, you might overestimate an article's significance, improperly making the interpretation of a whole passage dependent on a supposed technical use of the article. On the other hand, you might *underestimate* the importance of a particular article! Because of these dangers, you should recognize that my sketch of Greek article usage emphasizes what is normal in Greek. Often this results in no "quickie" interpretive insights. Rather, one simply recognizes that the article, say, in the phrase ὁ κόσμος, is the normal Greek practice in a certain situation before moving on to interpret the rest of the passage. On the other hand, if you know normal practices of article usage well, it makes the unusual employment of an article or omission of an expected article more noticeable. This helps you know when to focus upon the article during interpretation.

In general, Greek article usage was just as refined and subtle as usage of the English definite article, sometimes even more so. In many cases, ὁ (ἡ, τό) was used much the same way as English "the," though with important differences. The differences should be obvious as you work through the sketch of article uses below. You should remember that in many cases, article use or omission may be a matter of Greek style, allowing some variation. There is no substitute for careful observation and experience when evaluating the importance of a particular Greek article.

You will want to look up "anarthrous" (= "no article used") and "articular" (= "an article used") in the Glossary found in the *Primer* (pp. 231–37). Be sure to consult the Glossary for other grammatical terms as needed.

With Substantives

2. SPECIFIC. The Greek article, like the English definite article, may indicate that a specific or particular referent is in the author's mind, whether that referent is a person, an object, or a specific group. Usually, the author assumes that the reader knows what referent is meant, because it is commonly understood in the shared realm of discourse. The first example illustrates this phenomenon; there was a specific prophet expected by the Jews in John the Baptist's day.

○ **ὁ προφήτης** εἶ σύ· "Are you *the Prophet*?" (John 1:21). Not "*a* prophet," but a specific, expected prophet. John the Baptist answered that he was not *this* prophet, even though he was a prophet.

○ ἐν ἀρχῇ ἦν **ὁ λόγος**, "In the beginning was *the Word*" (John 1:1). *monadic*

○ ἦν δὲ ἄνθρωπος ἐκ **τῶν Φαρισαίων**, "Now there was a man from *the Pharisees*" (John 3:1). The Pharisees are presented as a distinct group recognized by both author and reader. To express this phrase anarthrously might have communicated that the group was an unknown sub-group within that sect: "a man from (some) Pharisees."

If the substantive refers to something which is unique in the human realm ("the world," "the sun"), or it is the dominant referent in the author's linguistic community ("the Scripture," "the Temple" "the Lord"), the article will normally be used. The referent is necessarily specific, since there is only one prominent item recognized. Some grammars refer to this as the "monadic" use of the article.

○ τὸ φῶς ἐλήλυθεν εἰς **τὸν κόσμον**, "The light has come into *the world*" (John 3:19). κόσμος is invariably articular in the NT unless some other rule of article use/non-use interferes.

○ πρόσωπον αὐτοῦ ὡς **ὁ ἥλιος**, "His face was like *the sun*" (Rev. 10:1). The sentence goes on: καὶ οἱ πόδες αὐτοῦ ὡς **στῦλοι πυρός**, "and his feet like pillars of fire." The anarthrous "pillars of fire" are parallel with monadic "*the* sun."

○ ὃς ἂν ὀμόσῃ ἐν **τῷ ναῷ** . . . "Whoever swears by *the Temple*" (Matt. 23:16). The Jewish linguistic community recognized one temple even though the surrounding world was dotted with pagan temples and shrines.

3. PREVIOUS REFERENCE. ("Anaphoric" or "Resumptive.") The article is frequently used to point back to a noun which was introduced earlier in the context. In English we often use a demonstrative pronoun to communicate this idea: "I saw a cloud yesterday. . . . Anyway, *that cloud* I saw was huge." This second occurrence of the noun is specific, because it points back to the same referent already mentioned. This construction is common in the NT and often explains why a noun which is first mentioned anarthrously is given an article in its subsequent occurrences.

○ ἐν αὐτῷ **ζωὴ** ἦν, καὶ **ἡ ζωὴ** ἦν τὸ φῶς τῶν ἀνθρώπων, "In him was life, and *this life* (just mentioned) was the light of men" (John 1:4).

○ **ἀντίχριστος** ἔρχεται . . . οὗτος ἐστιν **ὁ ἀντίχριστος**, "An antichrist is coming . . . this is *the* antichrist (that I mentioned earlier)" (1 John 2:19, 22).

○ **Σαῦλος** . . . **ὁ** δὲ **Σαῦλος**, "*Saul* . . . . Now the *Saul* (I mentioned earlier) . . ." (Acts 8:3 and 9:1). The article of previous reference is often found in historical narrative where the author is helping the reader keep track of people in the narrative.

○ ἡ θλῖψις **ὑπομονὴν** κατεργάζεται, **ἡ** δὲ **ὑπομονὴ δοκιμήν**, **ἡ** δὲ **δοκιμὴ ἐλπίδα**. **ἡ** δὲ **ἐλπὶς** οὐ καταισχύνει, "Tribulation produces endurance, and *this endurance* (produces) character, and *this character* (produces) hope. And *this hope* does not disappoint" (Rom. 5:3-5). The articles interlock the nouns together in a chain.

4. GENERIC. An article may be used with a noun that is typical of a class or group. This use does not always correspond to English, although the articular expression: "*the* man on the street" does not refer to a specific individual, but is like the Greek "generic" article. Look for contexts where a general reference to groups is expected, even proverbial statements. This use, of course, is the opposite of "specific" discussed above.

○ ἄξιος γὰρ **ὁ ἐργάτης** τοῦ μισθοῦ αὐτοῦ, "For *the worker* (is) worthy of his wage" (Luke 10:7). A semi-proverbial statement referring not to a specific worker, but to a representative of all workers.

○ δεῖ οὖν **τὸν ἐπίσκοπον** ἀνεπίλημπτον εἶναι, "Therefore, it is necessary that *an overseer* be beyond reproach" (1 Tim. 3:2). Here we could render with "the overseer," but the point is that this articular noun is the representative of a group.

○ χρείαν εἶχεν ἵνα τις μαρτυρήσῃ περὶ **τοῦ ἀνθρώπου**, "He was not in need of anyone to testify (to him) about *mankind*" (John 2:25).

5. WITH NOUNS MODIFIED BY GENITIVE PRONOUNS. The article is normally employed with nouns that are modified by a genitive personal pronoun. In these instances, the article is appropriate because "our eyes" or "his righteousness" are specific, particular referents. Note that the article alone can function in place of such a possessive pronoun, so that **τοῖς** ὀφθαλμοῖς in the first example below can mean "with *our* eyes."[1] (See §11 for this use of the article.) Since this is the case, the *pronoun* could be viewed as redundant, not the article.

○ ὃ ἑωράκαμεν **τοῖς** ὀφθαλμοῖς **ἡμῶν**, "Which we have seen with *our eyes*" (1 John 1:1).

○ **τὸ** θυγάτριόν **μου** ἐσχάτως ἔχει, "*My little girl* is deathly ill" (Mark 5:23).

○ ὡς υἱὸς ἐπὶ **τὸν** οἶκον **αὐτοῦ**, "as Son over *his house*" (Heb. 3:6).

6. WITH ABSTRACT NOUNS. The article was often employed in Greek with abstract terms where English would not normally use one. Sometimes the article was used with such nouns for previous reference (§3). Other times, it is a function of the *generic* idea (§4; so BDF §258).

○ **ἡ γνῶσις** φυσιοῖ, **ἡ** δὲ **ἀγάπη** οἰκοδομεῖ, "*Knowledge* puffs up, but *love* edifies" (1 Cor. 8:1).

○ **ἡ χάρις** καὶ **ἡ ἀλήθεια** διὰ Ἰησοῦ Χριστοῦ ἐγένετο, "*Grace* and *truth* came through Jesus Christ" (John 1:17).

○ πεπληρωμένοι πάσης **τῆς γνώσεως**, "filled with *all knowledge*" (Rom. 15:14).

7. WITH PROPER NAMES. The article may be omitted or included with Greek proper names, although they are usually anarthrous. An article was used when the person was well-known or previously mentioned in context (§3). Names which do not decline may be articular in order to clarify the name's case function (see examples 2 and 3). θεός often acts as a proper name and is articular.

> "Scholarship has not yet solved completely the problem of the article with proper names." J. H. Moulton

○ ἡμεῖς δὲ **τοῦ Μωϋσέως** ἐσμὲν μαθηταί· ἡμεῖς οἴδαμεν ὅτι **Μωϋσεῖ** λελάληκεν ὁ θεός, "We are disciples of *Moses*; we know that God has spoken to *Moses* (John 9:28-29). The first occurrence may be articular because Moses was well-known, or, in conjunction with the word order, because it adds stress to the name, "We are disciples of *Moses* (not just of *anyone)*."

○ Ἀβραὰμ ἐγέννησεν **τὸν Ἰσαάκ**, Ἰσαὰκ δὲ ἐγέννησεν **τὸν Ἰακώβ**, "Abraham bore *Isaac*, and *Isaac* bore *Jacob*" (Matt. 1:2). The genealogy in Matthew proceeds this way throughout; the

---

[1]This phenomenon, by the way, accounts for many variant readings in the NT manuscripts. For example, οἱ ἄνδρες, ἀγαπᾶτε **τὰς** γύναικες, "Husbands, love *your* wives" (Eph. 5:25) is found as: ἀγαπᾶτε τὰς γυναῖκες **ὑμῶν** in some manuscripts.

article clarifies which name is to be taken as the accusative, the others are nominative (cf. ἐκ τῆς Ῥούθ in v. 5).

○ οὗτοι υἱοί εἰσιν Ἀβραάμ . . . προευηγγελίσατο **τῷ Ἀβραάμ**, "These are sons of *Abraham* . . . [the Scripture] proclaimed the gospel earlier *to Abraham*" (Gal. 3:7-8). The second occurrence of the name may be articular because of a previous reference, or to clarify that this indeclinable name is to be taken as dative in its second occurrence.

○ ὁ λόγος ἦν πρὸς **τὸν θεόν**, "The Word was with *God*" (John 1:1).

8. WITH NOMINATIVE ACTING AS VOCATIVE. In the Greek of the Koine period, a noun in the nominative case was often substituted for an anarthrous vocative noun (there is no vocative article form). When this occurred, the nominative noun was always articular: **οἱ ἄνδρες**, ἀγαπᾶτε τὰς γυναῖκας, "*Husbands,* love your wives" (Eph. 5:25). See the discussion and examples below under "[Nominative] Used as Vocative" (§24).

9. SUBSTANTIZING. The article can turn various parts of speech such as adjectives, prepositional phrases, participles, or bits of quoted sentences[2] into virtual nouns. You know this idiom from the substantive use of Greek adjectives and participles (*Primer*, §§10.5, 20.7).

○ **τὰ** ἐν τῷ κόσμῳ, "the things in the world" (1 John 2:15). The idea is that the prepositional phrase becomes a virtual substantive adjective: "the in-the-world things."

○ ὁ μὴ **ἐσθίων** τὸν **ἐσθίοντα** μὴ κρινέτω, "Let *the person who does not eat* not judge *the one who eats*" (Rom. 14:3). Two substantive participles.

○ ἡ ἀγάπη **τῷ πλησίον** κακὸν οὐκ ἐργάζεται, "Love effects no harm *to one's neighbor*" (Rom. 13:10). πλησίον is a preposition, "near," made into a noun, "neighbor."

10. WITH CERTAIN PRONOUNS. The Greek article occurs with nouns modified by an adjectival demonstrative pronoun. The noun is necessarily definite or specific, which explains the rationale for the employment of the article. This is a matter of Greek style; the article serves merely as reinforcement for the demonstrative and is not translated, and it is not to be confused with cases where the pronoun is predicate (cf. *Primer* §17.4). See the Reader on 1 John 1:5.

○ ἐσμεν ἐν **τῷ** κόσμῳ **τούτῳ**, "we are in *this world*" (1 John 4:17).

○ **ταύτην τὴν** ἐντολὴν ἔχομεν, "we have *this commandment*" (1 John 4:21).

In a similar fashion, the article serves as a marker of distinct, definite meanings of modifying pronouns (ὁ ἄνθρωπος αὐτός, "the man himself"; ὁ αὐτὸς ἄνθρωπος, "the same man") or of certain adjectives (πᾶς ὁ ἄνθρωπος, "every man"; ὁ πᾶς ἄνθρωπος, "the whole man"). These are matters of style dictated by the individual pronoun or adjective which should each be checked in BAGD.

---

[2]The use of the article with quotes is not very frequent; see Wallace, pp. 237–39; cf. BDF §267.

Pronominal Uses

11. AS POSSESSIVE PRONOUN. If the idea of possession is clear from context, the article itself functioned as a possessive pronoun appropriate for that context.

- ⭕ οἱ ἄνδρες, ἀγαπᾶτε **τὰς** γυναῖκας, "Husbands, love *your* wives" (Eph. 5:25). ("Husbands, love *the wives*" is clearly not intended!)

- ⭕ μὴ ἀφιέτω **τὸν** ἄνδρα, "Let her not leave *her* husband" (1 Cor. 7:13).

- ⭕ Ἀνοίξας δὲ Πέτρος **τὸ** στόμα, "Then Peter opened *his* mouth" (Acts 10:34).

> "In short, there is no more important aspect of Greek grammar than the article to help shape our understanding of the thought and theology of the NT writers." Daniel Wallace

12. AS PERSONAL PRONOUN. In narrative contexts especially, the Greek article served as a sort of shorthand for a personal pronoun when the author felt that the identity of the referent was clear from context. Usually the article was employed with δέ or μέν. Less frequently, the idea of alternation is communicated in some contexts with a μέν . . . δέ series: "the one . . . the other" or "one this . . . another that."

- ⭕ Φαρισαῖοι ἔλεγον τοῖς μαθηταῖς αὐτοῦ . . . **ὁ** δὲ ἀκούσας εἶπεν, "The Pharisees were saying to his disciples . . . and after *he* heard (about it), he said . . ." (Matt. 9:11-12).

- ⭕ εἶπεν τῇ μητρὶ αὐτῆς· τί αἰτήσωμαι; **ἡ** δὲ εἶπεν, "She said to her mother, 'What should I ask for?' And *she* [the mother] said . . ." (Mark 6:24).

- ⭕ **οἱ** δὲ εἶπαν αὐτῷ, "Then *they* said to him . . ." (Matt. 2:3-5).

- ⭕ ἕκαστος ἴδιον ἔχει χάρισμα ἐκ θεοῦ, **ὁ** μὲν οὕτως, **ὁ** δὲ οὕτως, "Each has his own gift from God, *one* this sort, and *another* that sort" (1 Cor. 7:7); alternation.

- ⭕ ἔδωκεν **τοὺς** μὲν ἀποστόλους, **τοὺς** δὲ προφήτας, "He gave *some* as apostles, *others* as prophets . . ." (Eph. 4:11); alternation again.

13. AS RELATIVE PRONOUN. Many times a construction with the Greek article, especially articular participles, must be translated by an English relative pronoun: πᾶς **ὁ** ἀγαπῶν, "everyone *who* loves" (1 John 4:7). In these cases, the Greek article is not really functioning as a relative pronoun, but the idea is similar and that is how we must render it into English.[3] There are also instances when a second article is used with a noun or other substantive to tie an additional adjective, prepositional phrase, or participle to the noun. The basic format is: **ὁ** ἄρτος **ὁ** ζῶν, "the living bread" (John 6:51). The redundant second article may be separated from the noun it modifies by intervening words as some of the examples show.

- ⭕ τοῦτό μού ἐστιν τὸ σῶμα **τὸ** ὑπὲρ ὑμῶν, "This is my body *which* is for you" (1 Cor. 11:24).

---

[3]But see Rom. 2:21-23 where a relative clause occurs in parallel with articles (cf. Moule, p. 106).

- ὁ λόγος γὰρ **ὁ** τοῦ σταυροῦ τοῖς μὲν ἀπολλυμένοις μωρία ἐστίν, "For the word (*which* is) of the cross is foolishness to those who are perishing" (1 Cor. 1:18). The relative pronoun would be awkward in English. In classical Greek the format ὁ λόγος **ὁ** τοῦ σταυροῦ was common, but in Koine the redundant article was being phased out: ὁ λόγος τοῦ σταυροῦ was normal. In this verse the redundant article is used because of the intervening γάρ.

- ὁ δὲ αὐτὸς θεὸς **ὁ** ἐνεργῶν τὰ πάντα ἐν πᾶσιν, "But (it is) the same God *who* effects all in everyone" (1 Cor. 12:6).

- τὰ παθήματα τῶν ἁμαρτιῶν **τὰ** διὰ τοῦ νόμου, "The passions of sinful acts *which* (arose) through the law" (Rom. 7:5).

- ἵνα . . . ἡ διακονία μου **ἡ** εἰς Ἰερουσαλὴμ εὐπρόσδεκτος τοῖς ἁγίοις γένηται, "In order that my service *which* (is) for Jerusalem might be acceptable to the saints" (Rom. 15:31). Here the relative pronoun need not appear in English: "my service for Jerusalem." The article was needed in Greek to avoid confusion; without it, the prepositional phrase might be taken with the verb and mean something quite different: "In order that my service might be acceptable in Jerusalem to the saints."

14. AS A DEMONSTRATIVE PRONOUN. The Greek article functioned as a demonstrative pronoun much earlier in Greek as evidenced in Homer: **τὴν** δ᾽ ἐγὼ οὐ λύσω, "but I will not release *this* [woman]" (from Smyth §1100). The article was still used in place of the demonstrative pronoun "this," "that," etc. in the Koine period. In some cases the article was a "softer" expression than the demonstrative pronoun, sometimes called the "deictic" use, for pointing to something at hand: "this one here."

- ἔργα αὐτοῦ πονηρὰ ἦν **τὰ** δὲ τοῦ ἀδελφοῦ αὐτοῦ δίκαια, "His works were evil, but *those* (works) of his brother were righteous" (1 John 3:12).

- ἀπόδοτε πᾶσιν τὰς ὀφειλάς, **τῷ** τὸν φόρον τὸν φόρον . . . "Pay off your debts to all: *to that* (person to whom you owe) the tax, (pay) the tax . . ." (Rom. 13:7).

- ἔρημός ἐστιν **ὁ** τόπος, "*This* place is deserted" (Matt. 14:15).

In Certain Constructions

(canonical)

15. WITH TWO NOUNS IN GENITIVE RELATION. (Apollonius' canon.) Two nouns joined in a genitive phrase are either both articular or both anarthrous: **ὁ** λόγος **τῆς** ζωῆς, "the word of life" or, λόγος ζωῆς "word of life"; but not, **ὁ** λόγος ζωῆς, or, λόγος **τῆς** ζωῆς. This principle holds true even if the noun in the genitive is *indefinite* in meaning. In other words, whether a noun in the genitive has an article or not is usually determined by whether the noun it is joined to—the "head noun"—has an article or not. In such cases, the specificity of the genitive noun must be determined by careful consideration of the phrase as a whole and from context.

- περὶ **τοῦ** λόγου **τῆς** ζωῆς, "concerning *the* word of *life*" (1 John 1:1). The latter is an abstract noun that might have been anarthrous otherwise. Compare: ῥήματα ζωῆς αἰωνίου ἔχεις, "You have *words* of eternal *life*" (John 6:68); both nouns are anarthrous.

- ἡ δὲ δύναμις **τῆς** ἁμαρτίας ὁ νόμος, "*The* power *of sin* (is) the law" (1 Cor. 15:56).

○ τῷ μὲν νοΐ δουλεύω **νόμῳ θεοῦ** τῇ δὲ σαρκὶ **νόμῳ ἁμαρτίας**, "On the one hand, in my mind I am slave to (the) law of God. On the other hand, in my flesh, (I am slave to) *a principle of sin*" (Rom. 7:25). There is a subtle employment of articles and vocabulary here! Compare: ἐν **τῷ** νόμῳ **τῆς** ἁμαρτίας, "in *the principle of sin*" (Rom. 7:23).

16. WITH SINGULAR PARALLEL NOUNS. (Granville Sharp's canon; see especially Wallace, pp. 270–90.) In an idiom that is somewhat similar to English, one article used with two *singular* nouns in a series suggests that they both refer to the same person or object, whereas two articles suggest that two people or objects are referenced. Compare: "*the* Lord and Savior" (= one person), with "*the* Lord and *the* Savior" (= two persons). The lack of a second article does not always indicate one referent with two titles; rather, it merely asserts that both (or more) referents are somehow closely joined. As Wallace carefully observes, this principle did not affect *plural* nouns in the same way, even though the two groups might have a close affinity.[4] This is not a principle to be applied mechanically but is a subtle point of article usage to be applied carefully in context.

○ ἐν δικαιοσύνῃ **τοῦ** θεοῦ ἡμῶν καὶ σωτῆρος Ἰησοῦ Χριστοῦ, "in the righteousness of our God and Savior Jesus Christ" (2 Pet. 1:1; cf. Titus 2:13); one person.

○ ὁ ἀρνούμενος **τὸν** πατέρα καὶ τὸν υἱόν, "the one who denies *the Father* and *the Son*" (1 John 2:22); two persons.

○ **ὁ** θεὸς καὶ πατὴρ τοῦ κυρίου ἡμῶν Ἰησοῦ Χριστοῦ, "*The God and Father* of our Lord Jesus Christ" (Eph. 1:3).

○ Ἐγὼ Ἰωάννης, **ὁ** ἀδελφὸς ὑμῶν καὶ συγκοινωνὸς ἐν **τῇ** θλίψει καὶ βασιλείᾳ καὶ ὑπομονῇ, "I John, *your brother* and *fellow-participant* in the tribulation and kingdom and endurance" (Rev. 1:9). Two examples of the principle: (1) brother and fellow-participant are closely associated; and, (2) the tribulation-kingdom-endurance group are unified.

17. WITH PREDICATE NOMINATIVES. (Colwell's canon;[5] see especially Wallace, pp. 256–70.) When a noun is used as a predicate nominative in a predicate statement, the presence or absence of an article with that noun may be determined by word order rather than by whether the noun is definite or not. Colwell identified the normal pattern as: (1) Definite predicate nouns that *follow* the copulative verb (usually εἰμί, "to be") tend to have the article expressed: ἐγώ εἰμι **τὸ** φῶς τοῦ κόσμου, "I am *the* Light of the world" (John 8:12). The definite, predicate noun φῶς follows the copulative verb εἰμί, hence the article τό was expressed. (2) Definite predicate nouns that *precede* the copulative verb tend to omit the article, even though they are specific in meaning: **φῶς** εἰμι τοῦ κόσμου, "I am *(the)* Light of the world" (John 9:5). Here, Jesus is clearly not saying: "I am a light (among many) of the world"; this is the same assertion he made in v. 8:12. And notice that the noun φῶς can be considered definite because it is joined with an articular τοῦ κόσμου (cf. §15 above).

Colwell's canon should be handled carefully—one must always leave room for variations in style, conflicts with other rules of article usage, the anarthrous noun focusing on a quality, etc. And we should stress this: the canon shows that a pre-verbal anarthrous predicate noun *may* be definite in

---

[4]For example, **τῶν** ἀποστόλων καὶ προφητῶν in Eph. 2:20 and **τοὺς** ποιμένας καὶ διδασκάλους in Eph. 4:11.

[5] E. C. Colwell, "A Definite Rule for the Use of the Article in the Greek New Testament," *Journal of Biblical Literature* 52 (1933): 12-21.

meaning, not that it *always* is definite; φῶς in 1 John 1:5 is one example where the anarthrous predicate is not definite but focuses on the noun's quality (see the Reading Notes). Colwell's canon is a helpful description of an important Greek idiom, but it must be used with care.[6] It's a canon with one "n" not two.

○ **θεὸς** ἦν ὁ λόγος, "The word was *God*" (John 1:1); not "*a god*."

○ εἰ ὁ θεὸς **πατὴρ** ὑμῶν ἦν ἠγαπᾶτε ἂν ἐμέ, "If God were *your Father*, you would love me" (John 8:42). The fact that πατήρ is anarthrous is determined by its function as the predicate noun; it is still definite in conjunction with ὑμῶν. Not "a father of yours."

○ **βασιλεύς** εἰμι τῶν Ἰουδαίων, "I am *the* King of the Jews" (John 19:21). Like the previous example, βασιλεύς is confirmed to be definite according to Apollonius' canon explained above (§15).

○ Ὁ δὲ ἑκατόνταρχος καὶ οἱ μετ᾽ αὐτοῦ τηροῦντες τὸν Ἰησοῦν . . . ἐφοβήθησαν σφόδρα, λέγοντες· ἀληθῶς **θεοῦ υἱὸς** ἦν οὗτος, "Then the centurion and those where were guarding Jesus with him . . . became exceedingly afraid and said, 'Truly he was *the Son of God*'" (Matt. 27:54).

○ **πατὴρ** δ᾽ ὁ Ζεύς, "Now Zeus is *our father*" (Plutarch, *Roman Questions* 40 [274B]).

Anarthrous Constructions

18. ANARTHROUS SUBSTANTIVES. Substantives may be expressed anarthrously in order to bring out the character or quality of the referent. The noun refers to an individual who shares qualities with others in its class. Be careful here, though, because many nouns may be definite even when they are anarthrous in Greek.

○ Μωϋσῆς μὲν πιστὸς . . . ὡς **θεράπων** . . . Χριστὸς δὲ ὡς **υἱός**, "Moses was faithful . . . as *a servant* . . . but Christ as *a son*" (Heb. 3:5-6).

○ τίς γὰρ υἱὸς ὃν οὐ παιδεύει **πατήρ**; "What son is there whom his father, *as a father*, does not chasten?" (Heb. 12:7; translation Moulton, 83).

○ ὁ θεὸς **ἀγάπη** ἐστίν, "God is *love*" (1 John 4:8).

19. THE ARTICLE AND PREPOSITIONS. An anarthrous noun used with some prepositions may still be definite. The principle is: an anarthrous substantive after a preposition *may* be definite or not, but an articular substantive has some kind of specific referent. This should not be considered to be an invariable grammatical "rule," for there are frequent exceptions. It seems instead to be a pattern based upon style and a general tendency with some prepositions and some nouns. Compare a similar phenomenon in English: "I am going *to the beach*"; "The ship went *to sea*." Why would we

---

[6]I am not aware of studies of this construction outside the NT, yet one can observe it elsewhere. I have noticed it particularly in the LXX of the Psalms; e.g., **υἱός** μου εἶ σύ, "You are my Son" (Ps. 2:7; cf. 15[16]:2); σὺ δέ, κύριε, **ἀντιλήμπτωρ** μου εἶ, "And you, O Lord, are my Helper" (Ps. 3:4).

not say: "I am going *to beach*," or, "The ship went *to the sea*"? The last example below goes into some depth in order to illustrate the NT situation.

○ ἐν ἀρχῇ, "in *the* beginning" (John 1:1).

○ ἀπ᾽ ἀρχῆς, "from *the* beginning" (1 John 1:1).

○ διὰ νόμου, "through *the* law" (Rom. 4:13).

○ ἐκ νεκρῶν, "from *the* dead" is a common phrase in the NT and νεκρῶν is anarthrous in all occasions except in Col. 1:18 (πρωτότοκος ἐκ **τῶν** νεκρῶν, "firstborn from the dead") and Eph. 5:14 (an OT reference: ἀνάστα ἐκ **τῶν** νεκρῶν, "arise from the dead"). And it is noteworthy that anarthrous ἐκ νεκρῶν occurs elsewhere in both Colossians (Col. 2:12) and Ephesians (Eph. 1:20). Anarthrous ἐκ νεκρῶν occurs in Mark 6:14—nothing exceptional here. Yet Matthew in his parallel chose a synonymous preposition and the article: ἀπὸ **τῶν** νεκρῶν (Matt. 14:2). Perhaps ἀπό is used with an article more often? Well, Matthew does use the articular expression ἀπὸ **τῶν** νεκρῶν twice elsewhere (Matt. 27:64 and 28:7), but Luke has anarthrous ἀπὸ νεκρῶν (Luke 16:30)! All these phrases would be translated alike in English: "from *the* dead." Compare also these two equivalent expressions: περὶ δὲ **τῆς** ἀναστάσεως **τῶν** νεκρῶν, "concerning *the* resurrection of *the* dead" (Matt. 22:31), and ἐξ ἀναστάσεως νεκρῶν, "from *the* resurrection of *the* dead" (Rom. 1:4; Acts 26:23).

Conflicts of Interest

20. WHEN RULES COLLIDE. There are many situations which occur in the actual use of any language where grammatical rules conflict and an author must puzzle out how to express his thoughts "properly." The same is true in the Greek NT. This phenomenon accounts for many of the exceptions to the rules of normal article usage sketched out above.[7] As a result, when you encounter an article use or non-use which seems to conflict with these rules, you must not assume too hastily that there is some point of emphasis or nuance here; see if there is some conflict of article usage at work which explains the discrepancy. With time and experience, you will be able to discern the difference between "article use collision" and an author's suggestive and subtle nuance. The following are a few examples of rule conflict; some others are noted in the Reading Notes as encountered.

○ ἐν ἀρχῇ **τοῦ** εὐαγγελίου, "in *the* beginning of *the* gospel" (Phil. 4:15). We expect ἐν **τῇ** ἀρχῆς in this situation, because of "Apollonius' canon" (§15 above). This exception occurs because ἀρχῆς is the object of a preposition (§19 above), and it therefore needs no article even though it is definite.[8] Paul here *could* have dropped the article before εὐαγγελίου to conform to "Apollonius' canon" and the reader would still have regarded "gospel" as though it were articular "*the* gospel," not "*a* gospel." Thus we find: ἀπ᾽ ἀρχῆς κόσμου, "from *the* beginning of *the* world" (Matt. 24:21); not "from *the* beginning of *a* world."

---

[7]Other exceptions are caused by an author's idiomatic style; you must remember that Koine Greek was spoken over a large geographical area with regional "flavors" much like the varieties of English, Spanish, or French spoken around the world today.

[8]Cf. S. Hull, "Exceptions to Apollonius' Canon in the New Testament," *Trinity Journal* 7 (1986): 3-16.

○ **φῶς** εἰμι **τοῦ** κόσμου, "I am *(the)* Light of the world" (John 9:5). Again, Apollonius' canon leads us to expect that both φῶς and κόσμου be articular, however φῶς is anarthrous, even though definite, because of Colwell's canon (above §17). Colwell and Apollonius butted heads and Colwell won.

○ **τεκνία μου**, ταῦτα γράφω ὑμῖν, "*My dear children,* I am writing these things to you" (1 John 2:1). As pointed out in §5 above, the article is normally used with a possessive pronoun in Greek; we expect **τὰ** τεκνία μου. However, τεκνία is in the vocative case (see below §26) which *has no article form!*

Nominative Case §§21–25

21. INTRODUCTION. (Wallace, pp. 36–64; Young, pp. 9–15; Porter, pp. 83–87.) The nominative functions principally as the subject of a finite verb. Predicate nominatives are frequent as well, but the other uses here and in the reference grammars are less common in the NT.

22. SUBJECT. A substantive in the nominative case was most commonly used as the subject of a verb, whether the voice of the verb was active, middle, or passive. With copulative verbs (usually εἰμί) a nominative personal pronoun was often supplied *without emphasis*, whereas the inclusion of the nominative personal pronoun with most other verbs signified some sort of emphasis. And remember that copulative verbs were often implied rather than expressed: τί [ἐστιν] τὸ ὄφελος; "What [is] the profit?" (James 2:14).

- **τὸ φῶς** ἐν τῇ σκοτίᾳ φαίνει, "*The light* is shining in the darkness" (John 1:5).

- **Χριστὸς** ἐγήγερται ἐκ νεκρῶν, "*Christ* has been raised from the dead" (1 Cor. 15:20).

- **αὐτός** ἐστιν ἐν τῷ φωτί, "*He* is in the light" (1 John 1:7). No emphasis for αὐτός. Compare the next example.

- ἀλλ᾽ ἐρεῖ **τις**, **Σὺ** πίστιν ἔχεις **κἀγὼ** ἔργα ἔχω, "But *someone* will say, '*You* have faith, while *I* have works" (James 2:18). There are three subject nominatives in this example. The personal pronouns, σύ and ἐγώ [embedded in κἀγώ] are emphatic, in order to underscore the contrast between the two subjects.

23. PREDICATE. The predicate noun, pronoun, adjective, or other substantive in a predicate sentence with a copulative verb (εἰμί, γίνομαι, or ὑπάρχω) was placed in the nominative case. The same is true in English: "I am *he*," not, "I am *him*"; "It is *I*," not, "It is *me*."

- ὁ θεὸς **φῶς** ἐστιν, "God is *light*" (1 John 1:5).

- αὕτη ἔστιν **ἡ ἀγγελία**, "This is *the message*" (1 John 3:11).

- ὁ νόμος **παιδαγωγὸς** ἡμῶν γέγονεν, "The law became *our guardian*" (Gal. 3:24).

24. AS VOCATIVE. A noun in the nominative case is sometimes used for direct address instead of the vocative (§§26–27 below). This substitution probably resulted because the nominative and vocative forms are identical in most cases (see vocative forms below in §26). Nominatives used as vocatives are modified by the article (see §8 above).

- οἱ **ἄνδρες**, ἀγαπᾶτε τὰς γυναῖκας, "*Husbands*, love your wives" (Eph. 5:25).

- ναὶ **ὁ πατήρ**, ὅτι οὕτως εὐδοκία ἐγένετο ἔμπροσθέν σου, "Yes *Father*, for thus it was well pleasing in your sight" (Matt. 11:26).

- τὰ **τέκνα**, ὑπακούετε τοῖς γονεῦσιν, "*Children*, obey your parents" (Col. 3:20).

25. HANGING NOMINATIVE. (*Nominativus pendens.*) Sometimes a word in the nominative case begins a clause as introduction to a referent which occurs later in the clause in another case. The nominative "hangs" grammatically without any clear function in relation to the verb. This is a form of "anacoluthon," a grammatical break in midstream. The nominative was similarly used in titles and other special parts of speech as well.[9]

○ ὁ γὰρ **Μωϋσῆς οὗτος** . . . οὐκ οἴδαμεν τί ἐγένετο αὐτῷ, "For *this Moses* . . . we don't know what happened *to him*" (Acts 7:40).

○ καὶ **ὁ νικῶν** . . . δώσω αὐτῷ ἐξουσίαν, "And *the one who conquers* . . . I will give to him authority" (Rev. 2:26).

○ Ἀποκάλυψις Ἰησοῦ Χριστοῦ, "The *revelation* of Jesus Christ" (Rev. 1:1). This is the nominative in a title.

---

[9]Cf. Wallace, pp. 49–55 for some finer distinctions relating to independent uses of the nominative.

Vocative Case §§26–27

26. INTRODUCTION. (Wallace, pp. 65–71; Young, pp. 15–16; Porter, pp. 87–88.) The vocative case was only briefly mentioned in the *Primer* (§3.5), hence you should memorize the sample forms from the three declensions given here. Notice that most of these vocatives are identical in form with the nominatives in their respective declensions.

Vocative Case Forms

	SINGULAR	PLURAL
First Declension	φωνή	φωναί
	καρδία	καρδίαι
Second Declension	λόγε	λόγοι
	τέκνον	τέκνα
Third Declension	γύναι	γυναῖκες
	πάτερ	πατέρες
	βασιλεῦ	βασιλεῖς

27. VOCATIVE. The vocative case was used predominately for words in direct address: "Sir," "Lord," "Madam," etc. The inclusion of the particle ὦ, "O," often added an element of heightened emotion or rhetorical sharpness. See §24 above for the nominative used in place of the vocative.

○ **κύριε**, θεωρῶ ὅτι προφήτης εἶ σύ, "*Sir*, I perceive that you are a prophet" (John 4:19).

○ ἐξομολογοῦμαί σοι, **πάτερ**, κύριε τοῦ οὐρανοῦ καὶ τῆς γῆς, "I praise you, *Father, Lord* of heaven and of earth" (Matt. 11:25). See verse 26 where ὁ πατήρ is found as a nominative used as a vocative (cf. §24 above).

○ **ὦ ἄνθρωπε**, μενοῦνγε σὺ τίς εἶ ὁ ἀνταποκρινόμενος τῷ θεῷ; "Well then! Just who are you, *O man*, to talk back to God!" (Rom. 11:20).

○ **γύναι**, τί κλαίεις; "*Woman*, why are you crying?" (John 20:15). "Woman" does not communicate well in English; it was a polite expression in Greek.

○ **ὦ γύναι**, μεγάλη σου ἡ πίστις, "*O woman*, great is your faith!" (Matt. 15:28).

Accusative Case §§28–34

28. INTRODUCTION. (Wallace, pp. 176–205; Young, pp. 16–22; Porter, pp. 88–92.) Most of the accusatives you will encounter in Greek function as the direct object of non-copulative verbs. The other uses below (and a few less important ones found in the cited reference grammars) are specialty uses which you will find only occasionally in the Greek of the NT era.

29. DIRECT OBJECT. The direct object of a verb is normally expressed in the accusative case (except for certain verbs which require direct objects in the genitive or dative case; see §§51 and 65). If the accusative direct object is cognate with the verb (i.e., the two were etymologically related), it is called a "cognate accusative." The cognate served to intensify the action, but is otherwise a normal direct object.

- **εἰρήνην** ἔχομεν πρὸς τὸν θεὸν, "We have *peace* with God" (Rom. 5:1).

- ἡ σκοτία **αὐτὸ** οὐ κατέλαβεν, "The darkness did not vanquish *it*" (John 1:5).

- **ὃ** ἀκηκόαμεν, "*what* we have heard" (1 John 1:1).

- ἐφοβήθησαν **φόβον** μέγαν, "They feared a great fear" (Mark. 4:41). This is a cognate accusative because φόβος and φοβέομαι are etymologically related.

30. DOUBLE ACCUSATIVE. Some verbs in Greek as well as in English take what is called a "double accusative."[10] The double accusative is a variety of the predicate statement, since the verbs "to be" or "to become" are implied. In some cases the English word "as" is used in translation of this construction. A double nominative was used with virtually the same function when the verb was passive: ἐτέθην **ἐγὼ κῆρυξ**, "*I* was appointed *as a herald*" (1 Tim. 2:7; 2 Tim. 1:11).

- **πατέρα** πολλῶν ἐθνῶν τέθεικά **σε**, "I have appointed *you* (to be) the *father* of many nations" or, "*as* the father of . . ." (Rom. 4:17; Gen. 17:5).

- **ὃν** ἔθηκεν **κληρονόμον** πάντων, "*Whom* he established *as heir* of all things" (Heb. 1:2).

- **ψεύστην** ποιοῦμεν **αὐτόν**, "We are making *him* out (to be) *a liar*" (1 John 1:10).

31. RESPECT. (Specification.) The accusative case was employed with or without a preposition (περί), to indicate the subject matter or another kind of limiting qualification on the statement. This function is virtually identical with that of the dative of respect (§56 below). You will see this meaning communicated with a preposition like περί much more frequently in the NT. English "concerning" or "with respect to" brings out the meaning of the accusative of respect sufficiently.

---

[10]The double accusative is different from a construction with two direct objects joined by a conjunction: "I am not writing *a new commandment* to you, *but an ancient commandment*" (1 John 2:7). And it is different from a word in apposition to a direct object: "We have an Advocate, (namely) Jesus Christ" (1 John 2:1). Likewise, do not confuse a statement in English such as, "He made *me a sandwich*," with the Greek double accusative construction. This is English shorthand for, "He made a sandwich *for me*" where "for me" is the equivalent of the Greek dative. If "He made *me a sandwich*," were a double accusative construction, the meaning would be, "He made me (to be) a sandwich"! (The "Cannibal Accusative"?!)

○ Μωϋσῆς γὰρ γράφει **τὴν δικαιοσύνην**, "For Moses writes *with respect to the righteousness* . . ." (Rom. 10:5). Compare: **ταῦτα** γράφω ὑμῖν, "I am writing *these things* to you" (1 John 2:1), where ταῦτα functions as the direct object of the verb. In Rom. 10:5 δικαιοσύνην is not the direct object—the thing written—but the subject matter of the writing.

○ **τὸν ἀριθμὸν** ὡς πεντακισχίλιοι, "[There were] about 5,000 (people) *with respect to number*" (John 6:10).

○ ἵνα ἐλεήμων γένηται καὶ πιστὸς ἀρχιερεὺς **τὰ** πρὸς τὸν θεόν, "in order that he might become a merciful and faithful High Priest *concerning the things* relating to God" (Heb. 2:17). The neuter article (τά) "substantizes" the prepositional phrase (see §9 above).

32. ADVERBIAL. Adjectives and pronouns sometimes function as adverbs when expressed as neuter accusatives. The adverbial meaning of these words can best be determined from context (and a good lexicon!).

○ ἔθετο ὁ θεὸς ἐν τῇ ἐκκλησίᾳ **πρῶτον** ἀποστόλους, **δεύτερον** προφήτας, **τρίτον** διδασκάλους, "God appointed in the church *first* apostles, *second* prophets, *third* teachers . . ." (1 Cor. 12:28). You learned πρῶτον as an adverb (*Primer* §30.1), but now you see that it is an adjective (πρῶτος, –η, –ον) expressed as an adverbial accusative.

○ τεκνία, ἔτι **μικρὸν** μεθ' ὑμῶν εἰμι, "Children, I will only be with you *for a little while* longer" (John 13:33).

○ **περισσότερον** αὐτῶν πάντων ἐκοπίασα, "I labored *all the more* than them all" (1 Cor. 15:11). (The genitive is used with comparisons [below §47].)

33. EXTENT. The accusative case is used adverbially with measurement nouns and phrases to indicate the extent of an action either in space or in time (duration). (The adverbial accusative in the previous section involves adjectives and pronouns more generally.) Compare this use with the adverbial uses of the genitive (§50) or the dative (§64) cases.

○ (EXTENT IN SPACE): ἐληλακότες οὖν ὡς **σταδίους εἴκοσι πέντε** ἢ **τριάκοντα**, "then, after they had gone about *twenty-five or thirty stades*" (John 6:19).

○ (EXTENT IN TIME): ἐμεῖνεν ἐκεῖ **δύο ἡμέρας**, "He remained there *for two days*" (John 4:40).

34. SUBJECT OF INFINITIVE. You will recall from the *Primer* that infinitives in Greek require their subject to be expressed in the accusative case rather than in the nominative (*Primer* §25.5). Perhaps this rule originated from the fact that infinitives themselves were often used as direct objects of finite verbs. Regardless of origin, though, this phenomenon will confuse you unless you learn it well now!

○ δεῖ **με** καὶ Ῥώμην ἰδεῖν, "It is necessary that *I* also see Rome" (Acts 19:21).

○ δεῖ **αὐτὸν** ἀποκτανθῆναι, "It is necessary that *he* be killed" (Rev. 11:5). The infinitive is passive, but its subject αὐτόν is still accusative.

○ εἰς τὸ εἶναι **αὐτὸν** πρωτότοκον ἐν πολλοῖς ἀδελφοῖς, "in order that *he* might be the Firstborn among many brothers" (Rom. 8:29). In this case, πρωτότοκος ("firstborn") is also in the accusative as a predicate noun. The rule is that predicates agree in case with their subjects; if the subject is accusative (here because of the infinitive construction), then the predicate is accusative also.

Genitive Case §§35-52

35. INTRODUCTION. (See Wallace, pp. 72–136; Young, Chap. 2; Porter, pp. 92–97.) The genitive case is the most flexible case in Greek. The bewildering variety of descriptions of the genitive found in our literature is reduced here to the most common types found in the NT. Remember that our purpose is not the mere assigning of labels to constructions but *understanding* them. Knowing the following categories will help you to understand certain Greek phrases more profoundly. At times, though, you will find certain equivocal genitive phrases. For instance, the simple phrase, τὸ εὐαγγέλιον **τοῦ Χριστοῦ** (Phil. 1:27; cf. Mark 1:1), may mean either, "the good news proclaimed about Christ (by someone else)" (objective genitive or genitive of connection) or "the good new that Christ proclaimed," (subjective genitive).[11] In such cases, it is best to keep an open mind and recognize that there are certain ambiguities in all languages.

36. POSSESSION. This is the simplest use of the genitive; it signifies ownership or possession of some object. In some cases, the possession is literal ownership of goods (the first example), and in many other cases it is a more figurative possession (the other two examples).

○ τὸν οἶκόν **σου**, "your house" (Matt. 9:6).

○ ἐπὶ πᾶσαν δύναμιν **τοῦ ἐχθροῦ**, "over all the power *of the enemy*" (Luke 10:19).

○ αἱ χεῖρες **ἡμῶν**, "our hands" (1 John 1:1).

37. PERSONAL RELATIONSHIP. This category covers family and other personal relations where the thought of "ownership" expressed by the previous genitive use would be inappropriate. In the NT, the genitive was sometimes used in a metaphorical construction with "son(s) of" or "child(ren) of" under Semitic influence.

○ υἱοί εἰσιν **θεοῦ τῆς ἀναστάσεως** υἱοί ὄντες, "They are sons *of God*, since they are sons *of the resurrection*" (Luke 20:36).

○ τῷ λαῷ **τοῦ θεοῦ**, "for the people *of God*" (Heb. 4:9).

○ ἤμεθα τέκνα φύσει **ὀργῆς**, "We were *children of wrath* naturally" (Eph. 2:3).

38. SUBJECTIVE. Along with the objective genitive (§41 below), this use involves a genitive substantive of any type connected to a substantive which conveys a verbal notion. For example, ἀγάπη in the phrase: ἡ **ἀγάπη** τοῦ θεοῦ (1 John 2:5) is joined to the genitive τοῦ θεοῦ and designates the verbal idea of "loving." Now you must decide whether the genitive communicates the person *performing* the action, "God loves someone," in which case God would be the *subject* of the verbal idea, hence the term "*subject*ive genitive." Or decide whether the genitive word expresses the person *receiving* the action, "someone loves God," this would be the *object* of the verbal idea, an "*object*ive genitive." If you paraphrase the genitive phrase as a verbal clause, it often helps to identify the meaning intended.

---

[11]See the discussion by Moisés Silva (*God, Language and Scripture* [Foundations of Contemporary Interpretation, IV; Grand Rapids: Zondervan, 1990], 109), who believes that there is intentional vagueness in this phrase, "that served simply to identify his (Paul's) message."

○ ἡ πίστις **σου** σέσωκέν σε, "*Your* faith has made you well" (Mark 5:34 and 10:52). Paraphrase as: "*You believed* and it made you well." Σου functions as the subject of πίστις when converted into a verb (ἐπίστευσας).

○ ἡ ἀγάπη **τοῦ θεοῦ** ἐν ἡμῖν, "the love *of God* in us" (1 John 4:9). The context shows that John is referring to God's love toward us (not vice versa). Paraphrase: ὁ θεὸς ἀγαπᾷ ἡμᾶς, "God loves us."

○ ἡ παρουσία **τοῦ υἱοῦ** τοῦ ἀνθρώπου, "the arrival *of the Son* of Man" (Matt. 24:27). Paraphrase: "The Son of Man arrives."

39. AGENCY. This use is the same as the subjective genitive except that the verbal idea of the lead substantive (often an adjective or passive participle) to which the genitive is attached is *passive* in meaning. You can paraphrase the idea with an active verb to see the connection with the subjective genitive. Otherwise paraphrase with a passive verb and with the preposition "by," as illustrated here:

> "[O]f itself the use of the genitive may have as many varieties as there are ways in which two notions may be associated." Max Zerwick

○ κατὰ πίστιν ἐκλεκτῶν **θεοῦ**, "in accordance with the faith *of God's* elect" (Titus 1:1). The adjective, ἐκλεκτῶν, carries a passive verbal idea: "people who have been chosen." The genitive, θεοῦ, signifies the agent of election: "people chosen *by God*." (The first genitive is subjective: πίστιν **ἐκλεκτῶν**, means "the elect believe.") A full, clumsy paraphrase is: "in accordance with the faith that those people exercise who have been elected by God."

○ οἱ εὐλογημένοι **τοῦ πατρός** μου, "those blessed *by* my *Father*" (Matt. 25:34). Active verb paraphrase: "those whom my Father has blessed."

○ κατὰ τὸ **ἑκάστου** ἔργον, "according to the work *of each one*" (1 Pet. 1:17). Paraphrase: "in accordance with the things done *by each one*."

○ ἐν οἷς ἐστε καὶ ὑμεῖς κλητοὶ **Ἰησοῦ Χριστοῦ**, "among whom you also are those who are called *by Jesus Christ*" (Rom. 1:6). Paraphrase: "those whom Jesus Christ has called."

40. SOURCE. (Origin.) The genitive of source or origin functions like a prepositional phrase with ἐκ or ἀπό, "from (the source of)." The meaning is often very close to the subjective genitive; for instance, τὰς ἐντολὰς **αὐτοῦ** (1 John 2:3) could mean: "the commandments that come *from him*" (source) or "he commanded (these things)" (subjective). There is little exegetical value in making a distinction between these two uses in this particular case.

○ τοῦτο οὐκ ἐξ ὑμῶν, **θεοῦ** τὸ δῶρον, "this (is) not from you, the gift (is) *from God*" (Eph. 2:8). The meaning is that the gift (of salvation by grace through faith) does not originate from human resources, but originates *from God*.

○ ἵνα ἡ ὑπερβολὴ τῆς δυνάμεως ᾖ **τοῦ θεοῦ** καὶ μὴ ἐξ ἡμῶν, "so that the surpassing greatness of the power might be *from God* and not from us" (2 Cor. 4:7). Notice that the simple genitive phrase, τοῦ θεοῦ, is paralleled by the prepositional phrase denoting source, ἐξ ἡμῶν.

○ ἐστὲ ἐπιστολὴ **Χριστοῦ**, "You are a letter *from Christ*" (2 Cor. 3:3).

41. OBJECTIVE. A substantive in the genitive may express the object of a verbal substantive to which it is joined. The first example below is clearly an objective rather than a subjective genitive, but, as mentioned in the second example below, there is considerable debate over a similar phrase in Paul.[12] As with the subjective genitive, the objective genitive is always joined with a lead substantive which has a verbal referent.

- ἔχετε πίστιν **θεοῦ**, "Have faith *(in) God*" (Mark 11:22). Here the noun in the genitive, θεοῦ, indicates the direct object of the verbal noun transformed into a verbal idea (πιστεύετε).

- δικαιοσύνη δὲ θεοῦ διὰ πίστεως **Ἰησοῦ Χριστοῦ**, "but the righteousness of God through faith *in Jesus Christ*" (Rom. 3:22). There is currently a lively scholarly debate about whether this interpretation is correct or not. Is the genitive Ἰησοῦ Χριστοῦ to be taken as a objective genitive (as translated here) or is it an subjective genitive: "Jesus Christ's faithfulness"?

- ὁ ἄρχων **τῶν βασιλέων** τῆς γῆς, "the ruler *over the kings* of the earth" (Rev. 1:5). The noun "ruler" designates ruling; the kings are the object over whom the "King of kings" rules. (Note the same objective genitive meaning for the English phrase "King *of kings*.") The second genitive, τῆς γῆς, can best be taken as an adjectival genitive: "*earthly* kings" (§42).

- φόβῳ **θανάτου**, "by the fear *of death*" (Heb. 2:15). Paraphrase as a verbal statement and the objective genitive becomes the accusative object: φοβοῦνται **θάνατον**, "they fear *death*."

42. ADJECTIVAL. ("Hebrew" genitive, attributive, qualitative.). An abstract noun in the genitive may function like an adjective for the substantive to which it is joined. We only use a limited number of similar constructions in English; for instance, "She was an author *of note*" (meaning "a notable author"). Hebrew, as you may know, has a restricted number of adjectives; it often uses a noun joined to another noun in the construct state with an adjectival meaning: "the mountain *of his holiness*" (Ps. 48:1); the noun "holiness" functions here as an adjective: "his *holy* mountain."

- κατὰ πνεῦμα **ἁγιωσύνης**, "according to the Spirit *of holiness*" (Rom. 1:4); the *Holy* Spirit.

- ἐν πνεῦμα **πραΰτητος**, "with a spirit *of gentleness*" (Gal. 6:1); a *gentle* spirit.

- ὁ πατὴρ **τῶν οἰκτιρμῶν** καὶ θεὸς πάσης παρακλήσεως, "the Father *of mercies* and God of all comfort" (2 Cor. 1:3). The first phrase is adjectival: "the *merciful* Father" whereas the second genitive is probably subjective: "the God *who comforts fully*."

- ἤγγιζεν ὁ χρόνος **τῆς ἐπαγγελίας**, "The time *of the promise* has arrived" (Acts 7:17); the *promised* time.

43. REVERSED ADJECTIVAL. (Antiptosis.[13]) The relation of an adjectival genitive (above) may be employed in reversed manner: the *lead noun* acts as an adjective to the noun in the genitive, not

---

[12]See Wallace, pp. 115–16 for a summary of the current debate.

[13]See E. W. Bullinger, *Figures of Speech Used in the Bible*, (London: Eyre & Spottiswoode, 1898; reprinted by Baker Book House, 1968), 507-509.

vice versa. This category is not always discussed in our grammars;[14] it is not excessively common, but it *is* interesting and often marks phrases an author wanted to accent.

○ τὴν ἐπαγγελίαν τοῦ πνεύματος, "*the promise* of the Spirit," meaning, "the *promised* Spirit," not "the *spiritual* promise" (Gal. 3:14). Expressed as an adjectival genitive, we would have: τὸ πνεῦμα τῆς ἐπαγγελίας which is found in Eph. 1:13, "the *promised* Spirit." There is no semantic difference between the two ways of stating the phrase; it is a matter of style.

○ ἵνα . . . καὶ ἡμεῖς ἐν καινότητι ζωῆς περιπατήσωμεν, "in order that we too may walk in *newness of life*" (Rom. 6:4). This striking phrase is the semantic equivalent of "new life" but much more rich.

○ βάθος γῆς, "*depth* of soil," meaning, "*deep* soil" (Matt. 13:5).

44. EXPLANATORY. (Epexegetical, Appositional.) A word in the genitive case may be the equivalent of the word with which it is joined. It functions like a word in apposition, which serves to explain the other word or supply supplementary information. There may be an underlying predication in this shorthand idiom equating the two words. You can supply "that is" or "i.e." in English to bring out the meaning.

> "The genitive case is one of the most crucial elements of Greek syntax to master." Daniel Wallace

○ ὁ . . . δοὺς τὸν ἀρραβῶνα τοῦ πνεύματος, "who gave the down-payment *of the Spirit*" (2 Cor. 1:22). The Holy Spirit is given to us as a down-payment. The underlying predication is: "the Holy Spirit is a sort of down-payment (of our inheritance)."

○ λήμψεσθε τὴν δωρεὰν τοῦ ἁγίου πνεύματος, "You will receive the gift *of the Holy Spirit*" (Acts 2:38). As in the previous example, the Holy Spirit is equated with the gift. One could translate: "the gift, that is, *the Holy Spirit*."

○ κατέβη εἰς τὰ κατώτερα μέρη τῆς γῆς, "He descended to the lower parts *of the earth*" (Eph. 4:9). As some scholars recognize, this does not mean "he descended to the underworld," but to the lower parts (from heaven's perspective), i.e., the earth (see Zerwick §45).

45. CONTENT OR MATERIAL. Like English constructions with "of," the genitive can specify the contents of a container ("basket *of bread*") or the material out of which it is made ("house *of cards*"). In many cases, the material or contents are metaphorical.

○ οὐδεὶς ἀγοράζει οὐκέτι γόμον χρυσοῦ καὶ ἀργύρου καὶ λίθου τιμίου καὶ μαργαριτῶν, "No one buys (their) cargo *of gold* and *of silver* and *of precious stone* and *of pearls* anymore . . ." (Rev. 18:11-12).

○ σύροντες τὸ δίκτυον τῶν ἰχθύων, "(They were) dragging the net *of fish*" (John 21:8).

○ ἐπὶ σκεύη ἐλέους, "upon vessels *of mercy*" (Rom. 9:23). A metaphor, "cups containing mercy"; compare σκεύη ὀργῆς, "vessels *of wrath*" (Rom. 9:22).

---

[14]Yet see Wallace, pp. 89–91 "Attributed Genitive," and Greenlee, p. 26; §C16 "Qualified Genitive."

○ λήμψεται τὸν στέφανον **τῆς ζωῆς**, "He will receive the crown *of life*" (James 1:12). Life is the composition of the crown. See also "crown *of gold*," or "a crown *of* twelve *stars*" (Rev. 12:1).

46. PARTITIVE GENITIVE. (Genitive of the whole.) When we use "of" in English to say: "one *of* the boats," it is the same form of expression as the Greek partitive genitive: ἓν τῶν πλοίων (Luke 5:3). The construction is marked when the lead substantive identifies *a part* (hence the term, *partitive*) and the word in the genitive identifies the whole. The substantives referring to the part can be numbers, indefinite pronouns, and adjectives and nouns which indicate various portions. Sometimes the preposition ἐκ is used with the same partitive meaning, even when the prepositional phrase is used by itself and the word for the part is not expressed but implied (cf. 1 John 2:19).

○ τινες **τῶν γραμματέων**, "some *of the scribes*" (Matt. 9:3).

○ οἱ λοιποὶ **τῶν ἀνθρώπων**, "the rest *of the men*" (Luke 18:11).

○ δύο **τῶν ἀκουσάντων**, "two *of those who listened*" (John 1:40).

○ πολλοὶ **ἐκ τῶν μαθητῶν** αὐτοῦ, "many *of his disciples*" (John 6:66); πολλοὶ **τῶν μαθητῶν** αὐτοῦ would mean the same thing.

○ ἠγόρασας τῷ θεῷ ἐν τῷ αἵματί σου **ἐκ πάσης φυλῆς** καὶ **γλώσσης** καὶ **λαοῦ** καὶ **ἔθνους**, "You purchased for God with your blood [some people] *from every tribe* and *language* and *people* and *nation*" (Rev. 5:9). Here the indefinite pronoun (τινές) is implied, and the preposition ἐκ has the partitive sense.

47. COMPARISON. The object of a comparison may be expressed in the genitive case. In English, we use "than" exclusively after comparisons, so the Greek idiom with the genitive takes some practice. Greek can also use ἤ, "than" instead of the genitive in comparisons as the first two examples below illustrate (cf. 1 John 4:4).

○ ὁ ἰσχυρότερός **μου**, "one stronger *than I*" (Mark 1:7). The alternate form of expression with ἤ would be: ὁ ἰσχυρότερος ἢ ἐγώ, but that would seem too clumsy in Greek.

○ μείζων ἐστὶν ὁ θεὸς **τῆς καρδίας** ἡμῶν, "God is greater *than our heart*" (1 John 3:20). The same thing could have been expressed with ἤ, "than": μείζων ἐστὶν ὁ θεὸς ἢ ἡ καρδία ἡμῶν.

○ ἀγαπᾷς με πλέον **τούτων**; "Do you love me more *than these*?" (John 21:15). πλέον is an adverbial accusative (above §32) qualifying the degree of "loving" (ἀγαπᾷς).

○ πολυτιμότερον **χρυσίου**, "more valuable *than gold*" (1 Pet. 1:7).

48. PRICE OR VALUE. Words indicating the price or value of an item may be expressed in the genitive without a preposition. This is an idiom with no English equivalent, so look for words denoting monetary values (especially [Roman] denarii and [Greek] drachmae) or the Greek word τιμή ("price," "value") as a clue that this use of the genitive is being employed.

○ **διακοσίων δηναρίων** ἄρτοι, "bread (valued at) *200 denarii*" (John 6:7).

○ συνεψήφισαν τὰς τιμὰς αὐτῶν καὶ εὗρον **ἀργυρίου** μυριάδας πέντε, "They counted up their price [magic books] and found (it to be) 50,000 *silver coins*" (Acts 19:19).

○ **τιμῆς** ἠγοράσθητε, "you were bought *at a [heavy] price*" (1 Cor. 7:23).

49. CONNECTION.[15] (General, Descriptive; see especially Wallace, pp. 79–81.) As Zerwick notes (§39), two words in a genitive relation may be related to one another in such a general way that classifying them into separate categories would be of little value. Hence the term here means that the two words are connected in some miscellaneous or vague way! For example, in Paul's phrase: ὁ δὲ θεὸς **τῆς ὑπομονῆς** καὶ **τῆς παρακλήσεως**, "Now the God *of endurance* and *of consolation*" (Rom. 15:4), could be classified as a sort of reverse subjective genitive: "the God who causes us to endure and who consoles us," but the idea comes through without minute classification of the genitive relation.

> "This [the genitive] is so immensely versatile and hard-working a case that anything like an exhaustive catalogue of its uses would be only confusing and unnecessarily dull."
> C. F. D. Moule

I find that an English translation with a hyphen often communicates the idea of a genitive of connection; for instance, Paul's frequent phrase, ἐξ ἔργων **νόμου**, "from works of law," (e.g., Gal. 3:2) is not always an objective genitive, "from doing the law," but means, "from doing what the law demands," and is communicated in the English translation: "from law-works" as opposed to "faith-hearing" (ἐξ ἀκοῆς **πίστεως**, Gal. 3:2).

One example of the genitive of connection, is that the genitive may specify the subject matter of a discourse. Smyth's "genitive of connection" has this "subject matter" meaning exclusively.

○ ἐξ ἔργων **νόμου**, "Was it by performing *the law*?" (Gal. 3:4). Or translate: "by *law-works*."

○ ὁ λόγος γὰρ ὁ **τοῦ σταυροῦ**, "For the word *of the cross*. . ." (1 Cor. 1:18). I.e., "the message *about* the cross." Compare "the word *of God*" which has a different genitive relation.

○ τὸ εὐαγγέλιον **τοῦ Χριστοῦ**, "the good news *about Christ*" (Phil. 1:29).

50. ADVERBIAL. A noun that refers to a time period may be expressed in the genitive to indicate *the time during which* the action of the verb occurs. Contrast this use with the adverbial (temporal) uses of the dative and accusative cases. Note that the genitive noun is not connected to another noun or substantive in the sentence, yet it functions as an adverb.

○ ἦλθεν πρὸς αὐτὸν **νυκτός**, "He came to him *during the night*" (John 3:2).

○ **νυκτὸς** καὶ **ἡμέρας** ἐργαζόμενοι, "Working *day* and *night*" (1 Thess. 2:9). This expression is used a half dozen times or so elsewhere in the NT.

---

[15]I have appropriated the label "genitive of connection" from H. W. Smyth's *Greek Grammar*. However, Smyth defines this genitive function more narrowly to those places where the genitive was used "to state the subject of a remark" (§1381). Some grammarians give this "subject matter" use a separate label (e.g., Young's "Communicative Content," p. 27). I'm not trying to muddy the waters here, but to make my labels meaningful and to reduce them to a manageable size.

○ ἵνα μὴ γένηται ἡ φυγὴ ὑμῶν **χειμῶνος**, "that your flight may not occur *during winter*" (Matt. 24:20).

51. WITH VERBS, ADJECTIVES, AND NOUNS. Some verbs take a direct object in the genitive case (see *Primer* §27.4). More similar to English, certain adjectives (like πλήρης "full of," or μέσος "middle of") are connected to words in the genitive. In most cases, the genitive is simply following its basic meanings; i.e., with μέσος the genitive has a partitive sense, meaning "in the middle *part* of." The genitive is found with some nouns, especially nouns of ruling ("ruler of"), filling ("fulness of"), etc. You will find that the standard lexicons like BAGD will indicate which verbs, adjectives, and nouns are usually qualified by words in the genitive case.

○ ἀκούσουσιν **τῆς φωνῆς** αὐτοῦ, "They will hear his *voice*" (John 5:28). Some students mistakenly render this: "hear *of* his voice." That is a different meaning and not the sense of the Greek idiom.

○ πλήρης **χάριτος** καὶ **ἀληθείας**, "full *of grace* and *of truth*" (John 1:14).

○ ἐν μέσῳ **τῆς θαλάσσης**, "in the middle *of the lake*" (Mark 6:47).

○ **διαθήκης νέας** μεσίτῃ, "to the mediator *of a new covenant*" (Heb. 12:24). The genitive in this case is objective, meaning, "he is the one who mediates *a new covenant*." The same construction can signify separation: μεσίτης **θεοῦ** καὶ **ἀνθρώπων**, "mediator *between God* and *men*" (1 Tim. 2:5).

52. GENITIVE ABSOLUTE. See *Primer* §21.5 for full description. Remember that the genitive absolute is simply an idiomatic use of the otherwise normal adverbial participle (*Primer* §20.5).

○ ἔτι **λαλοῦντος τοῦ Πέτρου** τὰ ῥήματα ταῦτα ἐπέπεσεν τὸ πνεῦμα τὸ ἅγιον ἐπὶ πάντας τοὺς ἀκούοντας τὸν λόγον, "*As Peter was* still *speaking* these words, the Holy Spirit fell upon all those who were listening to his speech" (Acts 10:44).

○ **ὀψίας** δὲ **γενομένης** προσῆλθον αὐτῷ οἱ μαθηταί, "*When evening arrived*, his disciples came to him" (Matt. 14:15).

○ ἔτι **ἁμαρτωλῶν ὄντων ἡμῶν** Χριστὸς ὑπερ ἡμᾶς ἀπέθανεν, "While *we were* still *sinners* Christ died for us" (Rom. 5:8). In this case the genitive absolute constitutes a predication where both the subject (ἡμῶν) and the predicate (ἁμαρτωλῶν) as well as the participle (ὄντων) are all expressed in the genitive case.

Dative Case §§53–65

53. INTRODUCTION. (See Wallace, pp. 137–75; Young, Chap. 3; Porter, pp. 97–100.) The dative case falls roughly into three general functions: special interest (advantage, disadvantage); instrumental (means, cause, etc.), and locative (location). There are also a few miscellaneous other uses distantly related to these three, but most Greek datives function as simple indirect objects of verbs.

54. INDIRECT OBJECT. (Special Interest.) An "indirect object" is a person or object which is indirectly affected by the verb. This can perhaps more helpfully be called a "special interest" in the action. For example, in the sentence, "I gave the fig *to Mary*," Mary, the indirect object, has some special interest in the action. In this case, Mary's interest could be described also as "advantage" (below), but it is safest to call most of these datives "indirect objects" and reserve the more specific terms for when the idea of advantage (or disadvantage) is clearly perceivable.

○ ταῦτα γράφω **ὑμῖν**, "I am writing these things *to you*" (1 John 2:1).

○ εἶπεν δὲ ὁ κύριος . . . **τῷ Παύλῳ**, "Then the Lord said . . . *to Paul*" (Acts 18:9).

○ διὰ τῆς χάριτος τῆς δοθείσης **μοι**, "through the grace given *to me*" (Rom. 12:3).

55. ADVANTAGE/DISADVANTAGE. The dative of indirect object (special interest) is utilized with the added nuance that the person specified in the dative receives either advantage or benefit from the action or disadvantage from the action. This nuance is only deduced from the context; try to paraphrase with the idea of advantage or disadvantage expressed and see if it clarifies the meaning or not. Use English expressions like "for the benefit of" for advantage, and "against," or "to the disadvantage of" for disadvantage.

○ μαρτυρῶ γὰρ **αὐτοῖς** ὅτι ζῆλον θεοῦ ἔχουσιν, "For I testify *on their behalf* that they do have a zeal for God" (Rom. 10:2).

○ μηδὲ παριστάνετε τὰ μέλη ὑμῶν ὅπλα ἀδικίας **τῇ ἁμαρτίᾳ**, "And don't present your members as weapons of unrighteousness *to advance the cause of sin*" (Rom. 6:13).

○ ἔρχομαί **σοι**, "I am coming *to your disadvantage*" (Rev. 2:5, 16). This is often interpreted as a simple indirect object, but the disadvantage seems clear from context (cf. Moule, p. 46).

○ μαρτυρεῖτε **ἑαυτοῖς**, "You are testifying *against yourselves*" (Matt. 23:31).

56. RESPECT. The dative can communicate in what respect the action occurs. This is a way of qualifying the limits or extent of the verb's idea. (The accusative has virtually the same possible meaning; above §31). Sometimes a person referenced in the dative has only a very loose involvement in the action, or a statement is given in the author's opinion. This is the so-called "ethical dative" (BDF §192), which does not occur frequently enough to warrant its own section. The English expression, "as far as I am concerned," or "as for me," is the closest English equivalent.

○ ἀπεθάνομεν **τῇ ἁμαρτίᾳ**, "we died *with respect to sin*" (Rom. 6:1). The dative (necessarily) qualifies the verb to show that physical death is not in view.

○ ἐστερεοῦντο **τῇ πίστει** καὶ ἐπερίσσευον **τῷ ἀριθμῷ**, "They were growing stronger *with respect to faith* and they were increasing *with respect to number*" (Acts 16:5).

○ ἵνα ᾖ ἁγία καὶ **τῷ σώματι** καὶ **τῷ πνεύματι**, "in order that she might be holy *in respect to* both *body* and *spirit*" (1 Cor. 7:34). English would use "in," a sort of "location" metaphor: "holy *in body* and *in spirit*."

○ **ἐμοὶ** γὰρ τὸ ζῆν Χριστός, "*As for me*, to live is Christ" (Phil. 1:21). The "ethical" dative.

○ τί **ἐμοὶ** καὶ **σοί**, γύναι· "Dear lady, why do you involve me?" (John 2:4;NIV). Obviously, "What to me and to you, woman?" is a translation with little to recommend it. Compare the demoniacs confronting Jesus: τί **ἡμῖν** καὶ **σοί**, υἱὲ τοῦ θεοῦ, "What do you want with us, Son of God?" (Matt. 8:29; NIV). In both examples the "ethical" dative communicates the idea: "What mutual concern do we have?"

57. POSSESSION. Logically related to the dative of respect, the dative may indicate possession, which is conceived as a special kind of relation or respect. This construction is often used with εἰμί either implied or expressed.

○ ὄνομα **αὐτῷ** Ἰωάννης, "the name *(belonging) to him* (was) John" (John 1:6). The Greek idea is: "the name *with respect to him* was John"; there was a special relation between the name "John" and him.

○ τί **σοι** ὄνομά ἐστιν; "What is *your* name?" (Luke 8:30).

○ θεὸς δὲ οὐκ ἔστιν νεκρῶν ἀλλὰ ζώντων, πάντες γὰρ **αὐτῷ** ζῶσιν, "But God is not (the God) of the dead, but of the living. For all live *(who belong) to him*" (Luke 20:38). This interpretation was advanced by Prof. C. E. Hill in, "'So, All His People Live.' A New Translation of Luke 20:38b" (unpublished paper).

58. MEANS. (Instrumental.) A common use of the dative without a preposition specifies what instrument or means was used to accomplish the action. Distinguish this use from the ὑπό + genitive construction which specifies the personal agent who performs the action. The dative is an impersonal means in most cases. The preposition ἐν may be supplied with the same meaning.

○ ὃ ἑωράκαμεν **τοῖς ὀφθαλμοῖς** ἡμῶν, "which we have seen *with our eyes*" (1 John 1:1).

○ ἐγω ἐβάπτισα ὑμᾶς **ὕδατι**, "*I* baptized you *with water*" (Mark 1:8). Some manuscripts have ἐν ὕδατι. See: ἐγὼ μὲν ὑμᾶς βαπτίζω **ἐν ὕδατι**, "I baptize you *with water*" (Matt. 3:11).

○ ἐλυτρώθητε . . . **τιμίῳ αἵματι** . . . Χριστοῦ, "You were ransomed *with the costly blood* of Christ" (1 Pet. 1:18-19).

59. CAUSE. The cause of an action is conceptually related to *means*, hence sometimes nouns in the dative case refer to cause. More commonly, however, this relation is expressed in Greek by διά + accusative, "because of."

○ τῇ **ἀπιστίᾳ** ἐξεκλάσθησαν, "They were broken off *because of disbelief*" (Rom. 11:20).

○ ἵνα **τῷ σταυρῷ** τοῦ Χριστοῦ μὴ διώκωνται, "in order that they may not be persecuted *because of the cross* of Christ" (Gal. 6:12).

○ μή πως **τῇ περισσοτέρᾳ λύπῃ** καταποθῇ ὁ τοιοῦτος, "Lest such a one somehow be consumed *because of excessive grief*" (2 Cor. 2:7).

60. AGENT. The personal agent of an action is normally expressed with a passive verb and the ὑπό + genitive construction, but a simple dative may be used with this meaning in rare instances.

○ εἰ δὲ **πνεύματι** ἄγεσθε, "If you are being led *by the Spirit* . . ." (Gal. 5:18). The more common construction is found, for example: ὁ Ἰησοῦς ἀνήχθη εἰς τὴν ἔρημον ὑπὸ τοῦ πνεύματος, "Jesus was led into the desert *by the Spirit*" (Matt. 4:1; but see Luke 4:1: ἤγετο ἐν τῷ πνεύματι).

○ ἔμπροσθεν τῶν ἀνθρώπων πρὸς τὸ θεαθῆναι **αὐτοῖς**, "before men in order to be seen *by them*" (Matt. 6:1).

○ ἐσφραγίσθητε **τῷ πνεύματι** τῆς ἐπαγγελίας τῷ ἁγίῳ, "You were sealed *by the promised Holy Spirit*" (Eph. 1:13). (The genitive is adjectival [above].)

61. MANNER. (Associative.) A word in the dative may function as an adverb to specify the manner with which the action is performed. Translate these dative words with an English adverb if possible, or with an appropriate prepositional phrase.

○ ὡς οὐδὲν ὑπεστειλάμην . . . διδάξαι ὑμᾶς **δημοσίᾳ**, "How I did not shrink back from . . . teaching you *publicly*" (Acts 20:20). This is close to the dative of location (below "in public [places]").

○ **ἐπιθυμίᾳ** ἐπεθύμησα τοῦτο τὸ πάσχα φαγεῖν μεθ᾽ ὑμῶν, "I have longed *with (great) longing* to eat this Passover with you" (Luke 22:15).

○ ὁ δὲ **πολλῷ** μᾶλλον ἔκραζεν· "And he was crying out *much more*" (Mark 10:48). The phrase, πολλῷ μᾶλλον, occurs most often in Paul. The dative, πολλῷ, is technically the classical "dative of degree of difference," or "dative of measure," but it can be conceived of here as an idiomatic unit functioning adverbially. For the translation of ὁ δέ see §12 above.

62. ASSOCIATION. (Comitative.) The dative is used to identify someone else who is involved in performing an action along with the subject(s). In English we use the preposition "with" for this function; for example, "I am walking *with John*." In Greek, the dative alone or with the prepositions σύν, μετά, and πρός either independently or as prepositional prefixes on verbs may be used.

○ Μὴ γίνεσθε ἑτεροζυγοῦντες **ἀπίστοις**· τίς γὰρ μετοχὴ **δικαιοσύνῃ** καὶ **ἀνομίᾳ**, ἢ τίς κοινωνία **φωτὶ** πρὸς σκότος; "Do not be unequally yoked *with unbelievers*. For what partnership (is there) for *righteousness with lawlessness*? Or what fellowship does *light* have with darkness?" (2 Cor. 6:14). All four dative nouns are datives of association, and the prepositional phrase, πρὸς σκότος, has the same function.

○ συνταφέντες **αὐτῷ** ἐν τῷ βαπτισμῷ, ἐν ᾧ καὶ συνηγέρθητε . . . συνεζωοποίησεν ὑμᾶς σὺν αὐτῷ, "You were buried *with him* in baptism, in whom you were also co-raised . . . he raised you along with him" (Col. 2:12-13). The pronoun αὐτῷ is the object of the preposition συν– attached to the lead verb.

63. LOCATION. The dative without a preposition sometimes indicates the location where an action occurs, especially in certain set phrases (κύκλῳ, "in a circle"). Some grammars tell us that this idiom is rare in the NT, but there are a few more possibilities than they normally cite. Nevertheless, most occurrences of the dative of location will employ the preposition ἐν (and possibly ἐπί): ἡ ἀλήθεια οὐκ ἔστιν **ἐν ἡμῖν**, "the truth is not *in us*" (1 John 1:8). And: ἐπιμένωμεν **τῇ ἁμαρτίᾳ**, "shall we remain *in sin*" (ἐπί is prefixed to the verb) (Rom. 6:1).

○ ὕψωσεν **τῇ δεξιᾷ** αὐτοῦ, "He ascended *to his right hand*" (Acts 5:31).

○ ἐπιγνοὺς ὁ Ἰησοῦς **τῷ πνεύματι** αὐτοῦ ὅτι οὕτως διαλογίζονται ἐν ἑαυτοῖς, "After Jesus perceived *in his spirit* that they were reasoning in this fashion among themselves . . ." (Mark 2:8). One could argue that this is a dative of means, but it does not seem likely to me.

○ ἐστιν ἀλήθεια . . . ἀνανεοῦσθαι δὲ **τῷ πνεύματι** τοῦ νοὸς ὑμῶν, "It is true . . . that (you) are also being renewed *in the spirit* of your mind" (Eph. 4:23). This dative could not be means, since inner renewal does not take place by means of our mental effort, but rather is the location where inner renewal begins (see also Rom. 12:2).

64. TIME WHEN. The dative alone (or with ἐν) can communicate when the action occurs. This is a type of locative dative, i.e., the location in time.

○ **τῇ τρίτῃ ἡμέρᾳ** ἐγερθήσεται, "he will be raised *on the third day*" (Matt. 17:23).

○ ἐπορεύθη ὁ Ἰησοῦς **τοῖς σάββασιν**, "Jesus traveled *on the sabbath* (Matt. 12:1).

○ ἵνα μὴ γένηται ἡ φυγὴ ὑμῶν χειμῶνος μηδὲ **σαββάτῳ**, "that your flight may occur neither during winter nor *on a sabbath*" (Matt. 24:20); see §50 above for the adverbial genitive χειμῶνος.

65. DIRECT OBJECT. Some verbs such as ἀκολουθέω, ἀποκρίνομαι, λατρεύω, πιστεύω, and προσκυνέω require that their direct objects be expressed in the dative case. See *Primer* §27.4 for NT examples.

Pronouns §§66–71

66. INTRODUCTION. (See Wallace, pp. 315–54; Young, pp. 71–80; Porter, Chap. 8.) You have already learned the basics of Greek pronoun usage from the *Primer* so there is no reason to repeat that introductory material here. The following table shows where certain pronominal uses can be found in the *Primer* for you to review.

Syntax of Pronouns	Primer Section
Personal pronouns	§16.5
Emphatic αὐτός	§16.6
Attributive αὐτός	§16.6
Reflexive pronouns	§16.7
Pronominal adjectives	§16.8
Demonstrative pronouns	§17.4
Interrogative pronouns	§17.5
Indefinite pronouns	§17.6
Relative pronouns	§24.5
Indefinite use of relative pronoun	§24.6

Furthermore, in many cases, a Greek pronoun functions the same as its English counterpart, which makes detailed study of the Greek pronouns tedious and unnecessary. Hence, what follows is not a comprehensive treatment of Greek pronouns, but rather a highlighting of those instances where the pronoun will be of particular interest for exegesis or where English and Greek pronominal usage differs. For a more thorough treatment of pronouns, please consult one of the grammars cited earlier; and consult BAGD for unusual meanings of a particular pronoun.

67. PERSONAL PRONOUNS.

(a) NOMINATIVE. The nominative personal pronoun of all three persons is not required with finite verbs, since the personal reference is supplied with the verb ending: λύω "*I am loosing*"; ἀκούετε "*You* (all) are listening"; etc. This makes the nominative personal pronoun redundant and unnecessary, hence it normally has a different role in the statement than mere identification of the personal agent of the active or middle verb or the personal recipient of a passive verb. In the other ("oblique") cases, though, the pronoun is required for explicit expression of the person: ἡ φωνή **μου**, "*my* voice"; γράφω **ὑμῖν**, "I am writing *to you*"; etc.[16] So then, look for some kind of emphasis in the nominative personal pronouns, whether of contrast between different agents, stress on unexpected personal involvement, etc. The exception to this emphatic use is the predicate statement where sometimes an author felt that the nominative personal subject was necessary to clarify his meaning.

(b) OBLIQUE CASES. In cases other than the nominative, the personal pronouns are unremarkable, except for the fact that the first and second person forms come with "emphatic" forms in the singular: ἐμοῦ, σοῦ, ἐμοί, σοί, κτλ. (see *Primer* §16.2) (as well as

---

[16]This difference in function between the nominative and oblique cases of the personal pronouns is represented in the first person paradigm by a difference in form. ἐγώ comes from a different root than (ἐ)μου, (ἐ)μοι, and (ἐ)με. "[T]he lack of integration of the forms of the personal pronouns in particular into a proper paradigm follows from the lack of functional integration," Andrew L. Sihler, *New Comparative Grammar of Greek and Latin* (New York and Oxford: Oxford University Press, 1995), 370.

possessive adjective forms [ἐμός, σός, ἡμέτερος, ὑμέτερος]). The "emphatic" forms are normally used after prepositions without emphasis (μετ' ἐμοῦ, ἐν ἐμοί, κτλ.). But used by themselves—which is not all that common in the NT—there is some sort of emphasis or focus intended: πίστεως ὑμῶν τε καὶ **ἐμοῦ**, "your faith as well as *my own*" (Rom. 1:12); **ἐμοὶ** γὰρ τὸ ζῆν Χριστὸς, "Now *as for me,* to live is Christ" (Phil. 1:21).

(c) THIRD PERSON. The third person pronoun (αὐτός, αὐτή, αὐτό) did not start life as a personal pronoun but as an intensive pronoun adding emphasis or focus to other words. This meaning survives when it is placed in the predicate position with a noun: ὁ ἄνθρωπος **αὐτός**, "the man *himself."* We even find this meaning with other pronouns: καὶ **ἐγὼ αὐτὸς** ἄνθρωπός εἰμι, "*I* am *myself* also a man" (Acts 10:26); καὶ ἐξ **ὑμῶν αὐτῶν** ἀναστήσονται ἄνδρες, "And men will arise *even from your very midst*" (Acts 20:30). In the attributive position, αὐτός refers to the identity of the noun: ὁ **αὐτὸς** ἄνθρωπος, "the *same* man." Finally, the simple form αὐτός sometimes substitutes for the reflexive pronoun (see below).

68. REFLEXIVE PRONOUNS. There is nothing particularly mysterious about reflexive pronouns: βάλε **σεαυτὸν** κάτω, "throw *yourself* down" (Matt. 4:6). The singular form is an interesting blend of the personal pronoun and intensive αὐτός; hence, ἐμε + αυτόν → ἐμαυτόν; σε + αυτόν → σεαυτόν. The following instance shows how this development may have taken place: αὐτὴ προστάτις πολλῶν ἐγενήθη καὶ **ἐμοῦ αὐτοῦ**, "She became a patroness of many people, even *of myself*" (Rom. 16:2). When ἐμοῦ αὐτοῦ is written in the ancient style: EMOYAYTOY we can see more easily how contracted EMAYTOY developed (try saying ἐμουαυτου fast ten times). Yet there are places where the reflexive pronoun itself was represented by the simple intensive pronoun: οὐκ ἐπίστευσεν **αὐτὸν** αὐτοῖς, "He did not entrust *himself* to them," where ἑαυτόν could be expected.

69. RELATIVE PRONOUNS. The standard rule for relative pronouns is that when an antecedent (or postcedent—see *Primer* §24.5) is expressed, the relative pronoun agrees with it in gender and number but not necessarily in case. The case of a relative pronoun is determined by its own function in the statement, not by the case of the antecedent which normally has its own, separate function. There are times, though, when the case of the relative pronoun is assimilated into the case of its antecedent; this is called *attraction:* ὃς δ' ἂν πίῃ ἐκ τοῦ ὕδατος **οὗ** ἐγὼ δώσω αὐτῷ, οὐ μὴ διψήσει εἰς τὸν αἰῶνα, "Whoever drinks from the water *which* I will give him, will in no way ever get thirsty" (John 4:14; note that there are *four* pronouns in this sentence!). The relative pronoun οὗ agrees with its antecedent in number and gender (neuter singular) but also in case (genitive), even though οὗ should be accusative as the direct object of δώσω. There are even a few instances where the case of the *antecedent* has been attracted to the case of the relative pronoun, called "inverse attraction."

70. RARE DEMONSTRATIVE PRONOUN. ὅδε, ἥδε, τόδε is an older, more vivid demonstrative pronoun found particularly in classical drama and poetry. (The form itself is a combination of the article and conjunctive δέ: ὅδε = ὁ + δε.) In our literature, though, it occurs eight times as a prophetic formula: **τάδε** λέγει τὸ πνεῦμα τὸ ἅγιον, "*These things* says the Holy Spirit" (Acts 21:11) and seven times in the messages to the seven churches in Revelation 2–3. τάδε lends an old-fashioned tone in these passages—like "thus saith the Lord" in English—and is a clear allusion to τάδε λέγει as found a hundred odd times in the LXX as introduction to prophetic pronouncements.

71. MISCELLANEOUS PRONOUNS. There are a number of other miscellaneous pronouns in Greek, particularly variations of the relative and of the interrogative pronouns: οἷος, "of such a kind"; ὁποῖος, "of what sort"; ὅσος, "as much as"; πόσος, "how many, how much?"; ποταπός, "what sort?" These words are not that difficult, so it is best to consult BAGD for the specific meaning of these and other such forms when encountered in NT reading.

Adjectives §§72–76

72. INTRODUCTION. (See Wallace, pp. 291–314; Young, pp. 80–83; Porter, Chap. 6.) As in the last lesson, you have already covered the essential syntax in the *Primer,* in this case, the syntax of adjectives. This gives you an opportunity to review and to master adjective uses now if you have not already done so. The following table shows where adjective syntax was covered in the *Primer* for your review.

Syntax of Adjectives	Primer Section
Predicate Adjectives	§10.5
Attributive Adjectives	§10.5
Substantive Adjectives	§10.5
Comparative Degree	§29.4
Superlative Degree	§29.5
Adjectives as Adverbs	§29.6

As in the last lesson, the following brief discussion will cover adjective syntax which is important enough to highlight again and some minor uses not found in the *Primer.* For a more thorough treatment of adjectives, please consult one of the grammars cited earlier in this paragraph, and be sure to consult BAGD on a regular basis also.

73. OTHER FORMS. We are considering adjectives proper in this lesson, but many other kinds of words, particularly participles, adverbs, and prepositional phrases, may be put to use as virtual adjectives: ἡ χάρις ἡ **δοθεῖσά** μοι, ἡ **ἄνω** κλήσις, and ἡ **ἐν Ἐφέσῳ** ἐκκλησία. Even other nouns may modify a noun adjectivally when bound together in a genitive relation: τὸ πνεῦμα τῆς **ἁγιωσύνης** is the equivalent of τὸ πνεῦμα τὸ **ἅγιον.** In English, these sorts of qualifying statements are often expressed as relative clauses: "the grace *which was given* to me"; then, by a process of shorthand, the relative pronoun and verb are dropped: "the grace *given* to me." Greek does not use relative clauses nearly to the extent that English does; Greek prefers the article instead: ἡ χάρις **ἡ** δοθεῖσά μοι. But Greek does have a shorthand way of expressing these kind of clauses by dropping the substantive if it is clearly perceived in context: οἱ ἐν Ἐφέσῳ (ἄνθρωποι), "the (people) who are in Ephesus" (see [substantive use of article] §9 above).

74. DEGREE. Adjectives are said to have "degree" relating to whether they are positive, comparative, or superlative—other notions like the "elative" sense (see below) are not referred to as "degree." As in English, the different degree forms of Greek adjectives are frequently built upon a common root: **σοφός,** "wise"; **σοφώτερος,** "wiser"; **σοφώτατος,** "wisest." But the most common adjectives *do not* use the same root for all of their degree forms: μικρός, "small"; ἐλάχιστος, "smallest" (not μικρότιστος as we expect), and κακός, "bad"; χείρων, "worse." In my opinion, there is a tendency in all languages, for people to change and adapt the words they use most frequently so that they become irregular in paradigm forms, while rarer words stay regular. I suppose we just get tired of saying things the same way all the time. After all, there is nothing inherently wrong with "good," "gooder," and "goodest" as any two-year old can attest; yet for some reason, we prefer "good," "better," and "best." The same goes for καλός, καλλίων, κράτιστος.[17]

75. DEGREE CHANGES. It is important to learn the degree forms; however, you should know that there was considerable movement toward simplification going on in Greek during the NT period. As

---

[17]In earlier Greek the regular forms καλώτερος and κάλλιστος are found for καλός.

a result, adjectives of one degree were frequently adapted to communicate another degree. It may be helpful to picture this adaptation by thinking of the degrees as a pyramid with the positive degree on the bottom and the superlative on the top. In this case, the different degrees of adjectives were often adapted "up" but not "down" as follows:

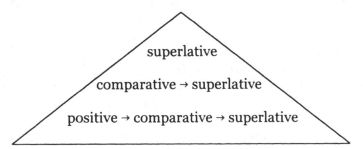

The illustration shows that a positive Greek adjective sometimes functioned as either a comparative or a superlative, the comparative sometimes functioned as a superlative (but not a positive), and the superlative, thankfully, played the part of itself only. Think of the movement as "up" the pyramid.[18] Hence, for example, when you encounter καλός ("good," "excellent"), it might be adapted to mean "better" or "best" in a particular context.[19] Likewise, a comparative form like μείζων ("greater," "bigger") might mean "best" or "biggest." Let one NT example suffice to illustrate: ὁ **μικρότερος** ἐν πᾶσιν ὑμῖν ὑπάρχων οὗτός ἐστιν **μέγας**, "That one who is *the least* among you, this is the one who is *greatest*" (Luke 9:48). In this example both the comparative form μικρότερος and the positive form μέγας function as superlatives. For further examples and help on this point consult the reference grammars cited above and BAGD for specific words.

76. ELATIVE SENSE. In the classical era of Greek (roughly 500–350 BC, leaving Homer, Hesiod, and a few other others out of the picture), adjectives of the superlative degree also regularly conveyed an "elative" sense. For example, ὕψιστος could mean "highest" (superlative) or "very high" (elative). This is still true in the NT era, but an adjective of the comparative degree also sometimes functioned with an elative sense; for instance, σπουδαιότερος in 2 Cor. 8:17 does not mean "more eager [than someone]" but "very eager." If the comparative adjective has this elative meaning, it is most likely used absolutely—that is, there is no comparison phrase with ἤ ("than") or no genitive of comparison (see above §47).[20]

---

[18]This may be a debatable proposition; however, our grammarians are a bit confusing on this point. Porter says: "Some argue that the comparative and superlative forms can be shifted down a category each, so that the superlative form is sometimes comparative in force and the comparative is sometimes positive in force" (p. 122), for which he cites Moule, p. 97. However, when Moule says that "N.T. Greek shows a tendency to push the degrees *down*" (emphasis added), he explains that "the positive tends to do duty for the comparative, and the comparative for the superlative." In other words, Moule and I agree, but one of us is standing on his head. To top it off, Wallace's examples of the "downward" movement of the degrees are sometimes debatable as he prudently admits (especially pp. 303–5). In any case, the presentation of degree shifting presented above can be accepted as an adequate rough guideline for this phenomenon.

[19]E.g., Matt. 18:8 where καλόν means "better." Indeed, the comparative form of καλός does not occur in the NT, but the idea "better than" does.

[20]See Wallace, pp. 300–301, and especially p. 301 for helpful discussion of a significant text.

Participles §§77–83

77. INTRODUCTION. (Wallace, pp. 612–55; Young, Chap. 10; Porter, Chap. 10.) I have explained the elementary functions of Greek participles as well as I can in the *Primer*. I recommend that you review Lessons 19–21 of the *Primer* now before reading this *Sketch* any further. The basic material there will apply to most of the participles you encounter in the New Testament. And, since *one in every twenty words* in the Greek New Testament is a participle, you will encounter a lot of them! The uses of participles sketched below are the minor uses not covered in the *Primer*. This sketch does not cover the attributive or substantive participle uses which have already been adequately described and are not as versatile as the adverbial participle.[21] The label "adverbial" does not quite fit some of the participle functions below, although these participles are placed in the "adverbial" position (not governed by an article). As with other sections, the sketch here should be supplemented by reading the appropriate sections in the reference grammars cited at the beginning of this paragraph.

78. ADVERBIAL PARTICIPLE SEMANTICS. The discussion of adverbial participles in the *Primer* dealt exclusively with those which have a temporal (time) relationship with the main verb. Present participles were analyzed as expressing an event which was contemporaneous with the main event ("while") and the aorist adverbial participle as expressing an event prior to the main action ("after"). This temporal relationship is by far the most common for adverbial participles, yet sometimes certain logical relations may be implicit between the participle and the main verb.[22] In essence, the participle can imply any relation which may exist between two clauses. The following are the most important relations with examples: temporal, manner, means, causal, purpose, result, conditional, and concessive.

○ TEMPORAL. See *Primer* §20.5.

○ MANNER (MODAL). ἐπορεύοντο **χαίροντες**, "they went off *rejoicing*" (Acts 5:41). The participle expresses an activity or mental state which describes "how" the main event occurs. This is the "manner" or "mode" (hence the term "modal" in our literature) in which the main event is carried out. Sometimes this is translated with an English clause introduced with "by" as in this example: ὡς Σάρρα ὑπήκουσεν τῷ Ἀβραάμ . . . ἧς ἐγενήθητε τέκνα **ἀγαθοποιοῦσαι**, "As Sarah obeyed Abraham . . . whose children you have become *by your well-doing*" (1 Pet. 3:6). Because "by" is often used in translation, it is easy to confuse a participle of manner with the one of "means" discussed next.

○ MEANS. Χριστὸς ἡμᾶς ἐξηγόρασεν ἐκ τῆς κατάρας τοῦ νόμου **γενόμενος** ὑπὲρ ἡμῶν κατάρα, "Christ redeemed us from the curse of the law *by becoming* a curse on our behalf" (Gal. 3:13). The participle clause expresses an event which was the means for accomplishing some

---

[21]Called the "circumstantial" participle in classical Greek grammar.

[22]To analyze an adverbial participle as having a logical relation does not necessarily mean that a residual temporal relationship does not exist as well. For instance, in the example of "means" from Gal. 3:13 above, the aorist participle γενόμενος expresses the means by which Christ accomplished our redemption, and logically the means comes before the effect, so there may be a temporal priority with the aorist participle also. The other examples can often be analyzed in the same way. Note especially the use of *future* participles to express purpose (which is future from the time of the main event, not from the time of speaking or writing). The same can be said of English equivalents. "*Seeing* a lion, Antiev scrambled up a tree." It seems that either "*Because he saw* a lion" (causal) or "*When he saw* a lion" (temporal) can substitute for the participle in this English example. Both are implied.

result. By performing one action, another action is accomplished. Translate with an English phrase introduced with "by."

○ CAUSAL (REASON). ὁ δὲ **θέλων** δικαιῶσαι ἑαυτὸν εἶπεν πρὸς τὸν Ἰησοῦν· καὶ τίς ἐστίν μου πλησίον; "But he, *because he wanted* to justify himself, said to Jesus, 'And just who is my neighbor?'" (Luke 10:29). The adverbial participle may specify the reason or rationale that the main event takes place. Likewise it may refer to the natural causation of the main event, though all of these ideas are summarized as "causal" and rendered with "because" as in our example. An example of the "rationale" or "explanatory" idea is: ἀλλήλους ἀγαπήσατε ἐκτενῶς, **ἀναγεγεννημένοι** οὐκ ἐκ σπορᾶς φθαρτῆς ἀλλὰ ἀφθάρτου, "Love one another fervently, *for you were born again* not from corruptible seed but incorruptible" (1 Pet. 1:22–23).

○ PURPOSE. νομικός τις ἀνέστη **ἐκπειράζων** αὐτὸν λέγων· διδάσκαλε, τί ποιήσας ζωὴν αἰώνιον κληρονομήσω; "A certain lawyer arose *in order to test* him and said, 'Teacher, what should I do that I might inherit life eternal?'" (Luke 10:25). You have learned various constructions used in Greek to communicate purpose (e.g., ἵνα + subjunctive); the adverbial participle may also communicate the purpose (i.e., intended result) of the main event. (See also the future participles in §§82–83 below.)

○ RESULT. εἰ δὲ προσωπολημπτεῖτε, ἁμαρτίαν ἐργάζεσθε **ἐλεγχόμενοι** ὑπὸ τοῦ νόμου ὡς παραβάται, "And if you show favoritism, you are committing sin, *so that you are condemned* by the law as transgressors" (James 2:9). When there is an idea of *intention* in a result relationship, we call that a *purpose* clause (above). Otherwise, it is called a result relationship because the event which resulted from the main event may or may not have been intended (*not* in the James 2:9 example!). The participle may specify the result of the main verb occurring.

○ CONDITIONAL. πῶς ἡμεῖς ἐκφευξόμεθα τηλικαύτης **ἀμελήσαντες** σωτηρίας, "How should *we* escape *if we should neglect* such a great salvation?" (Heb. 2:3). The participle may express a condition required for the main event to take place or to be true. This participle can substitute for any of the types of conditional statements in Greek with all their variety of semantic functions.

○ CONCESSIVE. ὃς ἐν μορφῇ θεοῦ **ὑπάρχων** οὐχ ἁρπαγμὸν ἡγήσατο τὸ εἶναι ἴσα θεῷ, "Who, *even though existing* in the form of God, he did not consider his equality with God to be robbery" (Phil. 2:6). A concessive clause expresses a reason for the main event *not* to happen or to be true, yet it happens or is true anyway. The concession is a species of condition which normally leads to a certain conclusion or event, which, when granted in this case, leads to a different conclusion or result even though the condition exists. Another example is: ὃν οὐκ **ἰδόντες** ἀγαπᾶτε, "Whom, *even though you have not seen* [him], you love" (1 Pet. 1:8). The implication here is that not seeing someone may normally stand in the way of loving him. The participle may express concession (otherwise introduced by καὶ εἰ, καὶ ἐάν, or the contracted form κἄν, "even if").

79. PARALLEL (ATTENDANT CIRCUMSTANCE). The Greek participle has the ability to take on the function of the main verb. The Greeks preferred to employ participles in this way, rather than repeating the mood of the main verb and joining these verbs with a conjunction like καί. The "parallel" participle, then is a sort of chameleon, functioning in whatever mood the main verb is, whether it is indicative, imperative, etc. The most common example of this sort is the familiar ἀποκριθεὶς εἶπεν, "*he answered* (and) said" from the Gospels (e.g., Matt. 12:39). Here the participle ἀποκριθείς[23] functions as an indicative parallel with εἶπεν. Obviously, the meaning, "*after he answered*, he said" is not what the author has in mind. This parallel participle is particularly found in certain authors, and is frequent when a string of imperatives is being given.[24] For example:

○ Διὸ **ἀναζωσάμενοι** τὰς ὀσφύας τῆς διανοίας ὑμῶν **νήφοντες** τελείως **ἐλπίσατε** ἐπὶ τὴν φερομένην ὑμῖν χάριν ἐν ἀποκαλύψει Ἰησοῦ Χριστοῦ, "Therefore, *gird up* the loins of your mind, *be sober,* [and] *set your hope* entirely in the grace which is being brought to you at the revelation of Jesus Christ" (1 Pet. 1:13).

In this example, the first two participles function as imperatives parallel with ἐλπίσατε.[25] This is stylistically more refined than imperatives ἀναζώσασθε . . . καὶ νήφετε . . . καὶ ἐλπίσατε would have been. Look at the well known "Great Commission" passage for another example of this use of the participle (Matt. 28:19–20).[26]

80. COMPLEMENTARY.[27] In a few places in the New Testament, a participle may complete the idea of another verb, whereas this is normally the role of an infinitive (*Primer* §25.6). For example:

○ ὀλίγον ἄρτι εἰ δέον [ἐστὶν] **λυπηθέντες** ἐν ποικίλοις πειρασμοῖς, "If it is necessary *to grieve* for a little while in various trials" (1 Pet. 1:6).

This participle idiom is particularly used with verbs meaning "to stop" (οὐκ ἐπαύοντο **διδάσκοντες**, "they did not stop *teaching*" [Acts 5:42]) or "to continue" (ἐπέμενον **ἐρωτῶντες** αὐτόν, "they continued *to question* him" [John 8:7]).

81. INDIRECT DISCOURSE. The term "indirect" signifies that the writer is not quoting the thoughts or words of someone directly, but paraphrasing. This often involves a change of person in the reported statement. For instance, we encountered *direct discourse* in 1 John 2:4: ὁ λέγων ὅτι Ἔγνωκα αὐτόν, "The person who says, '*I have known* him'" (cf. note 2:4a) where first person ἔγνωκα represents a direct reference to the person's speech.[28] *Indirect discourse,* on the other hand, would have changed the verb to the third person in this instance: ὁ λέγων ὅτι **ἔγνωκεν** αὐτόν, "The person who says *that he has known* him." In Greek, indirect discourse is frequently communicated

---

[23]ἀποκρίνομαι 1A D (Passive form) Ptcp m n sg.

[24]Some grammarians speak of an imperatival function of participles; however, the examples they use are simply parallel participles whose imperatival force has been picked up from the main verb.

[25]ἐλπίζω A A Impv 2 pl.

[26]For some reason, Daniel Wallace restricts parallel participles to aorist participles which are expressed before the main verb (Wallace, pp. 640–45; esp. p. 645 for Matt. 28:19–20). This analysis is too rigid. The parallel participle by its very nature is a flexible idiom. Notice the alternation of tense forms in the example given above from 1 Pet. 1:13 (ἀναζωσάμενοι is aorist and νήφοντες is present). The inherent nature of each event influenced the choice of tense form, and they are both obviously parallel in meaning with the imperative. In my opinion, the tense form of parallel participles represents the tense form which would have been used in the imperative or whatever mood with which they are parallel.

[27]Called the "supplementary" participle in classical Greek grammar.

[28]What may be confusing at first is that ὅτι in Greek may mark *either* direct or indirect discourse. With direct discourse, ὅτι functions as quotation marks and is not translated into English; with indirect discourse it is translated as "that."

much like in English; with ὅτι, "that," and an indicative verb.[29] In a few places, though, Greek allows the use of a participle in the accusative case (because it is virtually the direct object of the verb of speaking, thinking, perception, etc.). An example is:

○ ἀκούσας δὲ Ἰακὼβ **ὄντα** σιτία εἰς Αἴγυπτον, "When Jacob heard *that there was* grain in Egypt" (Acts 7:12).

Another good example of this construction is found in 1 John 4:2 (see note 4:2d above).

82. FUTURE FORM. The future participle was not covered in the *Primer* because there are only a dozen specimens in the NT. This form was found more often in literary Greek of the earlier periods but was passing out of use by the NT era. The form itself follows a logical format with the primary participle endings (–ων, –ουσα, –ον or –ομενος, –ομενη, –ομενον) placed on the future stem. Hence, for ποιέω the future stem is ποιησ– to which is attached –ων for the masculine nominative singular yielding ποιήσων (Acts 24:17). And for εἰμί the future (deponent) form ἔσομαι (*Primer* §10.2) is used to yield the future participle ἐσόμενον (Luke 22:49). Other examples are: ἄξων (ἄγω) (Acts 22:5); γενησόμενον (γίνομαι) (1 Cor. 15:37); and, ἀποδώσοντες (ἀποδίδωμι) (Heb. 13:17).

83. FUTURE PARTICIPLE SEMANTICS. The meaning of future participles can be divided into two categories: (a) purpose; (b) temporal. A future adverbial participle, as was common in classical Greek, may communicate the purpose of another event. This participle may be translated with an English infinitive (which is our main way of expressing purpose):

○ ἴδωμεν εἰ ἔρχεται Ἡλίας **σώσων** αὐτόν, "Let us see whether Elijah will come *to save* him" (Matt. 27:49).

○ οὐ πλείους εἰσίν μοι ἡμέραι δώδεκα ἀφ' ἧς ἀνέβην **προσκυνήσων** εἰς Ἰερουσαλήμ, "No more than twelve days from which I went up to Jerusalem *to worship*" (Acts 24:11).

Secondly, the future participle may be used, especially as a substantive, to refer to an event which is future from the time of the main setting:

○ ᾔδει γὰρ ἐξ ἀρχῆς ὁ Ἰησοῦς τίνες εἰσὶν οἱ μὴ πιστεύοντες καὶ τίς ἐστιν **ὁ παραδώσων** αὐτόν, "For Jesus had known from the beginning who were those who did not believe and who it was *who would betray* him" (John 6:64). Notice the difference in semantics between the present participle πιστεύοντες and the future παραδώσων.

○ ὡς θεράπων εἰς μαρτύριον **τῶν λαληθησομένων**, "as a servant for a testimony *of those things which would (later) be spoken*" (Heb. 3:5).

---

[29]We saw the other main way Greek communicates indirect discourse with an infinitive in 1 John 2:9; see *Sketch* §94 below for further discussion and examples of this construction.

Infinitives §§84–95

84. INTRODUCTION. (Wallace, pp. 587–611; Young, Chap. 11; Porter, Chap. 11.) As in previous lessons, you should review the basic information already given in the *Primer* (Lesson 25). In *Primer* §25.6, I introduced five infinitive uses which cover most of those found in the NT. I will review these five uses very briefly and then explain some other minor uses in a little more detail. As before, this sketch should be supplemented by reading the appropriate sections in the reference grammars cited at the beginning of the paragraph.

85. OVERVIEW. Infinitives are difficult to categorize. They are hybrid forms which share the function of *nouns* (they may have case functions, be modified by articles and adjectives, etc.) and of *verbs* (they can take subjects and objects, have tense and voice formations, be modified by adverbs, etc.). And in many cases, the Greek infinitive acts just like the English infinitive, for instance, as the complement of certain verbs: μέλλω **γράφειν**, "I am about *to write*." Yet there are some Greek uses which have no English equivalent. For example, infinitives in prepositional phrases cannot be translated word-for-word: διὰ τὸ αὐτὸν **γινώσκειν**, *not* "on account of the him to know" but "because he *knew*" (John 2:24). This makes practice with some uses of the infinitives imperative, particularly since infinitives are found about 2,300 times in the New Testament. Study the examples given below and in the reference grammars carefully. Also note that the infinitive, like other non-indicative mood verb forms, is negatived by μή rather than οὐ.[30]

86. INFINITIVES AND THE ARTICLE. One of the characteristics of Greek infinitives which seems so foreign to the beginning student is that they often come with an article. Paul's famous ἐμοὶ γὰρ **τὸ** ζῆν Χριστός is just one example of how a wooden translation approach causes only confusion: "To me for *the* to live Christ" is how an interlinear rendering would read.[31] If you think, though, about what an infinitive is, the article is perfectly logical: an infinitive is a type of *noun,* and nouns take articles for various reasons. A Greek infinitive may take an article for a few reasons, but it usually did so merely because it was part of a construction which customarily included the article, especially in the prepositional constructions (διὰ τὸ + infinitive, ἐν τῷ + infinitive, κτλ.). In these instances, the article (besides being "proper" according to stylistic expectations) served to identify the case function of the indeclinable infinitive and to clarify that the infinitive was to be taken with the preposition. In the example from John 2:24 cited above, διὰ **τὸ** αὐτὸν γινώσκειν, "because he knew," the neuter article clarifies that the (always neuter) infinitive goes with διά not the pronoun αὐτόν. If the article were missing, διὰ αὐτὸν γινώσκειν, the more likely meaning would be "to know *because of him*," i.e., αὐτόν as the object of διά. In the end, the Greek article with an infinitive is rarely translated into English, but is to be appreciated for its clarifying importance.

87. COMPLEMENTARY. (*Primer* §25.6.) An anarthrous infinitive "completes" another verb. This is the most common use of the infinitive and one we have seen in 1 John a few times already.

○ οὐ δύναται **ἁμαρτάνειν**, "he cannot *live in sin*" (1 John 3:9).

○ ὀφείλομεν ἀλλήλους **ἀγαπᾶν**, "We ought *to love*" (1 John 4:11).

---

[30]E.g., τὸ **μὴ** γινώσκειν, "to not know" rather than τὸ οὐ γινώσκειν.

[31]One could just as easily fault English infinitives for causing confusion with its constituent *preposition* "to": *to* see, *to* fall, *to* be going, etc. This "to" is obviously not the same as: "He gave it *to* her," but it could be so confused by a beginning student of English.

○ ὀφείλομεν ὑπὲρ τῶν ἀδελφῶν τὰς ψυχὰς **θεῖναι**, "We ought *to lay down* our lives for our brothers" (1 John 3:16).

88. PURPOSE. (*Primer* §25.6.) There are a number of constructions with the infinitive which communicate the purpose of the main action or state: the anarthrous infinitive alone, εἰς τὸ + infinitive, πρὸς τὸ + infinitive, τοῦ + infinitive, and rarely ὥστε or ὡς + infinitive.[32] In some cases the author's personal style determined which purpose infinitive construction to choose. For instance, τοῦ + infinitive is a distinguishing feature of Matthew and Luke's style. In any case, the meaning of these constructions is identical with the more common ἵνα + subjunctive purpose construction: all express the purpose (= intended result) of another action or state.

○ οὐκ ἦλθον **καταλῦσαι** [τὸν νόμον] ἀλλὰ **πληρῶσαι**, "I did not come *to destroy* [the law], but *to fulfill* [it]" (Matt. 5:17).

○ ὁ πέμψας με **βαπτίζειν** ἐν ὕδατι, "He who sent me *to baptize* with water" (John 1:33).

○ καὶ σημεῖον ἔλαβεν περιτομῆς σφραγῖδα . . . **εἰς τὸ εἶναι** αὐτὸν πατέρα πάντων τῶν πιστευόντων, "He received the sign of circumcision . . . *in order that* he *might be* the father of all who believe" (Rom. 4:11).

89. RESULT. (*Primer* §25.6.) If an event occurs as a result of another, yet it was not necessarily intended, we call this a *result* clause. An infinitive expressed in the same constructions identified under "purpose" (see the previous section) may also express result if *intent* (the main component of a purpose statement) is not in view. ὥστε + infinitive and the simple anarthrous infinitive in particular was used to express result in Greek.

○ νυνὶ δὲ κατηργήθημεν ἀπὸ τοῦ νόμου . . . **ὥστε δουλεύειν** ἡμᾶς ἐν καινότητι πνεύματος, "But now we have been released from the law . . . *so that* we *may serve* in newness of the Spirit" (Rom. 7:6).

○ ἰδοὺ ἐνίκησεν ὁ λέων ὁ ἐκ τῆς φυλῆς Ἰούδα . . . **ἀνοῖξαι** τὸ βιβλίον, "Look! The lion from the tribe of Judah has conquered . . . *so that he may open* the scroll" (Rev. 5:5).

○ **εἰς τὸ εἶναι** αὐτοὺς ἀναπολογήτους, "*so that* they *are* defenseless" (Rom. 1:20).

○ Διὸ παρέδωκεν αὐτοὺς ὁ θεὸς . . . **τοῦ ἀτιμάζεσθαι** τὰ σώματα αὐτῶν, "Therefore, God delivered them over . . . *that* [they] *should dishonor* their bodies" (Rom. 1:24).

90. CAUSAL. (*Primer* §25.6.) An author may express the reason why another event occurs with an infinitive clause, almost exclusively in the "διὰ τὸ + infinitive" construction. (ὅτι + finite verb is a much more common way to express cause in Greek.)

○ **διὰ τὸ μὴ ἔχειν** ῥίζαν ἐξηράνθη, "It dried up *because it did not have* roots" (Mark 4:6).

---

[32]See particularly Wallace, p. 591, n. 5 for examples of ὥστε and ὡς.

○ **διὰ τὸ εἶναι** αὐτὸν ἐξ οἴκου καὶ πατριᾶς Δαυίδ, "*Because he was* from the house and lineage of David" (Luke 2:4).

○ οὐκ ἔχετε **διὰ τὸ** μὴ **αἰτεῖσθαι** ὑμᾶς, "You do not have *because you do not ask*" (James 4:2).

91. TEMPORAL. (*Primer* §25.6.) There are three relative time relations: prior, contemporary, and subsequent time. We have seen that the Greek adverbial participle clause commonly communicates the first two.[33] The Greek infinitive in various prepositional phrases (and with the conjunction πρίν or πρὶν ἤ) may also express temporal relations with the main event of the sentence.

○ PRIOR TIME. The infinitive with the prepositional phrase πρὸ τοῦ or (about 10 times) an infinitive with the conjunction πρίν or πρὶν ἤ indicate an event prior to the main action or state. **πρὸ τοῦ** σε Φίλιππον **φωνῆσαι** ὄντα ὑπὸ τὴν συκῆν εἶδόν σε, "*Before* Philip *called* you, when you were under the fig tree, I saw you" (John 1:48; notice the contemporaneous present adverbial participle phrase with ὄντα). ὅτι **πρὶν** ἀλέκτορα **φωνῆσαι** δὶς τρίς με ἀπαρνήσῃ, "*Before* a rooster *crows* twice, you will deny me thrice" (Mark 14:72).

○ CONTEMPORARY TIME. The infinitive with ἐν τῷ marks the style of some writers to express an event contemporary with another event. Ἐν δὲ **τῷ πορεύεσθαι** αὐτοὺς αὐτὸς εἰσῆλθεν εἰς κώμην τινά, "And *while they were traveling,* he entered a certain village" (Luke 10:38).

○ SUBSEQUENT TIME. An infinitive with μετὰ τό indicates an event occurring after another. **Μετὰ** δὲ **τὸ σιγῆσαι** αὐτοὺς ἀπεκρίθη Ἰάκωβος, "And *after they quieted down,* James answered" (Acts 15:13).

92. FOLLOWING ἐγένετο. (*Primer* §25.6.) Particularly in Luke's writings, the infinitive may be used following an introductory ἐγένετο δέ or καὶ ἐγένετο to indicate the lead event in a narrative: "then it came to pass that. . . ."

○ Ἐγένετο δὲ ἐν σαββάτῳ **διαπορεύεσθαι** αὐτὸν διὰ σπορίμων, "Then it happened that he *was passing* through some grain fields on the Sabbath" (Luke 6:1).

○ ἐγένετο δὲ ἐν ἑτέρῳ σαββάτῳ **εἰσελθεῖν** αὐτὸν εἰς τὴν συναγωγὴν καὶ **διδάσκειν**, "Then it came to pass on another Sabbath that he *entered* into a synagogue and *was teaching*" (Luke 6:6).

93. NOMINAL. The term "nominal" simply means that the infinitive acts particularly like a noun. Since all infinitives have nominal qualities, this category contains those uses which are more noun-like than the others, *viz.* when the infinitive acts like the subject of an active or passive verb, or as the direct object of a verb.

○ SUBJECT. δεῖ **λυθῆναι** αὐτὸν μικρὸν χρόνον, "It is necessary that *he be released* for a brief time" (Rev. 20:3). One may regard δεῖ as a verb requiring a complementary infinitive (see above), however technically infinitive λυθῆναι is the subject of δεῖ: "*to be released* is

---

[33]The aorist adverbial expresses time prior to the main verb, and the present adverbial participle contemporaneous time; cf. *Primer* §20.5.

necessary." ὑμῖν δέδοται **γνῶναι** τὰ μυστήρια τῆς βασιλείας τῶν οὐρανῶν, "*To know* the mysteries of the kingdom of heaven has been granted to you" (Matt. 13:11). The infinitive γνῶναι is the subject of the passive verb δέδοται.

○ DIRECT OBJECT. ὥσπερ γὰρ ὁ πατὴρ ἔχει ζωὴν ἐν ἑαυτῷ, οὕτως καὶ τῷ υἱῷ ἔδωκεν ζωὴν **ἔχειν** ἐν ἑαυτῷ, "Just as the Father has life in himself, so also he has granted to the Son *to have* life in himself" (John 5:26). Infinitive ἔχειν functions as the direct object of ἔδωκεν.

94. INDIRECT DISCOURSE.[34] Indirect discourse is the act of a reporter of someone's words, thoughts, or perceptions "indirectly," whereas *direct discourse* quotes the words verbatim.[35] In Greek, one can express the reported discourse either with a ὅτι clause and the indicative or with an infinitive clause. In 1 John 2:6, for instance, we have ὁ **λέγων** ἐν αὐτῷ **μένειν**, "He who says that *he remains*," but John could just as well have said ὁ λέγων **ὅτι** ἐν αὐτῷ **μένει**.[36] The translation and the meaning are the same. To spot indirect discourse, look for any verb of speaking or mental or sensory perception to introduce the indirect statement: to say that, to think that, to notice that, to hear that, to forget that, to remember that, etc. In the examples which follow, I have highlighted both the infinitive and the verb of speaking or perception.

○ ὁ **λέγων** ἐν τῷ φωτὶ **εἶναι**, "He who says that *he is* in the light" (1 John 2:9).

○ ἐραυνᾶτε τὰς γραφάς, ὅτι ὑμεῖς **δοκεῖτε** ἐν αὐταῖς ζωὴν αἰώνιον **ἔχειν**, "You scour the Scriptures, because you imagine that you *have* eternal life in them" (John 5:39).

○ **ἠρώτων** αὐτὸν **μεῖναι** παρ' αὐτοῖς, "They kept asking that he *stay* with them" (John 4:40).

○ **ἤκουσαν** τοῦτο αὐτὸν **πεποιηκέναι** τὸ σημεῖον, "They heard that he *had performed* this sign" (John 12:18).

○ ὁ **λέγων** μὴ **μοιχεύειν** μοιχεύεις; "You who say that one *shouldn't commit adultery*, are you an adulterer?" (Rom. 2:22).

95. EPEXEGETICAL. When you see the term "epexegetical"[37] in grammatical discussion, just remember that this bulky terms means "explanatory." Hence, an infinitive may *explain something* about a substantive or adjective in the sentence. When it does, it is labeled "epexegetical," or better, "explanatory." This idiom is present also in English, so it presents no particular problems for exegesis or translation.

○ ἐζήτει εὐκαιρίαν **τοῦ παραδοῦναι** αὐτόν, "He was looking for an opportunity *to betray* him" (Luke 22:6).

---

[34]The infinitive of indirect discourse is, in fact, the *direct object* of the introductory verb, but it warrants separate treatment, so I chose not to cover it in the previous section.

[35]Cf. note 2:9b and §81 above (the participle in indirect discourse).

[36]Notice that the verb of speaking here (λέγων) comes in the form of a *substantive participle*. The mood of the verb of speaking or perception makes no difference, the content of the speech, thoughts, etc. still constitute indirect discourse.

[37]From Greek ἐπί and ἐξάγω "to bring out, explain."

○ ὦ ἀνόητοι καὶ βραδεῖς τῇ καρδίᾳ **τοῦ πιστεύειν** ἐπὶ πᾶσιν οἷς ἐλάλησαν οἱ προφῆται, "O you! So foolish and slow-hearted *to believe* in all the things the prophets spoke" (Luke 24:25).

○ ταῦτα παράθου πιστοῖς ἀνθρώποις, οἵτινες ἱκανοὶ ἔσονται καὶ ἑτέρους **διδάξαι**, "Convey these matters to faithful men who will be fit *to teach* others as well" (2 Tim. 2:2).

Prepositions §§96–102

* case came before preposition.

96. INTRODUCTION. (Wallace, pp. 355–89; Young, Chap. 6; Porter, Chap. 9.[38]) Frankly, prepositions are not the stuff of the Great American Novel![39] But prepositions are very, very common—a little less than one per verse in the New Testament (over 10,000 occurrences in all), and they are often semantically quite important. In this lesson we will not go into long technical discourse on prepositions. Nor will I give you a catalogue of their meanings (the grammars cited earlier do that for you as well as the lexicons like BAGD). Rather, we will briefly review their basic features and point out some important aspects of how prepositions might impact exegesis. Needless to say, a part of speech so common deserves *some* attention!

> "It is best to consider the prepositional phrase as a syntactical unit that must be analyzed as a whole in light of various factors: (a) the possible nuances of the preposition with objects in certain cases, (b) the possible case functions, (c) the relative frequencies of the uses, (d) the influence of the literary and situational contexts, especially the force of the verb and the object of the preposition, (e) whether the object noun is an event word, and (f) the distinctive prepositional usage of New Testament and Hellenistic Greek in general." Richard Young

You should consult the lexicons and other reference works for the range of meanings conveyed by an individual preposition, because some of them are *very* flexible and broad-ranging in meaning. And sometimes the meaning of a statement hinges upon the correct interpretation of the preposition. For instance, Jesus' well known statement: ἰδοὺ γὰρ ἡ βασιλεία τοῦ θεοῦ **ἐντὸς** ὑμῶν ἐστιν, "For behold, the kingdom of God is *?* you" (Luke 17:21). The "improper" preposition ἐντός has been translated in a variety of ways dramatically affecting the meaning of the statement: "*within* you", "in your *midst*," and "*within* your *reach*."[40] In this case and in many others, the preposition must be analyzed in light of key contextual factors (see the accompanying box).

97. OVERVIEW. Prepositions are relational words. They clarify relationships between different items in a sentence. Most often, prepositional phrases, usually comprising the preposition, an optional article, and a substantive object, clarify some aspect of an event conveyed by a verb form—prepositions are usually adverbial. Furthermore, it helps to understand that the possible relations which prepositions might express fall roughly into three main divisions: spatial, temporal, and logical relations. We will pause over these three categories in a moment.

98. PREPOSITIONS AND CASE. You will remember from the *Primer* that many prepositions communicate relationships in conjunction with the case of their object. Change the case of the object and you change the meaning of the preposition.[41] For instance, διά with the genitive conveys movement *through* an object (διὰ τοῦ ὕδατος, "*through* the water"), but with the accusative it expresses the logical grounds for something (διὰ τὸ ὕδωρ, "*because of* the water"). Likewise, ὑπό with the accusative can point to a location *under* an object as the diagram shows, but with the genitive it expresses the personal agent of a passive verb, *by*.

---

[38]See also Murray J. Harris, "Appendix: Prepositions and Theology in the Greek NT," *New International Dictionary of New Testament Theology,* vol. 3 (C. Brown, ed.; Grand Rapids: Zondervan, 1978), 1171–1215.

[39]*Κατά in All Its Semantic Permutations: The Novel.*

[40]See BAGD, p. 269 under ἐντός.

[41]There are a few exceptions to this, most notably, ἐπί often means the same thing whether its object is genitive, dative, or accusative.

Before the New Testament era, Greeks did not use prepositions quite as often. Instead, the cases alone bore the main load for communicating relationships. This is still true in New Testament times, of course, but prepositions were used more often to make a speaker or author's meaning more explicit. For instance, in the phrase **ἐν** ἡμέρᾳ κρίσεως, "*on Judgment Day*" (Matt. 10:15) Matthew uses the preposition, but the simple dative was also possible as we find with τῇ τρίτῃ ἡμέρᾳ, "*on the third day*" (Matt. 17:23).

Some grammarians conclude from the foregoing that Greek prepositions only or primarily make the meaning of the cases more explicit. While this seems true in many cases, it is not true in many others. For instance, the coming Paraclete will convict the world, among other things, περὶ κρίσεως, "*concerning judgment*" in John 16:8. The preposition περί with a genitive object modifying a verb of saying or writing specifies the subject matter of the discourse, *concerning*. Yet this is not an adverbial meaning of the genitive case; this is a function of the accusative (or dative) case: ἐλέγξει τὸν κόσμον . . . **κρίσιν**, "*he will convict the world . . . [concerning] judgment.*"[42] The preposition περί in this example is not highlighting the genitive case, but giving new meaning to it. The best way to consider Greek prepositions and the cases, is to view prepositions as functioning *in conjunction* with the cases in a variety of ways.

99. SPATIAL RELATIONS. Prepositions may specify the relation of an event or object with a location in space or in relation with another object ("He went *into* the city"; "The Lord was *in* a synagogue"; "They went *down* the mountain"). There is nothing particularly mysterious about this use of prepositions; the student must simply know which Greek prepositions communicate which of the possible spatial relationships.

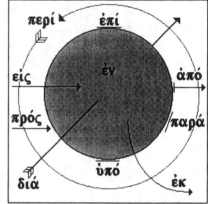

The diagram on the right illustrates some of the spatial relations expressed by the most common prepositions.[43] I say, *some* of the relations, because few prepositions convey only one meaning. For example, πρός frequently communicates movement *(up) to* or *toward* an object (but not movement *into* an object like εἰς). This is illustrated in the diagram by an arrow going up to the edge of the circle. Yet πρός does not mean this only. In John 1:1 we read that ὁ λόγος ἦν **πρὸς** τὸν θεόν. The gloss "into" does not work at all here, but rather, "in the presence of" or "with." Secondly, the diagram does not account for changes in the meaning of the prepositions in the various cases as mentioned above. All this shows that mnemonic devices like this diagram will help you to get a handle on some of the abstract meanings of prepositions, but they cannot substitute for careful study of an individual preposition in its various contexts.

100. TEMPORAL RELATIONS. The temporal relations of prepositions all relate to the three possible temporal notions: *prior* (πρό); *contemporaneous* (ἐν, ἐπί, κτλ.); and *posterior* (μετά). Further variations come when the relative duration is expressed: contemporary at a particular point in time *at the time of* (ἐπί), contemporary *throughout* a length of time (εἰς); or contemporary *from that point on* (ἐκ). The only other point to notice about prepositional temporal notions is that they tend to be expressed as spatial metaphors and so they bear a resemblance to spatial use of the same prepositions. For instance, ἐν expresses the spatial notion of *in that place*. In its temporal meaning, a unit of time is metaphorically presented as a place in time and ἐν means *in that place in time*. This is not a unique feature of Greek.

---

[42]This is the accusative "of respect or specification"; see *Sketch* §31.

[43]Others like ἀνά, "up"; κατά, "down"; ἔξω, "outside of"; κτλ. are not represented here.

101. LOGICAL RELATIONS. It would be rather tedious to catalogue all the possible logical relations which prepositions communicate: means, accompaniment, result, subject matter, reason, benefits, substitution, disadvantage, manner, etc. Let it merely be said that Greek prepositions can communicate all other types of relationships logically possible. Some of them will become especially familiar to you. For instance, εἰς with an abstract noun is a very handy shorthand way of expressing a purpose (ἵνα + subjunctive) or result clause (ὥστε + infinitive). Consider this example: οὗτος ἦλθεν **εἰς μαρτυρίαν** ἵνα μαρτυρήσῃ περὶ τοῦ φωτός, "He came *in order to bear testimony,* to bear witness concerning the light" (John 1:7). The prepositional phrase εἰς μαρτυρίαν is the equivalent of ἵνα μαρτυρήσῃ which follows; both communicate purpose. The prepositional phrase gives the author a stylistically pleasing way of expressing the same thing while avoiding verbatim redundancy.

102. A NOTE ON STYLE. There is a feature of Greek style with regard to prepositions worth at least a mention. If a verb contains a prepositional prefix, the same preposition is often repeated in the clause with its object. There is no emphasis on the preposition, it is simply a stylistic option to repeat it in Greek even though this repetition is not necessary.

- **ἐξ** ἡμῶν **ἐξ**ῆλθαν ἀλλ᾽ οὐκ ἦσαν ἐξ ἡμῶν, "They *left from* us, but they were not of us" (1 John 2:19).

- καὶ οὐκ ἤφιεν ἵνα τις **διενέγκῃ** σκεῦος **διὰ** τοῦ ἱεροῦ, "And he would not allow that anyone *carry* a jar *through* the temple" (Mark 11:16).

- ἐγένετο δέ . . . **περιαστράψαι** φῶς ἱκανὸν **περὶ** ἐμέ, "Then it came about . . . that a great light *shown all around* me" (Acts 22:6).

- ὁ ἐγείρας Χριστὸν ἐκ νεκρῶν ζῳοποιήσει καὶ τὰ θνητὰ σώματα ὑμῶν διὰ τοῦ **ἐν**οικοῦντος αὐτοῦ πνεύματος **ἐν** ὑμῖν, "He who raised Christ from the dead will also make your mortal bodies alive through his Spirit who *(in)dwells in* you" (Rom. 8:11).

1. range
2. Significance
3. Context
4. Other uses in NT

Words and Phrases §§103–106

103. INTRODUCTION. We are departing from Greek syntax at the end of this sketch in order to introduce some principles for the study of Greek words and phrases. The latter is included, because in many cases you will need to study words as integrally bound into a larger phrase unit rather than individually.[44] From this point on, however, I will simply refer to "word study," but the reader should understand that this means the study of either individual words or of phrase units.

Other terms you should know are "gloss," "meaning," and "referent." It is common to see statements such as: "The word σκεῦος *means* 'jar.'" It is better, however, to see that the word "jar" is an English word substitute, a *gloss,* for σκεῦος, but that the gloss "jar" does not fully explain the *meaning* of σκεῦος. The meaning of σκεῦος or of any other word is a full explanation of the word's *referent*—the object, concept, event, etc. to which the word refers—in any one context. The meaning of a Greek word is normally expressed in at least one full sentence. Louw & Nida's lexicon (L&N) provides such descriptions of word meanings and is its chief advantage over BAGD, although the latter is still our primary reference work for Greek words. Hence, an attempt to communicate the *meaning* of σκεῦος would be something like this:

> A pottery *vessel* or *jar* used for storage or transportation of liquids or solids. Small, delicate σκεύα were made of colored glass and typically held perfumes. Very large σκεύα were made from stone and used for long-term storage of grain, olives, oil, dried fruit or fish, or of other foodstuffs. There were highly decorated, painted σκεύα and plain, unglazed σκεύα for common household use (cf. Rom. 9:21).

You can see that this description is much more helpful than simply giving the gloss, "jar," since ancient σκεύα and today's "jars" are not necessarily made from the same materials or used for the same purposes. Yet my description of the word's meaning does give two glosses (in italics) for translation purposes. In my experience, Greek students are too often satisfied with finding mere English glosses for Greek words, when, as exegetes, they should be more interested in word *meanings*. Glosses are needed by translators, but meaning is the *sine qua non* of the Bible interpreter.

104. WHY STUDY A WORD? This may seem like a silly question, but if you set out on a journey to nowhere in particular you are sure to end up there: nowhere in particular. Greek (and Hebrew) word study manuals often sketch out a standard procedure for the analysis of any word. But this often leads to unnecessary busywork. Different words need different kinds of study based upon several factors, including the student's prior knowledge. What follows is a sketch of the different occasions inspiring a Greek word study. These occasions significantly shape the nature and procedure of a word study.

○ THE REFERENTS VARY. Any one word in Greek—or in any other language for that matter—may point to a wide variety of referents. Hence, the study of some words simply aims at determining the referent which the author intends with his word(s). I suppose a classic example is ὁ λόγος in John 1:1. Do we gloss this as "Word," "Speech," "Reason" (i.e., the rational faculty), or as one of the other possible glosses of λόγος? The first stage of the word study is to determine the *semantic range* of the word, which simply means a collection of the various meanings to which a word (or phrase, remember) may have in any context. This is the commonest type of word study and may simply require consultation of a Greek lexicon

---

[44] This point was made in §1:6h when we looked at ποιεῖν τὴν ἀλήθειαν which might be well to review.

or two. The student then determines the most appropriate meaning according to the relevant contexts of the passage where the word occurs.

○ THE REFERENT IS NOT UNDERSTOOD. This is probably the most common reason for studying an ancient word. The student does not know the referent of a word. Perhaps the word itself is a new vocabulary item. Sometimes the ancient referent is different from the modern referent (e.g., σκεῦον and "jar"), or the referent no longer exists (e.g., the "Asiarchs" of Acts 19:31), or there were even varying referents in antiquity for this one word (e.g., Jewish γραμματεῖς were nothing like the γραμματεύς at Ephesus—see the note below). This latter problem is especially true of NT money values. What is the value of the "50,000 silver coins" in Acts 19:19?[45] Furthermore, certain words have different cultural connotations. A "cynic" today does not identify the member of a philosophical party as in ancient Greece, where the etymology of this word (from κύων, "dog") was not forgotten.[46] Whatever the reason for not understanding a word, the Greek student must sometimes not only be a linguist to perform a proper word study but also an ancient historian competent not only in the culture and society of ancient Palestine, but of Rome and of the Greek world as well.[47] This is a big task, but one which will provide a lifetime of enriching study and reward.

> "The capacity of a word to have two or more different meanings is technically known as polysemy (Gk. πολύς, 'many' + σῆμα, 'sign, meaning'). In other words a particular form of a word can belong to different fields of meaning, only one of which need be its semantic contribution to a single sentence or context. . . . Incidentally, it is polysemy that makes a strictly literal translation such a futile exercise. This approach erroneously assumes that each word has a single meaning, and that this meaning has a precise equivalent meaning in a word of the receptor language. It is far better to determine what the potential senses of a word are, and then use all available contextual clues to select the sense that best fits the context." David Alan Black

○ THE REFERENT IS NOT PROPERLY REPORTED. What I mean by this is that our standard NT lexicons may not report a meaning accurately for a given word or phrase, or they may have missed the intended meaning. Often, students approaching Greek word study for the first

---

[45]Commentators typically regard these as Roman denarii (or Attic drachma) and assume that the value of each coin was equal to the daily wage of a common laborer (from texts like Matt. 20:9). But the location of Acts 19:19 is Ephesus where the Rhodian drachma was the standard (one quarter less valuable than the Attic drachma and the denarius). Furthermore, there is no evidence that one drachma was the daily wage in *Ephesus* (rather than in Palestine). That is a little like assuming that wages in modern Los Angeles are the same as in Mexico City. (It is not even true that wages and prices are uniform throughout the United States, which has a uniform money standard.)

[46]Our literature today rightly cautions against relying on the etymology of a word to determine its meaning. However, there are times—for instance, when various kinds of word play or the use of a rare word are encountered—when the etymology of a word was prominent in an author's mind and part of its meaning. That ancient authors like Plutarch were keenly interested in word etymologies is patent to anyone who reads them.

[47]For example, there is scholarly disagreement over the precise function and duties of the "Asiarchs" in Acts 19:31. However, there is no doubt that these were men of the highest social status at Ephesus. How their friendship may have influenced the protective action of the Ephesian γραμματεύς (Acts 19:35) is an intriguing question. Note as another example that the office of the Ephesian γραμματεύς of Acts 19 was nothing like the Jewish γραμματεῖς ("scribes") in the Gospels. The former was similar to a city mayor, while the latter were teachers and scholars.

time imagine that they will be blazing new trails of meaning in their personal study. While I personally encourage trail-blazing whenever possible, the truth is that over the last five centuries or so of Greek study in the West, we know the range of meanings pretty well for almost all New Testament words, even though it is true that lexicons are fallible and need revision in some few places.[48] To revise them requires specialized study in ancient sources. Pursue this specialized study as well as you can! But you should not hastily assume that our lexicons are wrong or inadequate.

105. How to Study a Word? I don't really want to answer this question fully here, because it is treated fully and well elsewhere. But let me sketch out a procedure which will act as a rough guide, while you will remember from the discussion above that the purpose and occasion of the word study will significantly determine the specifics of how you study a particular word. And other parts of exegesis like establishing the original text are assumed here.

- ❍ STEP ONE: Determine the rough translation value of the word or phrase in question. A translation will often help here, though the more periphrastic versions may actually obscure the meaning of an individual word by setting it in a different sort of English phrase.

- ❍ STEP TWO: Consult BAGD. This should be your first stop—and for most words, your last stop—for every Greek word study. The advantages of this tool are numerous despite its well-known disadvantages. Particularly, you can usually begin to understand a referent from the many glosses provided in the BAGD articles, though it could do a better job of organization, and it would be helpful to focus on meanings rather than glosses.

- ❍ STEP THREE: It is a good idea to consult L&N also. This lexicon differs from all others for ancient Greek by focusing on a word's *meanings*. L&N is also particularly helpful in helping you understand a word's potential meanings by placing each meaning in a complete semantic field. This makes L&N one of the few tools at our disposal for seeing a particular word in light of its synonyms and antonyms.

- ❍ STEP FOUR: LSJ[49] is regarded as the standard lexicon for classical Greek. However, this text covers the Greek of all ancient periods including the LXX and NT. It is always a good idea to check LSJ on a word. There are some few times when BAGD may have missed something, and the history of a word's use might be of some interest as long as one does not impute historical meanings into a NT word which did not actually exist.

- ❍ STEP FIVE (after you consult BAGD, L&N, LSJ, and other lexicons as needed): Your goal in an individual study will vary from here on out. For words which refer to objects, things, people, etc. you may need to move from here to a Bible dictionary or Bible encyclopaedia to

---

[48]For instance, the glosses for χώριον in BAGD ("place," "piece of land," "field," etc.) do not quite communicate the meaning of this term in Acts 4:34. The disciples who were selling their χώρια held multiple *plantations* or absentee *estates* (cf. LSJ). They were not selling their subsistence fields and practicing *primitive communism*; they were selling off their sources of luxury income. I am familiar with this term from an ancient inscription where the annual revenues from a χώριον was willed to a certain actors guild. The guild acted as the absentee land-owner; cf. the parables of Jesus where "estates" were entrusted to an οἰκονόμος ("overseer," "steward," or "manager") by the owner.

[49]There are actually three editions of the Liddell-Scott lexicon: small, medium-sized, and enormous versions. "Liddell" rhymes with "middle," so these three lexicons are affectionately known as: "Little Liddell," "Middle Liddell," and "BIG Liddell." When I refer to LSJ here, however, I mean only Big Liddell.

get a further handle on the ancient referent. For words which refer to concepts or qualities, a theological dictionary may be the next stop. In each case, have a clear goal and you will find that your study of the Greek language will reap rich rewards.

106. FOR FURTHER READING. The following is an annotated list of some particularly helpful references and guides for performing accurate Greek word studies.

- ○ Richard P. Belcher, *Doing an Effective Greek Word Study* (Columbia, S.C.: Richbarry, 1985). A pretty good "how to" pamphlet with step-by-step instructions on using the various reference tools.

- ○ David Alan Black, *Linguistics for Students of New Testament Greek* (Grand Rapids: Baker, 1988). General orientation to linguistic principles and their effects on the study of Greek. See especially Chapter Five: "Semantics: Determining Meaning."

- ○ David Alan Black, *Using New Testament Greek in Ministry* (Grand Rapids: Baker, 1993). See especially his suggestions for tools (Chapter 2).

- ○ Donald A. Carson, *Exegetical Fallacies* (Grand Rapids: Baker, 1984). See especially Chapter One: "Word Study Fallacies" for some errors of method to avoid.

- ○ Gordon Fee, *New Testament Exegesis* (Philadelphia: Westminster, 1983). Contains a section on "how to" for word studies.

- ○ J. P. Louw, *Semantics of New Testament Greek* (Philadelphia: Fortress, and Chico, CA: Scholars Press, 1982). General orientation. A bit more technical than Black's book.

- ○ Moisés Silva, *God, Language and Scripture* (Grand Rapids: Zondervan, 1990). A good theoretical orientation on how language works in general—not a "how to" book, though.

Syntax Sketch Outline

The Greek Article §§1-20 (pp. 83–92)

1. INTRODUCTION.

2. SPECIFIC. The Greek may indicate that a specific or particular referent is in the author's mind, whether that referent is a person, an object, or a specific group.

3. PREVIOUS REFERENCE. ("Anaphoric" or "Resumptive.") The article is frequently used to point back to a noun which was introduced earlier in the context.

4. GENERIC. An article may be used with a noun that is typical of a class or group.

5. WITH NOUNS MODIFIED BY GENITIVE PRONOUNS. The article is normally employed with nouns that are modified by a genitive personal pronoun.

6. WITH ABSTRACT NOUNS. The article was often employed in Greek with abstract terms where English would not use one.

7. WITH PROPER NAMES. The article may be omitted or included with Greek proper names, although they are usually anarthrous.

8. WITH NOMINATIVE ACTING AS VOCATIVE. A noun in the nominative case was often substituted for an anarthrous vocative noun (there is no vocative article form).

9. SUBSTANTIZING. The article can turn various parts of speech such as adjectives, prepositional phrases, participles, or bits of quoted sentences into virtual nouns.

10. WITH CERTAIN PRONOUNS. The Greek article occurs with nouns modified by an adjectival demonstrative pronoun.

11. AS POSSESSIVE PRONOUN. The Greek article itself may function as a possessive pronoun appropriate for that context.

12. AS PERSONAL PRONOUN. The Greek article served as a sort of shorthand for a personal pronoun in narrative passages especially.

13. AS RELATIVE PRONOUN. The Greek article is often translated into an English relative pronoun, especially with articular participles.

14. AS A DEMONSTRATIVE PRONOUN. The Greek article may function as a demonstrative pronoun.

15. WITH TWO NOUNS IN GENITIVE RELATION. (Apollonius' canon.) Two nouns joined in a genitive phrase are normally either both articular or both anarthrous.

16. WITH SINGULAR PARALLEL NOUNS. (Granville Sharp's canon.) One article used with two *singular* nouns in a series suggests that they both refer to the same person or object, whereas two articles suggest that two people or objects are referenced.

17. WITH PREDICATE NOMINATIVES. (Colwell's canon.) Word order in a predicate statement with two nouns may determine the specificity of a noun rather than the presence or absence of an article. (1) Definite predicate nouns that *follow* the copulative verb tend to have the article expressed. (2) Definite predicate nouns that *precede* the copulative verb tend to omit the article, even though they are specific in meaning.

18. ANARTHROUS SUBSTANTIVES. Substantives may be expressed anarthrously in order to bring out the character or quality of the referent.

19. THE ARTICLE AND PREPOSITIONS. An anarthrous noun used with some prepositions may still be definite.

20. WHEN RULES COLLIDE. There are many situations which occur in the actual use of Greek articles where the grammatical rules conflict resulting in exceptions to the rules.

Nominative Case §§21–25 (pp. 93–94)

21. INTRODUCTION.

22. SUBJECT. A substantive in the nominative case was most commonly used as the subject of a verb, whether the voice of the verb was active, middle, or passive.

23. PREDICATE. The predicate noun, pronoun, adjective, or other substantive in a predicate sentence with a copulative verb was placed in the nominative case.

24. AS VOCATIVE. A noun in the nominative case is sometimes used for direct address instead of the vocative case.

25. HANGING NOMINATIVE. (*Nominativus pendens.*) Sometimes a word in the nominative case begins a clause as introduction to a referent which occurs later in the clause in another case.

Vocative Case §§26–27 (p. 95)

26. INTRODUCTION.

27. VOCATIVE. The vocative case was used predominately for words in direct address.

Accusative Case §§28–34 (pp. 96–98)

28. INTRODUCTION.

29. DIRECT OBJECT. The direct object of a verb is normally expressed in the accusative case.

30. DOUBLE ACCUSATIVE. Some verbs in Greek as well as in English take two accusatives.

31. RESPECT. (Specification.) The accusative case was sometimes employed with or without a preposition to indicate the subject matter or another kind of limiting qualification on the statement.

32. ADVERBIAL. Adjectives and pronouns sometimes function as adverbs when expressed as neuter accusatives.

33. EXTENT. The accusative case is used adverbially with measurement nouns and phrases to indicate the extent of an action either in space or in time (duration).

34. SUBJECT OF INFINITIVE. Greek infinitives require their subject to be expressed in the accusative case rather than in the nominative.

Genitive Case §§35–52 (pp. 99–105)

35. INTRODUCTION.

36. POSSESSION. This simplest use of the genitive signifies ownership or possession of some object.

37. PERSONAL RELATIONSHIP. The genitive expresses family and other personal relations.

38. SUBJECTIVE. A genitive substantive of any type connected to a substantive which conveys a verbal notion may express the subject of that verbal idea.

39. AGENCY. As with the subjective genitive, a genitive may express the agent of a *passive* verbal idea of the lead substantive.

40. SOURCE. (Origin.) The genitive of source or origin functions like a prepositional phrase with ἐκ or ἀπό, "from (the source of)."

41. OBJECTIVE. A substantive in the genitive may express the object of a verbal substantive to which it is joined.

42. ADJECTIVAL. ("Hebrew" genitive, attributive, qualitative.) An abstract noun in the genitive may function like an adjective for the substantive to which it is joined.

43. REVERSED ADJECTIVAL. (Antiptosis.) The relation of an adjectival genitive (above) may be employed in reversed manner where the *lead noun* acts as an adjective to the noun in the genitive, not vice versa.

44. EXPLANATORY. (Epexegetical, Appositional.) A word in the genitive case may be the equivalent of the word with which it is joined.

45. CONTENT OR MATERIAL. A word in the genitive can specify the contents of a container or the material out of which the lead substantive is made.

46. PARTITIVE GENITIVE. (Genitive of the whole.) A partitive genitive occurs when the lead substantive identifies *a part* and the word in the genitive identifies the whole.

47. COMPARISON. The object of a comparison may be expressed in the genitive case.

48. PRICE OR VALUE. Words indicating the price or value of an item may be expressed in the genitive without a preposition.

49. CONNECTION. (General, Descriptive.) This is a catch-all category for when two words are connected by the genitive relation in some miscellaneous or vague way.

50. ADVERBIAL. A noun that refers to a time period may be expressed in the genitive to indicate the time during which the action of the verb occurs.

51. WITH VERBS, ADJECTIVES, AND NOUNS. Some verbs take a direct object in the genitive case.

52. GENITIVE ABSOLUTE. This is an idiomatic use of the adverbial participle where the subject of the participle event and the participle are expressed in the genitive case. The phrase usually identifies something grammatically independent of the main construction.

Dative Case §§53–65 (pp. 106–9)

53. INTRODUCTION.

54. INDIRECT OBJECT. (Special Interest.) A dative may refer to the indirect object of verb form.

55. ADVANTAGE/DISADVANTAGE. The dative of indirect object may have the added nuance that the person specified in the dative receives either advantage or disadvantage from the action.

56. RESPECT. The dative may communicate in what respect the action occurs.

57. POSSESSION. The dative may refer to a person who possesses a name or object.

58. MEANS. (Instrumental.) The dative without a preposition may specify what instrument or means was used to accomplish an action.

59. CAUSE. The dative may refer to the cause of an event.

60. AGENT. The dative may refer to the personal agent of an action in rare cases.

61. MANNER. (Associative.) A word in the dative may function as an adverb to specify the manner in which the action is performed.

62. ASSOCIATION. (Comitative.) The dative may be used to identify someone else who is involved in performing an action along with the subject(s).

63. LOCATION. The dative without a preposition may indicate the location where an action occurs.

64. TIME WHEN. The dative without a preposition may communicate when an action occurs.

65. DIRECT OBJECT. Some verbs require that their direct objects be expressed in the dative case.

Pronouns §§66–71 (pp. 110–11)

66. INTRODUCTION.

67. PERSONAL PRONOUNS. (a) Nominative. (b) Oblique Cases. (c) Third Person.

68. REFLEXIVE PRONOUNS.

69. RELATIVE PRONOUNS.

70. RARE DEMONSTRATIVE PRONOUN. ὅδε, ἥδε, τόδε.

71. MISCELLANEOUS PRONOUNS.

Adjectives §§72–76 (pp. 112–13)

72. INTRODUCTION.

73. OTHER FORMS.

74. DEGREE.

75. DEGREE CHANGES.

76. ELATIVE SENSE.

Participles §§77–83 (pp. 114–17)

77. INTRODUCTION.

78. ADVERBIAL PARTICIPLE SEMANTICS.

- TEMPORAL. The participle may refer to an event which is contemporary or previous (rarely posterior) to the main event.

- MANNER (MODAL). The participle expresses some activity or mental state which describes "how" the main action occurs.

- MEANS. The participle clause expresses an event which was the means for accomplishing some result.

- CAUSAL (REASON). The adverbial participle may specify the reason or rationale for why the main event takes place.

- PURPOSE. The adverbial participle may communicate the purpose (intended result) of the main event.

- RESULT. The participle may specify the result(s) of the main verb occurring.

- CONDITIONAL. The participle may express a condition required for the main event to take place or to be true.

- CONCESSIVE. The participle may express a concession for the occurrence or truth of the main event.

79. PARALLEL (ATTENDANT CIRCUMSTANCE). The Greek adverbial participle may take on the function of the main verb and act in parallel.

80. COMPLEMENTARY. In a few places in the New Testament, a participle may complete the idea of another verb (normally the role of an infinitive).

81. INDIRECT DISCOURSE. In a few places, Greek allows the use of a participle in the accusative case to communicate an event in indirect discourse.

82. FUTURE PARTICIPLE FORM.

83. FUTURE PARTICIPLE SEMANTICS. A future participle may communicate purpose or an event which is temporally subsequent to the main event.

Infinitives §§84–95 (pp. 118–22)

84. INTRODUCTION.

85. OVERVIEW. Infinitives are hybrid forms which share the function of nouns and of verbs.

86. INFINITIVES AND THE ARTICLE. A Greek infinitive may be modified by a neuter singular article.

87. COMPLEMENTARY. An anarthrous infinitive may complete another verb.

88. PURPOSE. The infinitive in a number of constructions may communicate the purpose of the main event.

89. RESULT. An infinitive expressed in the same constructions identified under purpose may also express the actual result of the main event.

90. CAUSAL. An author may express the reason why another event occurs with an infinitive clause.

91. TEMPORAL. The Greek infinitive in various phrases may express prior, contemporary, or subsequent temporal relations with the main event.

92. FOLLOWING ἐγένετο. The infinitive may be used following an introductory ἐγένετο δέ or καὶ ἐγένετο to indicate the lead event in a narrative.

93. NOMINAL. An infinitive may act particularly like a noun (subject, direct object, etc.).

94. INDIRECT DISCOURSE. In Greek, one can express indirect discourse with an infinitive clause.

95. EPEXEGETICAL. An infinitive may explain something about a substantive or adjective in the sentence.

Prepositions §§96–102 (pp. 123–25)

96. INTRODUCTION.

97. OVERVIEW. Prepositions are relational words which clarify relationships between different items in a sentence.

98. PREPOSITIONS AND CASE. Prepositions communicate relationships in conjunction with the case of their object.

99. SPATIAL RELATIONS. Prepositions may specify the relation of an event or object with a location in space or in relation with another object.

100. TEMPORAL RELATIONS. The temporal relations of prepositions all relate to the three possible temporal notions: prior, contemporaneous, and subsequent time.

101. LOGICAL RELATIONS. Various prepositions communicate a wide variety of logical relations.

102. A NOTE ON STYLE. Prepositions found on compound verbs are often repeated in the sentence without adding any emphasis.

Words and Phrases §§103–106 (pp. 126–29)

103. INTRODUCTION.

104. WHY STUDY A WORD? Different words need different kinds of study based upon several factors.

   ○ THE REFERENTS VARY. Any one word in Greek may point to a wide variety of referents.

   ○ THE REFERENT IS NOT UNDERSTOOD. A word study may arise if the student does not know the referent of a word, its connotations, its ancient form, etc.

   ○ THE REFERENT IS NOT PROPERLY REPORTED. In a very few cases, our standard NT lexicons may not report a meaning accurately for a given word or phrase, or they may have missed the intended meaning.

105. HOW TO STUDY A WORD? This is a rough guide for word study procedures.

   ○ STEP ONE: Determine the rough translation value of the word or phrase in question.

○ STEP TWO: Consult BAGD.

○ STEP THREE: Consult L&N for the word or phrase in its semantic field, synonyms, and antonyms.

○ STEP FOUR: Consult LSJ for a synoptic view of the word or phrase.

○ STEP FIVE: You should proceed from here guided by the purpose of the word study.

106. FOR FURTHER READING.

Cross Reference to Other Grammars

The following table of cross references to other popular beginning grammars is offered for those students who may not have my *New Testament Greek Primer* (P&R, 1995). The references are to chapters or to section numbers in the grammars. It goes without saying that the material in each chapter is not exactly the same in every book.

Reader Lesson	Primer Assignment	Black[1]	Machen[2]	Mounce[3]	Wenham[4]
1	2	5	V	5–7	8–9
	3	4	IV	5–7	5–7
	14	10	XXIX	25	34
2	11	17	XVII	10	28–29
	12	17	XXV	10	31
3	28	–	VII	–	10
	30	18	XXVI and §550	–	39
4	4	3	III, X	15–16	3
	5	7	XI, XII	21	13
	6	19	XXIII	17	4, 40
5	7	3	XIII	19	21–22
	8	7	XIV	23	24
	15	12–15	X, XVI	24	17, 23, 27, 35
6	9	7	XV	22	25
	23	24	XXVIII	33	18
7	16	9	VIII	11–12	19
	17	11	IX, XXVII	13	14–15
	24	22	XXVII	14	18
8	10	6	VI	9	11–12
	29	18	XXV, XXX	–	30, 32–33
9	19	20	XVIII	26–27	36
	20	20	XIX	28–29	36
	21	20	XX	30	37
10	18	19	XXIV	–	26
	25	21	XXII	32	20
11	13	8	VII	8	16
	22	23	XXI	31	38
12	26	25	XXXI, XXXII	34	41–42
	27	25	XXXIII	35	43–44

[1]David Alan Black, *Learn to Read New Testament Greek* (Nashville: Broadman & Holman, 1994).

[2]J. Gresham Machen, *New Testament Greek for Beginners* (Toronto: Macmillan, 1923).

[3]William D. Mounce, *Basics of Biblical Greek* (Grand Rapids: Zondervan, 1993).

[4]J. W. Wenham, *The Elements of New Testament Greek* (Cambridge: Cambridge University Press, 1970).

Greek Accents

The Greek accent system was invented in the early Byzantine period to preserve the old pronunciation and meaning of Greek. It is not a simple system because of the many exceptions to its rules. The following are general rules of accentuation which will guide you in gaining a rough understanding of how accents work in your Greek New Testament. (For an extensive treatment see D. A. Carson, *Greek Accents* [Grand Rapids: Baker Book House, 1985].)

Definitions

1. The three accent marks found in modern Greek texts convey no difference of meaning, though they are used in different situations. They are called: the *acute* (΄); the *grave* (`); and the *circumflex* (ˆ) (*Primer* §1.6).

2. The last three syllables of a Greek word are given these names: the *ultima* is the last syllable ("ultimate"); the *penult* is next to the last ("near the ultima"); and the *antepenult* is third from the last ("before the next to the last"). Accents occur only within these last three syllables (below). The following words illustrate:

antepenult	*penult*	*ultima*
ἄν–	θρω–	πος
πορ–	εὐ–	ομαι
οὐ–	ραν–	ός

3. The placement of an accent is sometimes determined by the length of the vowel or diphthong of the syllable. The following are always long: η, ῃ, ει, αυ, ευ, ου, υι, ᾳ, ω, and ῳ. And the following are *sometimes* long and sometimes short: α, αι, ι, οι, and υ (–αι and –οι are short when they are final; but, for instance, final –αις and –οις are long). Only epsilon (ε) and omicron (o) are always short.

General Rules

1. Greek words receive an accent on one of their last three syllables only, even if the word is longer than three syllables. Here are examples:

ἀ / κη / **κό** / α / μεν	— antepenult
μαρ / τυ / **ροῦ** / μεν	— penult
συν / α / γω / **γῆ**	— ultima

2. The acute accent may fall on any of the last three syllables; the circumflex may fall on the last two only (the penult and ultima, never the antepenult); and the grave comes only on the ultima. The following illustrates:

	antepenult	*penult*	*ultima*
acute	΄	΄	΄
circumflex		ˆ	ˆ
grave			`

3. The circumflex accent appears only on long vowels or diphthongs (final –αι and –οι are short remember); it does not occur on short vowels or diphthongs. For example: μαρτυροῦμεν, πνεῦμα, ὀφθαλμοῖς (compare ὀφθαλμοί), and ἀληθῶς.

4. If the ultima is *long,* then the accent falls only on the last two syllables, not on the antepenult. This is what sometimes causes an accent to move toward the end of a word. For instance, ἄνθρωπος has a *short* ultima and the accent falls on the antepenult; but ἀνθρώπου has a *long* ultima, so the accent moves to the penult. Notice that with ἀνθρώπου the accent used is the acute even though the vowel is long (ω); this is because the circumflex is not used on the penult (second to the last syllable) when the ultima is long. If the ultima is *short,* then the circumflex might be found on the penult; e.g., ἀγαπῶμεν.

An important exception to the rule just mentioned is the genitive of certain third declension nouns: πίστεως, πόλεων, ἀναστάσεως, κτλ. (The reason for this is probably "quantitative metathesis" earlier in this noun declension's career: from πόληος with a long penult and short ultima to πόλεως with a short penult and long ultima.)

5. Normally, a grave accent replaces the acute on the ultima if the word is followed by another word and not by a punctuation mark. Hence, in: πιστός· ἐάν τις, the word πιστός is followed by a punctuation mark so the acute is retained, but πιστὸς λόγος has the grave. An exception to this pattern is when the following word is enclitic: πιστός ἐστιν (1 John 1:9). For enclitics, see *Primer* §§16.4 and 17.3.

6. Within the following rules just sketched out, the following two tendencies operate: accents on *nouns* tend to stay on the syllable of the noun's lexical form if possible ("retentive accent"), while accents on *verbs* tend to recede to the beginning of the word as far as possible ("recessive accent"). The movement of an accent is largely caused by the length of the noun or verb's ultima or by the addition of syllables to a verb's lexeme as suffixes. The following forms illustrate the noun's retentive tendency and its movement forced by lengthening of the ultima: ἄνθρωπος (lexical form); ἄνθρωποι (short final diphthong); ἄνθρωπον (short ultima); ἀνθρώποις (long final diphthong); ἀνθρώπου (long ultima). And the following forms illustrate the verb's recessive tendency: λύω (lexical form); ἔλυον, λέλυκα, and ἐλύετο; but additional syllables as suffixes move the accent back: ἐλύομεν, λελύκατε, ἐλυόμεθα.

Greek-English Vocabulary

The numbers in parentheses refer to the Lesson where the word is introduced. The principal parts for these verbs (and for those in the *Primer*) can be found in the Comprehensive Verb List.

A

ἀγγελία, ἡ, message (2)
ἁγιάζω, I am sanctifying, consecrating (8)
ἁγνίζω, I am purifying (6)
ἀγνοέω, I am ignorant, do not know (12)
ἁγνός, –ή, –όν, pure (6)
ἀγοράζω, I am buying (7)
ἀγρός, ὁ, field; farms (5)
ἀδελφή, ἡ, sister (9)
ἀδικέω, I am doing wrong, harming (8)
ἀδικία, ἡ, unrighteousness (2)
αἰσχύνομαι, I am ashamed; I shame (6)
αἴτημα, –ατος, τό, request (12)
ἀκάθαρτος, –ον, unclean (6)
ἀκοή, ἡ, hearing; account (11)
ἀλαζονεία, ἡ, arrogance, pride (5)
ἀληθινός, –ή, –όν, true, genuine (4)
ἀληθῶς, truly (3)
ἁμαρωλός, –όν, sinful; sinner (1)
ἀμπελών, –ῶνος, ὁ, vineyard (11)
ἀναβλέπω, I am receiving sight; I am looking up (10)
ἀναγγέλλω, I am announcing, reporting (2)
ἀναγινώσκω, I am reading (6)
ἀναιρέω, I take away, destroy; take up (mid.) (11)
ἀνάστασις, –εως, ἡ, resurrection (2)
ἄνεμος, ὁ, wind (7)
ἀνθρωποκτόνος, ὁ, murderer (8)
ἀνομία, ἡ, lawlessness (7)
ἀντί, instead of, on behalf of (12)
ἀντίχριστος, ὁ, Antichrist (5)
ἄξιος, –α, –ον, worthy (3)
ἅπας, ἅπασα, ἅπαν, all, every (5)
ἄπιστος, –ον, unbelieving (11)
ἀποδίδωμι, I am repaying, giving away (1)
ἄρα, consequently, so then (1)
ἀρεστός, –ή –όν, pleasing (9)
ἀρνέομαι, I am denying (5)
ἀρνίον, τό, lamb, sheep (7)
ἄρτι, now, just (adv.) (4)
ἄρχων, –οντος, ὁ, ruler (4)
ἀσθένεια, ἡ, weakness, sickness (11)
ἀσθενέω, I am weak, sick (6)
ἀσθενής, –ές, weak, helpless (9)
ἀστήρ, –έρος, ὁ, star (11)
αὐξάνω, I increase, grow (11)
ἄχρι(ς), until (conj. and prep.+ gen.) (1)

B

βαρύς, βαρεῖα, βαρύ, heavy (11)
βαστάζω, I am bearing, enduring (9)
βιβλίον, τό, book, scroll (5)
βίος, ὁ, belongings; life (5)
βλασφημέω, I am blaspheming, reviling (5)
βούλομαι, I want, wish (4)

Γ

γαμέω, I am marrying (8)
γέ, indeed (10)
γενεά, ἡ, generation; family (2)
γνωρίζω, I am making known (10)
γνῶσις, –εως, ἡ, knowledge (7)
γρηγορέω, I am watching, awake (12)

Δ

δείκνυμι, I am showing, proving (6)
δέκα, ten (10)
δένδρον, τό, tree (10)
δέομαι, I am begging, praying (12)
δεύτερος, –α, –ον, second (2)
δέω, I am binding (2)
διάβολος, ὁ, Devil (4)
διαθήκη, ἡ, covenant; last will (6)
διακονέω, I am serving (4)
διακονία, ἡ, service, ministry (5)
διάκονος, ὁ, ἡ, servant; deacon (m. or f.) (7)
διάνοια, ἡ, understanding; mind (12)
διδαχή, ἡ, teaching (7)
διέρχομαι, I am going through; I am spreading (2)
δικαιόω, I am justifying, vindicating (4)
διότι, therefore; because (11)
δοκιμάζω, I am testing, proving (9)
δουλεύω, I am enslaved; I am serving (10)
δυνατός, –α, –ον, able; powerful (6)

E

ἐγγύς, near (7)
εἴδωλον, τό, idol (12)
εἰκών, –όνος, ἡ, image (11)
ἐκεῖθεν, from there, thence (4)
ἐκλέγομαι, I am choosing, electing (12)
ἐκλεκτός, –ή, –όν, chosen, elect (12)
ἐκπορεύομαι, I am going out (6)
ἐκχέω, I am pouring out, shedding (9)
ἐλεέω, I have mercy on (7)
ἔλεος, –ους, τό, mercy, compassion (9)
ἐλεύθερος, –α, –ον, free (11)
ἐλπίζω, I hope (7)
ἔμπροσθεν + gen., before, in presence of (1)
ἐνδύω, I am dressing, putting on (9)
ἕνεκα + gen., because of, on account of (9)
ἑορτή, ἡ, feast (10)
ἔξεστι, it is lawful, allowed (impersonal) (7)
ἐπαγγέλλομαι, I am promising (5)
ἐπεί, since, for (9)
ἐπιγινώσκω, I understand, know well (2)
ἐπιθυμία, ἡ, lust, longing (4)
ἐπιστολή, ἡ, letter, epistle (11)
ἐπιστρέφω, I am returning, turning (5)
ἐπιτίθημι, I am putting on; I am adding (4)
ἐπικαλέω, I am calling; I am appealing
    (mid.) (7)
ἐπιτιμάω, I am rebuking, warning (7)
ἐργάζομαι, I am working (3)
ἑτοιμάζω, I am preparing (3)
ἔτος, ἔτους, τό, year (1)
εὐθέως, immediately (adv.) (5)
εὐλογέω, I am blessing (2)
εὐχαριστέω, I am giving thanks (4)
ἐχθρός, –ά, –όν, hostile; enemy
    (substantive) (6)

Z

ζῷον, τό, living being, animal (11)

H

ἡγέομαι, I am leading, ruling; I am thinking,
    considering (8)
ἥκω, I have come; I am present (9)
ἥλιος, ὁ, sun (6)
ἡμέτερος, –α, –ον, our (1)

Θ

θαυμάζω, I am amazed, wondering (2)
θεάομαι, I am beholding, viewing (1)
θλῖψις, –εως, ἡ, tribulation, affliction (2)
θηρίον, τό, animal, wild beast (1)
θυγάτηρ, θυγατρός, ἡ, daughter (8)
θύρα, ἡ, door (4)
θυσία, ἡ, sacrifice, offering (8)
θυσιαστήριον, τό, altar (11)

I

ἰάομαι, I am healing (10)
ἴδε, look, behold (7)
ἱερεύς, –έως, ὁ, priest (7)
ἱκανός, –ή, –όν, enough; many (4)
ἱλασμός, ὁ, propitiation (3)
ἰσχυρός, –ά, –όν, strong (4)
ἰσχύω, I am able, strong (8)

K

καθαρίζω, I am cleansing (2)
καθαρός, –ά, –όν, clean (9)
καθεύδω, I am sleeping (12)
καθίζω, I am sitting (mid.); I am causing to
    sit (1)
καινός, –ή, –όν, new, different (3)
καλῶς, well (4)
καταγινώσκω, I am condemning, blame (9)
καταλείπω, I leave behind, abandon (11)
καταργέω, I am abolishing, nullifying (9)
κατεργάζομαι, I am accomplishing,
    producing (12)
κατηγορέω, I am accusing (12)
κατοικέω, I am living, dwelling (2)
καυχάομαι, I am boasting, glorying in (4)
κεῖμαι, I lie down; exist (11)
κελεύω, I am commanding (10)
κλαίω, I am weeping (3)
κλείω, I am shutting (8)
κοιλία, ἡ, stomach; womb (12)
κοινωνία, ἡ, fellowship (1)
κόλασις, –εως, ἡ, penalty, punishment (10)
κοπιάω, I am laboring, working hard (12)
κρατέω, I am seizing, grasping (1)
κρίμα, κρίματος, τό, judgment (9)
κρίσις, –εως, ἡ, judgment (1)
κωλύω, I hinder (12)
κώμη, ἡ, village (9)

Λ

λευκός, –ή, –όν, white (10)
λυπέω, I am grieving, hurting (10)

Μ

μανθάνω, I am learning (10)
μαρτυρία, ἡ, testimony, witness (5)
μάρτυς, –υρος, ὁ, witness (5)
μάχαιρα, ἡ, knife; sword (7)
μέλος, μέλους, τό, member, limb (6)
μέρος, –ους, τό, part, portion (3)
μεταβαίνω, I am passing over, transfer (8)
μετανοέω, I am repenting (6)
μετάνοια, ἡ, repentance (12)
μήποτε, lest, otherwise; perhaps (10)
μήτε, neither. . . nor, and not (6)
μικρός, –ά, –όν, small, little (1)
μιμνήσκομαι, I remember (12)
μισέω, I am hating (3)
μισθός, ὁ, wages, reward (8)
μνημεῖον, τό, monument, grave (3)
μονογενής, –ές, only-begotten, unique (10)
μυστήριον, τό, mystery (8)

Ν

ναί, yes (6)
ναός, ὁ, sanctuary, temple (2)
νεανίσκος, ὁ, young man (4)
νέος, –α, –ον, new, young (12)
νεφέλη, ἡ, cloud (10)
νικάω, I am conquering (8)
νική, ἡ, victory (11)
νοῦς, νοός, ὁ, mind; thought (11)

Ο

ὅθεν, from where, whence (5)
οἰκοδομέω, I am building; I am edifying (3)
οἶνος, ὁ, wine (6)
ὀλίγος, –η, –ον, little, small, few (3)
ὀμνύω, I swear an oath (10)
ὅμοιος, –α, –ον, similar, like (2)
ὁμοίως, likewise, similarly (7)
ὁμολογέω, I am confessing, professing (2)
ὀπίσω, behind (adv. or prep. + gen.) (5)
ὀργή, ἡ, anger, wrath (5)
οὗ, where, to which (11)
οὐαί, woe, alas (1)
οὐκέτι, no longer, no more (μηκέτι) (1)

οὔπω, not yet (6)
οὖς, ὠτός, τό, ear (5)
ὀφείλω, I ought, owe (3)

Π

παῖς, παιδός, ὁ or ἡ, boy, girl, child (11)
παλαιός, –ά, –όν, old, ancient (4)
πάντοτε, always (3)
παραγγέλλω, I am ordering, instructing (6)
παραγίνομαι, I am arriving, appearing (5)
παράγω, I am introducing; I am passing
    away (pass.) (4)
παράκλησις, –εως, ἡ, comfort (8)
παράκλητος, ὁ, advocate; helper (3)
παραλαμβάνω, I am taking; I am taking
    along (1)
πάρειμι, I am present (11)
παρέρχομαι, I am passing by; I am
    neglecting (8)
παρίστημι, I am presenting, approach (3)
παρουσία, ἡ, arrival, coming (6)
παρρησία, ἡ, boldness, confidence;
    openness (6)
πάσχα, τό, Passover (8)
πάσχω, I am suffering, experiencing (3)
πεινάω, I am hungry (12)
πειράζω, I am tempting, testing, trying (4)
πέντε, five (4)
πέραν, other side; across (12)
περιβάλλω, I am clothing, dressing (12)
περιτομή, ἡ, circumcision (5)
πίμπλημι, I fill, fulfill; it comes to pass
    (pass.) (11)
πλανάω, I am deceiving (2)
πλάνη, ἡ, deception; error (9)
πληγή, ἡ, blow; plague (12)
πλῆθος, –ους, τό, crowd; quantity (7)
πλήν, only, however (7)
πλούσιος, –α, –ον, rich, wealthy (9)
πλοῦτος, ὁ, wealth (12)
πνευματικός, –ή, –όν, spiritual (10)
πόθεν, from where? (8)
ποῖος, –α, –ον, what kind? what? (6)
πορνεία, ἡ, fornication, immorality (11)
πόσος, –η, –ον, how many?, how great? (9)
ποταπός, –ή, –όν, what kind (6)
ποτέ, once, formerly, ever (8)
ποτήριον, τό, cup (7)
ποῦ, where, where? (1)

πρόβατον, τό, sheep (4)
προσευχή, ἡ, prayer (5)
προσέχω, I devote myself to (11)
προσκαλέω, I am summoning, calling (mid. only) (8)
προσφέρω, I am offering, bringing to (1)
προφητεύω, I am prophesying (9)
πτωχός, –ή, –όν, poor (6)
πώποτε, ever, at any time (10)

Σ

σήμερον, today (3)
σκανδαλίζω, I am making (someone) stumble (8)
σκάνδαλον, τό, offense, stumbling block (4)
σκεῦος, σκεύους, τό, vessel, jar (12)
σκοτία, ἡ, darkness (2)
σκότος, –ους, τό, darkness (2)
σός, σή, σόν, your (9)
σπέρμα, σπέρματος, τό, seed (2)
σπλάγχνον, τό, compassion, feelings (8)
σταυρός, ὁ, cross (9)
σταυρόω, I am crucifying (1)
στρατιώτης, –ου, ὁ, soldier (10)
συνείδησις, –εως, ἡ, conscience (7)
συνέρχομαι, I am coming together (7)
συνίημι, I understand (10)
σφάζω, I am slaying (8)
σωτήρ, –ῆρος, ὁ, savior, benefactor (10)
σωτηρία, ἡ, salvation, health (2)

Τ

τεκνίον, τό, dear child, little child (3)
τέλειος, –α, –ον, complete, perfect (10)
τελειόω, I am completing, fulfilling (3)
τελέω, I am completing, fulfilling (9)
τέλος, –ους, τό, end, goal; tax (3)
τέσσαρες, –α, four (3)
τιμή, ἡ, honor; value (3)
τυφλόω, I am blinding (someone); I am blind (pass.) (4)

Υ

ὑπομονή, ἡ, endurance, perseverance; patience (6)
ὑποστρέφω, I am turning back, returning (5)

Φ

φαίνω, I am shining, appearing (4)

φανερός, –ά, –όν, clear, evident (7)
φανερόω, I am revealing; I am appearing (pass.) (1)
φεύγω, I am fleeing, escaping (8)
φιλέω, I love; kiss (11)
φίλος, ὁ, ἡ, friend (m. or f.); friendly (as adj.) (8)
φόβος, ὁ, fear (1)
φρονέω, I am thinking (10)
φυλακή, ἡ, guard, prison (1)
φυλάσσω, I am guarding (7)
φυλή, ἡ, tribe, people (7)
φωνέω, I am calling (2)

Χ

χαρίζομαι, I am granting; I am forgiving (12)
χάριν + gen., because of, for the sake of (often occurs *after* its object) (8)
χήρα, ἡ, widow (10)
χρεία, ἡ, need, necessity (1)
χρῖσμα, –ατος, τό, anointing (5)
χώρα, ἡ, field, rural area, countryside (9)
χωρίς + gen., apart from, besides (prep.) (3)

Ψ

ψεύδομαι, I am lying (2)
ψευδοπροφήτης, –ου, ὁ, false prophet (9)
ψεῦδος, –ους, τό, lie (5)
ψεύστης, –ου, ὁ, liar (2)
ψηλαφάω, I am touching, handling (1)

Ω

ὥσπερ, as, just as (5)

Comprehensive Verb List

The following verbs appear in both my *Primer* and in this *Reader*. Only the principal parts that occur in the NT are given, and only one English gloss is given.

PRESENT	FUTURE	AORIST	PERFECT	PERFECT M/P	AORIST PASSIVE	GLOSS
ἀγαπάω	ἀγαπήσω	ἠγάπησα	ἠγάπηκα	ἠγάπημαι	ἠγαπήθην	*love*
ἁγιάζω		ἡγίασα		ἡγίασμαι	ἡγιάσθην	*sanctify*
ἁγνίζω		ἥγνισα	ἥγνικα	ἥγνισμαι	ἡγνίσθην	*purify*
ἀγνοέω		ἠγνόησα				*be ignorant*
ἀγοράζω		ἠγόρασα		ἠγόρασμαι	ἠγοράσθην	*buy*
ἄγω	ἄξω	ἤγαγον		ἦγμαι	ἤχθην	*lead*
ἀδικέω	ἀδικήσω	ἠδίκησα			ἠδικήθην	*harm*
αἴρω	ἀρῶ	ἦρα	ἦρκα	ἦρμαι	ἤρθην	*raise*
αἰσχύνομαι					ἠσχύνθην	*be ashamed*
αἰτέω	αἰτήσω	ᾔτησα	ᾔτηκα		ᾐτήθην	*ask*
ἀκολουθέω	ἀκολουθήσω	ἠκολούθησα	ἠκολούθηκα			*follow*
ἀκούω	ἀκούσω	ἤκουσα	ἀκήκοα		ἠκούσθην	*hear*
ἁμαρτάνω	ἁμαρτανῶ	ἥμαρτον (ἡμάρτησα)	ἡμάρτηκα	ἡμάρτημαι	ἡμαρτήθην	*sin*
ἀναβαίνω	ἀναβήσομαι	ἀνέβην				*ascend*
ἀναβλέπω		ἀνέβλεψα				*receive sight*
ἀναγγέλλω	ἀναγγελῶ	ἀνήγγειλα			ἀνηγγέλην	*announce*
ἀναγινώσκω		ἀνέγνων			ἀνεγνώσθην	*read*
ἀναιρέω	ἀνελῶ	ἀνεῖλον			ἀνῃρέθην	*destroy*
ἀνίστημι	ἀναστήσω	ἀνέστησα/ ἀνέστην	ἀνέστηκα		ἀνεστάθην	*stand up*
ἀνοίγω	ἀνοίξω	ἀνέῳξα	ἀνέῳγα	ἀνέῳγμαι	ἀνεῴχθην	*open*
ἀπαγγέλλω	ἀπαγγελῶ	ἀπήγγειλα		ἀπήγγελμαι	ἀπηγγέλην	*announce*
ἀπέρχομαι	ἀπελεύσομαι	ἀπῆλθον	ἀπελήλυθα			*leave*
ἀποδίδωμι	ἀποδώσω	ἀπέδωκα			ἀπεδόθην	*repay*
ἀποθνῄσκω	ἀποθανοῦμαι	ἀπέθανον				*die*
ἀποκαλύπτω	ἀποκαλύψω	ἀπεκάλυψα	ἀποκεκάλυφα	ἀποκεκάλυμμαι	ἀπεκαλύφθην	*reveal*
ἀποκρίνομαι		ἀπεκρινάμην			ἀπεκρίθην	*answer*
ἀποκτείνω	ἀποκτενῶ	ἀπέκτεινα			ἀπεκτάνθην	*kill*
ἀπόλλυμι/–ω	ἀπολέσω/–ῶ	ἀπώλεσα	ἀπόλωλα		ἀπωλόμην	*destroy*
ἀπολύω	ἀπολύσω	ἀπέλυσα	ἀπολέλυκα	ἀπολέλυμαι	ἀπελύθην	*release*
ἀποστέλλω	ἀποστελῶ	ἀπέστειλα	ἀπέσταλκα	ἀπέσταλμαι	ἀπεστάλην	*send out*

PRESENT	FUTURE	AORIST	PERFECT	PERFECT M/P	AORIST PASSIVE	GLOSS
ἅπτομαι/–ω	ἅψομαι	ἡψάμην				*touch*
ἀρνέομαι	ἀρνήσομαι	ἠρνησάμην		ἤρνημαι		*deny*
ἄρχομαι	ἄρξομαι	ἠρξάμην			begin	
ἀσθενέω		ἠσθένησα	ἠσθένηκα			*be weak*
ἀσπάζομαι		ἀσπασάμην				*greet*
αὐξάνω	αὐξήσω	ηὔξησα			ηὐξήθην	*grow*
ἀφίημι	ἀφήσω	ἀφῆκα	ἀφέωμαι	ἀφέθην	forgive	
βάλλω	βαλῶ	ἔβαλον	βέβληκα	βέβλημαι	ἐβλήθην	*throw*
βαπτίζω	βαπτίσω	ἐβάπτισα		βεβάπτισμαι	ἐβαπτίσθην	*baptize*
βαστάζω	βαστάσω	ἐβάστασα				*bear*
βλασφημέω		βλασφήμησα			ἐβλασφημή–θην	*blaspheme*
βλέπω	βλέψω/ ὄψομαι	ἔβλεψα/εἶδον	ἑώρακα/ ἑόρακα		ὤφθην	*see*
βούλομαι					ἐβουλήθην	*want*
γαμέω		ἐγάμησα	γεγάμηκα		ἐγαμήθην	*marry*
γεννάω	γεννήσω	ἐγέννησα	γεγέννηκα	γεγέννημαι	ἐγεννήθην	*beget*
γίνομαι	γενήσομαι	ἐγενόμην	γέγονα	γεγένημαι	ἐγενήθην	*become*
γινώσκω	γνώσομαι	ἔγνων	ἔγνωκα	ἔγνωσμαι	ἐγνώσθην	*know*
γνωρίζω	γνωρίσω	ἐγνώρισα			ἐγνωρίσθην	*make known*
γράφω	γράψω	ἔγραψα	γέγραφα	γέγραμμαι	ἐγράφην	*write*
γρηγορέω		ἐγρηγόρησα				*watch*
δεῖ						*it is necessary*
δείκνυμι	δείξω	ἔδειξα	δέδειχα		ἐδείχθην	*show*
δέομαι					ἐδάρην	*beg*
δέχομαι	δέξομαι	ἐδεξάμην		δέδεγμαι	ἐδέχθην	*receive*
δέω		ἔδησα	δέδεκα	δέδεμαι	ἐδέθην	*bind*
διακονέω	διακονήσω	διηκόνησα			διηκονήθην	*serve*
διδάσκω	διδάξω	ἐδίδαξα			ἐδιδάχθην	*teach*
δίδωμι	δώσω	ἔδωκα	δέδωκα	δέδομαι	ἐδόθην	*give*
διέρχομαι	διελεύσομαι	διῆλθον	διελήλυθα			*go through*
δικαιόω	δικαιώσω	ἐδικαίωσα		δεδικαίωμαι	ἐδικαιώθην	*justify*
διώκω	διώξω	ἐδίωξα	δεδίωχα	δεδίωγμαι	ἐδιώχθην	*persecute*
δοκέω	δόξω	ἔδοξα		δέδογμαι	ἐδόχθην	*think*
δοκιμάζω	δοκιμάσω	ἐδοκίμασα		δεδοκίμασμαι		*test*

Present	Future	Aorist	Perfect	Perfect M/P	Aorist Passive	Gloss
δοξάζω	δοξάσω	ἐδόξασα		δεδόξασμαι	ἐδοξάσθην	*glorify*
δουλεύω	δουλεύσω	ἐδούλευσα	δεδούλευκα			*serve*
δύναμαι	δυνήσομαι				ἠδυνήθην/ ἠδυνάσθην	*be able to*
ἐγγίζω	ἐγγιῶ	ἤγγισα	ἤγγικα			*draw near*
ἐγείρω	ἐγερῶ	ἤγειρα		ἐγήγερμαι	ἠγέρθην	*raise*
εἰμί	ἔσομαι	ἤμην				*be*
εἰσέρχομαι	εἰσελεύσομαι	εἰσῆλθον	εἰσελήλυθα			*enter*
ἐκβάλλω	ἐκβαλῶ	ἐξέβαλον	ἐκβέβληκα	ἐκβέβλημαι	ἐξεβλήθην	*throw out*
ἐκλέγομαι		ἐξελεξάμην		ἐκλέλεγμαι		*elect*
ἐκπορεύομαι	ἐκπορεύσομαι					*go out*
ἐκχέω	ἐκχεῶ	ἐξέχεα		ἐκκέχυμαι	ἐξεχύθην	*pour out*
ἐλεέω	ἐλεήσω	ἠλέησα		ἠλέημαι	ἠλεήθην	*have mercy*
ἐλπίζω	ἐλθιῶ	ἤλπισα	ἤλπικα			*hope*
ἐνδύω		ἐνέδυσα		ἐνδέδυμαι		*dress*
ἐξέρχομαι	ἐξελεύσομαι	ἐξῆλθον	ἐξελήλυθα			*go out*
ἐπαγγέλλομαι		ἐπηγγειλάμην		ἐπήγγελμαι		*promise*
ἐπερωτάω	ἐπερωτήσω	ἐπηρώτησα			ἐπηρωτήθην	*question*
ἐπιγινώσκω	ἐπιγνώσομαι	ἐπέγνων	ἐπέγνωκα		ἐπεγνώσθην	*understand*
ἐπιστρέφω	ἐπιστρέψω	ἐπέστρεψα			ἐπεστράφην	*return*
ἐπιτίθημι	ἐπιθήσθ	ἐπέθηκα				*add*
ἔξεστι						*it is lawful*
ἐπικαλέω		ἐπεκάλεσα		ἐπικέκλημαι	ἐπεκλήθην	*call*
ἐπιτιμάω		ἐπετίμησα				*rebuke*
ἐργάζομαι		ἠργασάμην		εἴργασμαι		*work*
ἔρχομαι	ἐλεύσομαι	ἦλθον	ἐλήλυθα			*come*
ἐρωτάω	ἐρωτήσω	ἠρώτησα			ἠρωτήθην	*ask*
ἐσθίω	φάγομαι	ἔφαγον				*eat*
ἑτοιμάζω		ἡτοίμασα	ἡτοίμακα	ἡτοίμασμαι	ἡτοιμάσθην	*prepare*
εὐαγγελίζομαι		εὐηγγελισάμην /–σα		εὐηγγέλισμαι	εὐηγγελίσθην	*preach the gospel*
εὐλογέω	εὐλογήσω	εὐλόγησα	εὐλόγηκα	εὐλόγημαι		*bless*
εὑρίσκω	εὑρήσω	εὗρον	εὕρηκα		εὑρέθην	*find*
εὐχαριστέω		εὐχαρίστησα				*give thanks*
ἔχω	ἕξω	ἔσχον	ἔσχηκα			*have*

PRESENT	FUTURE	AORIST	PERFECT	PERFECT M/P	AORIST PASSIVE	GLOSS
ζάω	ζήσω/–ομαι	ἔζησα				*live*
ζητέω	ζητήσω	ἐζήτησα				*seek*
ἡγέομαι		ἡγησάμην		ἥγημαι		*lead*
ἥκω	ἥξω	ἧξα				*be present*
θαυμάζω		ἐθαύμασα			ἐθαυμάσθην	*be amazed*
θεάομαι		ἐθεασάμην		τεθέαμαι	ἐθεάθην	*behold*
θέλω	θελήσω	ἠθέλησα				*want*
θεραπεύω	θεραπεύσω	ἐθεράπευσα		τεθεράπευμαι	ἐθεραπεύθην	*heal*
θεωρέω	θεωρήσω	ἐθεώρησα				*look at*
ἰάομαι	ἰάσομαι	ἰασάμην		ἴαμαι	ἰάθην	*heal*
ἵστημι	στήσω	ἔστησα/ ἔστην	ἕστηκα		ἐστάθην	*stand*
ἰσχύω	ἰσχύσω	ἴσχυσα				*be strong*
καθαρίζω	καθαριῶ	ἐκαθάρισα				*cleanse*
καθεύδω						*sleep*
κάθημαι	καθήσομαι					*sit*
καθίζω	καθίσω	ἐκάθισα	κεκάθικα			*cause to sit*
καλέω	καλέσω	ἐκάλεσα	κέκληκα	κέκλημαι	ἐκλήθην	*call*
καταβαίνω	καταβήσομαι	κατέβην	καταβέβηκα			*go down*
καταγινώσκω						*condemn*
καταλείπω	καταλείψω	κατέλιπον		καταλέλειμμαι	κατελείφθην	*abandon*
καταργέω	καταργήσω	κατήργησα	κατήργηκα	κατήργημαι	κατηργήθην	*abolish*
κατεργάζομαι		κατειργασάμην		κατείργασμαι	κατειργάσ–θην	*accomplish*
κατηγορέω	κατηγορήσω	κατηγόρησα				*accuse*
κατοικέω		κατῴκησα				*dwell*
καυχάομαι	καυχήσομαι	ἐκαυχησάμην		κεκαύχημαι		*boast*
κεῖμαι						*lie down*
κελεύω		ἐκέλευσα				*command*
κηρύσσω	κηρύξω	ἐκήρυξα			ἐκηρύχθην	*announce*
κλαίω	κλαύσω	ἔκλαυσα				*weep*
κλείω	κλείσω	ἔκλεισα		κέκλεισμαι	ἐκλείσθην	*shut*
κοπιάω		ἐκοπίασα	κεκοπίακα			*labor*
κόπτω	κόψω	ἔκοψα	κέκοφα	κέκομμαι	ἐκόπην	*cut*
κράζω	κράξω	ἔκραξα	κέκραγα			*shout*
κρατέω	κρατήσω	ἐκράτησα	κεκράτηκα	κεκράτημαι		*seize*

Comprehensive Verb List

Present	Future	Aorist	Perfect	Perfect M/P	Aorist Passive	Gloss
κρίνω	κρινῶ	ἔκρινα	κέκρικα	κέκριμαι	ἐκρίθην	judge
κωλύω		ἐκώλυσα			ἐκωλύθην	hinder
λαλέω	λαλήσω	ἐλάλησα	λελάληκα	λελάλημαι	ἐλαλήθην	talk
λαμβάνω	λήμψομαι	ἔλαβον	εἴληφα	εἴλημμαι	ἐλήμφθην	take
λέγω	ἐρῶ	εἶπον	εἴρηκα	εἴρημαι	ἐρρέθην/ ἐρρήθην	say
λογίζομαι	λογίσομαι	ἐλογισάμην		λελόγισμαι	ἐλογίσθην	reckon
λυπέω		ἐλύπησα	λελύπηκα		ἐλυπήθην	grieve
λύω	λύσω	ἔλυσα	λέλυκα	λέλυμαι	ἐλύθην	loose
μανθάνω		ἔμαθον	μεμάθηκα			learn
μαρτυρέω	μαρτυρήσω	ἐμαρτύρησα	μεμαρτύρηκα	μεμαρτύρημαι	ἐμαρτυρήθην	testify
μέλλω	μελλήσω					be about to
μένω	μενῶ	ἔμεινα	μεμένηκα			remain
μεταβαίνω	μεταβήσομαι	μετέβην	μεταβέβηκα			pass over
μετανοέω	μετανοήσω	μετενόησα				repent
μιμνῄσκομαι				μέμνημαι	ἐμνήσθην	remember
μισέω	μισήσω	ἐμίσησα	μεμίσηκα	μεμίσημαι		hate
νικάω	νεκήσω	ἐνίκησα	νενίκηκα			conquer
οἰκοδομέω	οἰκοδομήσω	ᾠκοδόμησα		οἰκοδόμημαι	οἰκοδομήθην	build
ὀμνύω		ὤμοσα				swear
ὁμολογέω	ὁμολογήσω	ὡμολόγησα				confess
ὁράω	ὄψομαι	εἶδον	ἑώρακα/ἑόρακα		ὤφθην	see
ὀφείλω						ought
παραγγέλλω		παρήγγειλα		παρήγγελμαι		order
παραγίνομαι		παρεγενόμην				arrive
παράγω						introduce
παραδίδωμι	παραδώσω	παρέδωκα	παραδέδωκα	παραδέδομαι	παρεδόθην	betray
παρακαλέω	παρακαλέσω	παρεκάλεσα	παρακέκληκα	παρακέκλημαι	παρεκλήθην	exhort
παραλαμβάνω	παραλήμψο—μαι	παρέλαβον			παρελήμφθην	take
πάρειμι	παρέσομαι					be present
παρέρχομαι	παρελεύσο—μαι	παρῆλθον	παρελήλυθα			pass by
παρίστημι	παραστήσω	παρέστησα	παρέστηκα			approach
πάσχω		ἔπαθον	πέπονθα			suffer

148

PRESENT	FUTURE	AORIST	PERFECT	PERFECT M/P	AORIST PASSIVE	GLOSS
πείθω	πείσω	ἔπεισα	πέποιθα	πέπεισμαι	ἐπείσθην	persuade
πεινάω	πεινάσω	ἐπείνασα				be hungry
πειράζω		ἐπείρασα		πεπείρασμαι	ἐπειράσθην	tempt
πέμπω	πέμψω	ἔπεμψα			ἐπέμφθην	send
περιβάλλω	περιβαλῶ	περιέβαλον		περιβέβλημαι		clothe
περιπατέω	περιπατήσω	περιεπάτησα	περιπεπάτηκα			walk
περισσεύω	περισσεύσω	ἐπερίσσευσα				increase
πίμλημι		ἔπλησα				fill
πίνω	πίομαι	ἔπιον	πέπωκα		ἐπόθην	drink
πίπτω	πεσοῦμαι	ἔπεσον	πέπτωκα			fall
πιστεύω	πιστεύσω	ἐπίστευσα	πεπίστευκα	πεπίστευμαι	ἐπιστεύθην	believe
πλανάω	πλανήσω	ἐπλήνησα		πεπλάνημαι	ἐπλανήθην	deceive
πληρόω	πληρώσω	ἐπλήρωσα	πεπλήρωκα	πεπλήρωμαι	ἐπληρώθην	complete
ποιέω	ποιήσω	ἐποίησα	πεποίηκα	πεποίημαι		do
πορεύομαι	πορεύσομαι	ἐπορευσάμην		πεπόρευμαι	ἐπορεύθην	go
πράσσω	πράξω	ἔπραξα	πέπραχα	πέπραγμαι	ἐπράχθην	do
προσέρχομαι	προσελεύσο—μαι	προσῆλθον	προσελήλυθα			approach
προσεύχομαι	προσεύξομαι	προσηυξάμην				pray
προσέχω			προσέσχηκα			devote oneself to
προσκαλέω		προσεκάλεσα		προσκέκλημαι		summon
προσκυνέω	προσκυνήσω	προσεκύνησα				worship
προσφέρω						offer
προφητεύω	προφητεύσω	ἐπροφήτευσα				prophesy
σκανδαλίζω		ἐσκανδάλισα			ἐσκανδαλίσ—θην	make stumble
σπείρω		ἔσπειρα		ἔσπαρμαι	ἐσπάρην	plant
σταυρόω	σταυρώσω	ἐσταύρωσα		ἐσταύρωμαι	ἐσταυρώθην	crucify
συνάγω	συνάξω	συνήγαγον		συνῆγμαι	συνήχθην	gather
συνέρχομαι		συνῆλθον	συνελήλυθα			come together
συνίημι	συνήσθ	συνῆκα				understand
σφάζω	σφάξω	ἔσφαξα		ἔσφαγμαι	ἐσφάγην	slay
σῴζω	σώσω	ἔσωσα	σέσωκα	σέσω(σ)μαι	ἐσώθην	save
τελειόω		ἐτελείωσα	τετελείωκα	τετελείωμαι	ἐτελειώθην	fulfill

Comprehensive Verb List

PRESENT	FUTURE	AORIST	PERFECT	PERFECT M/P	AORIST PASSIVE	GLOSS
τελέω		ἐτέλεσα	τετέλεκα	τετέλεσμαι	ἐτελέσθην	complete
τηρέω	τηρήσω	ἐτήρησα	τετήρηκα	τετήρημαι	ἐτηρήθην	keep
τίθημι	θήσω	ἔθηκα	τέθεικα	τέθειμαι	ἐτέθην	put
τυφλόω		ἐτύφλωσα	τετύφλωκα			blind
ὑπάγω	ὑπάξω	ὑπήγαγον		ὑπῆγμαι	ὑπήχθην	pass by
ὑπάρχω	ὑπάρξω	ὑπῆρξα				exist
ὑποστρέφω	ὑποστρέψω	ὑπέστρεψα				return
ὑποτάσσω	ὑποτάξω	ὑπέταξα	ὑποτέταχα	ὑποτέταγμαι	ἐτάχθην	subject
φαίνω	ἐφανῶ	ἔφανα			ἐφάνην	shine
φανερόω	φανερώσω	ἐφανέρωσα		πεφανέρωμαι	ἐφανερώθην	reveal
φέρω	οἴσω	ἤνεγκα	ἐνήνοχα		ἠνέχθην	carry
φεύγω	φεύξομαι	ἔφυγον				flee
φημί		ἔφη				say
φιλέω		ἐφίλησα	πεφίληκα			love
φοβέομαι					ἐφοβήθην	fear
φρονέω	φρονήσω					think
φυλάσσω	φυλάξω	ἐφύλαξα				guard
φωνέω	φωνήσω	ἐφώνησα			ἐφωνήθην	call
χαρίζομαι	χαρίσομαι	ἐχαρισάμην		κεχάρισμαι	ἐχαρίσθην	grant
χαίρω	χαρήσομαι				ἐχάρην	rejoice
ψεύδομαι		ἐψευσάμην				lie
ψηλαφάω		ἐψηλάφησα				touch